JavaScript By EXAMPLE

que®

Stephen Feather
with contribution by **Luke Cassady-Dorion**

JavaScript By Example

Library of Congress Catalog No.: 96-68583

ISBN: 0-7897-0813-2

98 97 96 6 5 4 3 2 1

Interpretation of the printing code: the rightmost double-digit number is the year of the book's printing; the rightmost single-digit number, the number of the book's printing. For example, a printing code of 96-1 shows that the first printing of the book occurred in 1996.

Screen reproductions in this book were created using Collage Plus from Inner Media, Inc., Hollis, NH. Macintosh screen reproductions were created using Capture from Mainstay, Camarillo, CA.

President: *Roland Elgey*

Publisher: *Joseph B. Wikert*

Director of Marketing: *Lynn E. Zingraf*

Publishing Manager
Jim Minatel

Title Manager
Steven M. Schafer

Editorial Services Director
Elizabeth Keaffaber

Managing Editor
Sandy Doell

Acquisitions Manager
Cheryl D. Willoughby

Acquisitions Editor
Doshia Stewart

Editors
Kelli M. Brooks
Susan Shaw Dunn
Andy Saff

Product Marketing Manager
Kim Margolius

Assistant Product Marketing Manager
Christy M. Miller

Strategic Marketing Manager
Barry Pruett

Technical Editors
Faisal Jawdat
Garrett Pease
Marty Wyatt

Technical Review
Scott J. Walter

Technical Support Specialist
Nadeem Muhammed

Acquisitions Coordinator
Jane K. Brownlow

Software Relations Coordinator
Patty Brooks

Editorial Assistant
Andrea Duvall

Book Designer
Kim Scott

Cover Designer
Ruth Harvey

Production Team
Steve Adams
Christine Berman
Debbie Bolhuis
Jason Carr
Trey Frank
Dan Harris
Clint Lahnen
Bob LaRoche
Steph Mineart
Laura Robbins
Donna Wright

Indexers
Erika Millen
Craig Small
Tim Taylor

Composed in *Palatino* and *MCPdigital* by Que Corporation.

Dedication

I would like to dedicate this book to my parents, Robert and Diane Feather. They taught me when I was young and tolerated me as a teen. Now I want them to see that it was all worthwhile. Thank you to two of the world's greatest parents.

About the Authors

Stephen Feather is the owner of LoboSoft Software, a hardware and software consulting firm in Fayetteville, Georgia. He has nearly 15 years of experience in the computer industry. He majored in English and computer science at Pennsylvania State University and then studied system programming and MIS at Berry College. He has been involved in the Internet for nearly six years. He is well versed in C, C++, Pascal, and BASIC on a variety of platforms, including LINUX, Windows, Windows 95, OS/2, Windows NT, UNIX, and DOS. His interests in the Internet primarily lie in the interfacing of HTML, CGI, Java, ActiveX and/or JavaScript to server-side databases.

Luke Cassady-Dorion—the author of Chapter 19, "Verifying Form Input"—is currently studying computer science at Drexel University in Philadelphia. He is head of Java development at Odyssey Systems Corporation and founder of the Philadelphia Java Users' Group.

Acknowledgments

I first want to thank **Steve Schafer** of Que for his vision for this book. Without Steve's ideas, this book would not be on the shelf right now.

Next, I would like to thank **Ken Brothers** for his help in co-authoring this book. Ken is an independent consultant with more than nine years' experience in computers. He received his bachelor's from Grove City College, majoring in business/computer systems management and accounting. He recently received his master's in accounting from Grove City College. His computer experience includes three summers with Pandya Computers, Inc., working as a repair technician and consultant as well as performing in-house programming. Ken has independently consulted with LoboSoft Software for about a year. His knowledge of programming languages includes BASIC, COBOL, Pascal, C, C++, and Assembly Language, and he has DBMS experience with SQL, Paradox, Fox, and Microsoft Access. Operating systems he has worked with include DOS, Windows 95, UNIX, and LINUX.

Also, **Bill Tidwell** of Digital Services Consultants in Atlanta should be thanked for the Web space to test our scripts.

Bob Moore of Suburban Designs in Fayetteville, Georgia, designed the line art for this book.

Lastly, I would like to thank my wife and daughter for supporting me throughout this entire book.

We'd Like to Hear from You!

As part of our continuing effort to produce books of the highest possible quality, Que would like to hear your comments. To stay competitive, we *really* want you, as a computer book reader and user, to let us know what you like or dislike most about this book or other Que products.

You can mail comments, ideas, or suggestions for improving future editions to the address below, or send us a fax at (317) 581-4663. For the online inclined, Macmillan Computer Publishing has a forum on CompuServe (type **GO QUEBOOKS** at any prompt) through which our staff and authors are available for questions and comments. The address of our Internet site is **http://www.mcp.com** (World Wide Web).

In addition to exploring our forum, please feel free to contact me personally to discuss your opinions of this book: I'm **71034,3406** on CompuServe, and **sschafer@que.mcp.com** on the Internet.

Thanks in advance—your comments will help us to continue publishing the best books available on computer topics in today's market.

Steven M. Schafer
Title Manager
Que Corporation
201 W. 103rd Street
Indianapolis, Indiana 46290
USA

Overview

Contents

Appendixes

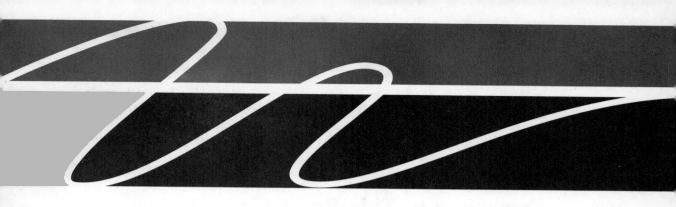

Introduction

JavaScript By Example is a "hands-on" book. In each chapter are numerous examples of how JavaScript can be used in normal everyday Web designs. By the end of this book, you should be able to understand how and what JavaScript can do for you.

What Is JavaScript?

JavaScript is an object-based scripting language that's used to develop client and Internet applications. JavaScript takes statements from an HTML page and, in turn, can perform a different action. JavaScript and its basics will be covered more in depth in Chapter 1, "Introducing JavaScript."

Who Should Use This Book?

This book is written for the beginning Web author who wants to keep up with the changing times. With JavaScript, you as the reader will be able to design Web pages with greater ease. After reading this book, you should agree that the possibilities are endless with what you can do with JavaScript.

What You Should Know Before Reading This Book

You should have an understanding of the Net and what's involved in designing Web pages. You also should have an intermediate understanding of HTML 2.0 and a basic understanding of HTML 3.0. If you need an HTML refresher course, an excellent book to consider is Que's *10 Minute Guide to HTML,* which explains HTML's basics very quickly. If you need a book with more examples and text, try Que's *Using HTML.* If you're just a little rusty on some parts of HTML, don't worry; the first few chapters of this book will review HTML and some other programming basics.

Overview of This Book

Because this is a beginning JavaScript book, the first six chapters review HTML and other programming basics to make sure that you have a firm grasp of these concepts. Chapters 7 through 16 go over the concepts needed to understand how to write JavaScript code. Chapters 17 through 23 show you some examples of how JavaScript can create very intriguing Web pages. Finally, Chapter 24 gives you the scoop on late-breaking information concerning the Netscape 3.0 beta and Microsoft Internet Explorer.

Conventions Used in This Book

Que has more than a decade of experience writing and developing the most successful computer books available. That experience has taught us what special features help readers the most. Look for these special features throughout the book to enhance your learning experience.

Several typeface and font conventions are used to help make reading the text easier:

- *Italic type* is used to emphasize points or to introduce new terms.
- Messages that appear on-screen, all program code, and programming commands, objects, methods, and functions appear in a special monospaced font:

```
<SCRIPT LANGUAGE="JavaScript">
```

- Text that appears in boldface type signifies a current URL on the Web:

  http://www.shareware.com/

  A URL-type statement that's not boldfaced means that it's simply an example; it's not a real URL on the Web.

This book also uses a special margin icon to alert you to *pseudocode* (an algorithm expressed in English to conceptualize the algorithm before coding it into programming language).

This book also contains tips, notes, cautions, and sidebars.

Tip: Tips suggest easier or alternative methods, to help you program more efficiently.

Note: Notes either point out information often overlooked in the documentation, or help you solve or avoid problems.

Caution: Cautions alert you to potentially negative consequences of an operation or action, especially if the latter could result in serious or even disastrous results, such as crashing the server.

Sidebars Provide Deeper Insight

This paragraph format provides technical, ancillary, or non-essential information that you may find interesting or useful. Sidebars are like extended notes, but you can skip over them without missing something necessary to the topic at hand.

Part I

JavaScript and Event Programming

CHAPTER 1

Introducing JavaScript

With the recent increase in interest in the Internet, it's no surprise that new Internet-related concepts and even programming languages are emerging. In this new era of connectivity, we find developers and programmers rushing to devise new methodologies for disseminating large amounts of information, with as little or no overhead as possible.

The World Wide Web has been one of these new resources. Every day, hundreds of new Web authors make their mark on the Internet. I assume that you're familiar with the Web and basic HTML (HyperText Markup Language). You'll be using a great deal of HTML throughout this book to build your scripts and to display their results.

What Is JavaScript?

Netscape, in an effort to further extend the functionality of its popular Navigator browser, developed a programming language that can be placed within Web pages. Originally called *LiveScript*, this new language was renamed *JavaScript* to capitalize on the popularity of the Java programming language developed by Sun Microsystems.

Before diving into exploring the power that JavaScript brings to the Web, it's worth the effort to examine exactly what JavaScript is and isn't.

JavaScript Is a Scripting Language

Computer applications can't be all things to all people, as hard as developers may try. To offset this, it's popular to allow the user to customize a program by writing little "program snippets" to do specialized things (such as spreadsheet macros). For the most part, these "mini-programs" aren't compiled (like regular programs are), but are interpreted line by line while the application is running. Programs such as these are called *scripts*, and the collection of commands and statements that can be used in a script is the *scripting language*.

JavaScript is a scripting language, its syntax looking much like C, C++, Pascal, or Delphi. JavaScript commands and functions are put in your Web document with your other text and HTML tags. When a user's browser retrieves your page, it "runs" your program and performs the appropriate operations.

> **Note:** Because the browser runs a JavaScript program after a document is retrieved, the browser must be capable of interpreting the language. Currently, only Netscape Navigator 2.0 or greater, Navigator Gold 2.0, and Internet Explorer 3.0 have this capability.

JavaScript Is Object-Based

Object-oriented program design attempts to deal with a program as a collection of individual parts (objects) that do different things, and not as a sequence of statements that perform a specific task. Objects of similar "type" are grouped together as *classes* (for example, an "apple" object is in the "fruit" class). The key here is that object-oriented languages allow you to build objects, but they don't have any built in.

An *object-based* language is an object-oriented language with a collection of objects built right into the language. For example, you don't have to build a "date" object in JavaScript—there's already one for you to use.

JavaScript Is Event-Driven

Whenever something "happens" on a Web page, an *event* occurs. Events can be just about anything—a button is clicked, the mouse is dragged, a page is loaded (or unloaded), a form is submitted, and so on. JavaScript is *event-driven* in that it's designed to react when an event occurs. How it reacts depends on what you program.

JavaScript Is Secure

JavaScript is designed to manipulate and present information through the browser, but it can't retrieve information from another file or save data to the Web server or the user's computer. This means it's not possible to write a JavaScript program that, say, would scan a computer's directories and retrieve (or erase) a user's files.

> **Note:** It is possible to write JavaScript that can monitor your browser session and record where you go and what you type (for example, a script that catches passwords for access to secure Web sites). To combat this, Netscape Navigator 2.01 (and Navigator Gold 2.01) offers users the option to deactivate JavaScript (in which case, any JavaScript code would simply be ignored). For users to do this, open the Options menu, choose Security Preferences, and select the Disable JavaScript check box.

JavaScript Is Platform-Independent

With regular computer programs, you know that you can't run a Windows version on a Macintosh (unless you're using an *emulator* to imitate the Windows environment). JavaScript, on the other hand, isn't bound to a particular computer, just to the browser that interprets it. Whether you have a Macintosh, Windows, or UNIX copy of Netscape Navigator, JavaScript will run.

> **Note:** In a few situations, certain functions don't work on all platforms (for example, the `random()` method as described in Chapter 10, "Math Methods"). When I go through the functions that make up JavaScript, I'll point out where these differences occur.

What JavaScript Is *Not*

Now that you've seen what JavaScript *is*, let's cover some of the things that it's *not*.

JavaScript Isn't Java

Too many people, including industry leaders, don't understand the differences between Java and JavaScript. Java, developed by Sun Microsystems, is a full-blown, object-oriented programming language, as opposed to JavaScript's compact, object-based structure. Java can be used to design stand-alone applications or to create mini-applications called *applets*.

Applets are platform-independent binaries. What does that mean? Java code, which is very similar to C, is compiled into binary form. This new applet can be run on any platform, provided that the platform has the software necessary to operate the applet. A Macintosh user, surfing the Web with a Java-compatible browser, can see and use the same applet that a user on a Windows 95 or UNIX computer can. Developers no longer are tied to compiling code for a specific platform.

Here are some other major differences between JavaScript and Java:

- Java is *compiled* into a "binary" file, which is given to the client (browser) to run; JavaScript, on the other hand, is passed to the client as text and *interpreted*.
- JavaScript is *object-based* (it has its own built-in objects). Java is *object-oriented* (objects are built from classes).
- JavaScript code is embedded within an HTML document as plain text. Java applets are referenced from a document, but the code is kept in a separate file in binary (computer) form.
- JavaScript is identified within a document by the `<SCRIPT>` tag. Java applets are embedded in a document using the `<APPLET>` tag.
- JavaScript uses *loose typing*, meaning that variables don't have to be declared, and a variable that was used as a string could be used as a number later. Java uses *strong typing*, which means that variables must be declared and used as a particular type (such as an integer or a string).
- JavaScript uses *dynamic binding*, which means that object references are checked at runtime. Java, on the other hand, uses *static binding*, in which object references must exist when the program is compiled.

JavaScript Isn't LiveWire

LiveWire and, subsequently, LiveWire Pro are new collections of products released by Netscape. LiveWire isn't just a scripting language. Although it does incorporate a new server-side, Java-compatible scripting language, that doesn't cover half of its features. LiveWire includes a WYSIWYG (what-you-see-is-what-you-get) editor/browser, a terrific graphical Web site manager, and (in the Pro version) support for SQL databases from Informix, Oracle, Sybase, and Microsoft. LiveWire will run only on a Netscape server.

JavaScript currently doesn't support direct database access. However, developers are now trying to build and access large databases using JavaScript.

JavaScript Isn't Perl

Perl is an interpreted language primarily used for reading, parsing, and printing text files. Quite often it's used to handle e-mail requests and forms. Perl looks and acts a great deal like C. Perl also can read abnormally large text files into a single string.

Whenever you're surfing the Net and see that the page you're interacting with has an extension such as .pl, that page most likely is a Perl script. You can use Perl to read form data and return the information enclosed in a readable format. Perl also can return dynamically created HTML pages. In addition to these functions, because Perl runs on the server rather than on the client, it can be given read-write access to the server's drives. This permits logging and visitor-tracking functions to be performed.

JavaScript currently can't read text files, nor can it parse incoming streams of data.

Why Use JavaScript?

Programmers who need to make calculations, read data from a table, and design custom HTML screens on the fly but who don't have access to the cgi-bin directory on their Internet providers' servers will be interested in JavaScript. Internet providers frown on allowing users access to the secured, server-side scripting directories. This presents a grave security risk—not only for the providers, but also for all the other users on that particular system.

Summary

JavaScript is an object-based scripting language designed to extend the capabilities of the Web. Developed by Netscape, it's similar in structure to C or C++ and is placed within a document to be interpreted by the browser. Event-driven, it can respond to the user's selections or actions, thus making a Web document "dynamic."

Review Questions

The answers to the review questions are in Appendix D.

1. What is JavaScript? What is it not?
2. What browsers currently support JavaScript?
3. What is Java?
4. How are JavaScript and Java similar? How are they different?
5. What's the difference between *object-oriented* and *object-based*?
6. What is an event? How does this relate to JavaScript?
7. What is a scripting language?
8. What is LiveWire?

Why Use JavaScript?

Summary

Review Questions

CHAPTER 2

JavaScript's Uniqueness and Limitations

What JavaScript brings to the Web table makes it a unique developer's tool. But this tool isn't without its limitations and quirks. Before you dive head first into learning what makes JavaScript tick, you need to be aware of some of these limitations and how to avoid or work around them.

A Unique Web Development Tool

As introduced in Chapter 1 (and detailed in the following chapters), JavaScript puts an enormous amount of control and flexibility into the hands of Web content developers. User-specific content, enhanced visual displays, and more seamless integration with browser plug-ins make JavaScript an excellent "glue" for binding the various pieces of a Web site into one cohesive information source.

Plugging into the Web

Plug-ins are helper applications that integrate into the browser and handle the display of specific kinds of files (for example, QuickTime movies or Macromedia Director files). They're called plug-ins because they "plug" (through installation) directly into the browser interface. Once they're installed, downloading a file of a type the plug-in handles no longer results in a separate program being run to display the file. Instead, the file is displayed *in place* within the Web document.

Among the built-in JavaScript objects is the `navigator` object, which holds various pieces of information on the features of the browser—including what plug-ins are

> currently installed. With this information, the designer can customize a page to display certain types of information, based on the browser's capabilities. Chapter 8, "JavaScript Objects," covers the `navigator` object in more detail.

All this added Web functionality is gained without the need to develop in more advanced programming languages, such as Sun's Java or Microsoft's VBScript. And the language itself (as you'll see) is simple and easy to learn, yet powerful. This is what makes JavaScript unique in the Web community—you no longer need to be a UNIX guru to develop eye-catching sites.

Granted, other tools are popping up like mad for Web design, offering features and services that rival or surpass JavaScript's (QuickTime VR, Shockwave, RealAudio, TrueSpeech…the list is growing almost daily). For the most part, however, to use these tools you need to buy a development environment (such as Director for Shockwave)—and those tools aren't cheap. Even Java development platforms are appearing—for a price. JavaScript capability comes with the browser; no additional software needs to be purchased.

Everything Has Its Limits

So JavaScript provides a powerful, flexible, free development environment for Web designers to use to their pages' content. This "Garden of Web-Eden," however, isn't without its weeds. These limitations fall into the following categories:

- Browser-related
- Platform-related
- Security-related

The following sections examine each of these categories.

Browser-Related Limitations

Because JavaScript code is run on the client (the browser), its interpreter must be implemented within the browser in order to work. Currently, the following browsers support JavaScript:

- Netscape Navigator 2.0
- Netscape Navigator Gold 2.0

As far as the browser interface is concerned, Navigator (shown in fig. 2.1) and Navigator Gold are identical, with Navigator Gold having the additional benefit of an incorporated WYSIWYG HTML editor. To avoid confusion, any references within this book to *Navigator* can apply to either browser unless specifically stated otherwise.

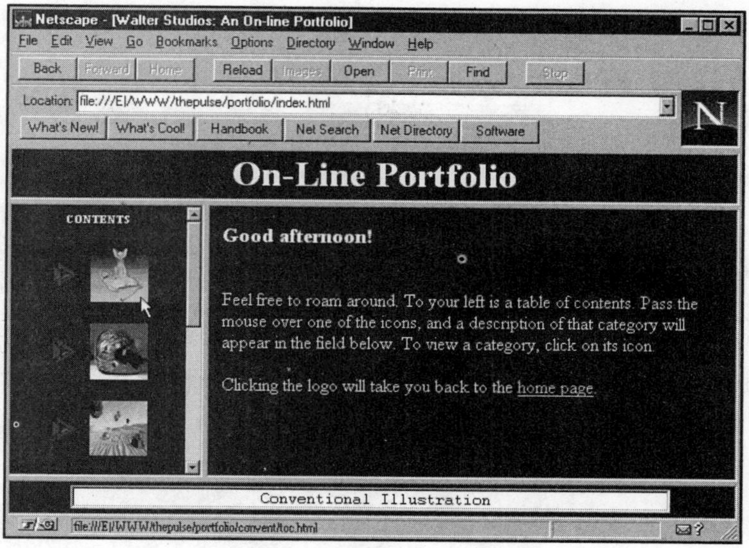

Figure 2.1
Netscape Navigator 2.0 supports JavaScript and the <FRAME> tag, making it possible to create "sectioned" pages. The input field at the bottom of the screen is a help window, displaying text sent to it from the contents bar on the left (with JavaScript).

Caution: Although the editor in Navigator Gold makes creating and maintaining Web pages much easier, it's *not* properly JavaScript-enabled, and will more than likely damage (or delete) any JavaScript code found in a page being edited. Also, it doesn't handle *framed page sets* (pages constructed by using the <FRAMESET> and <FRAME> tags); instead, it chooses to treat those pages as though it's a frame-disabled browser.

In a nutshell, you're better off using a plain-text editor to edit JavaScript pages. If you want to use Navigator Gold's editor initially to lay out your page, you can do so, but once you start adding JavaScript code to the page, switch to an editor that won't destroy your work.

Two additional browsers also support JavaScript, but they're both currently test releases and aren't guaranteed to totally support the language (or support it correctly):

- Netscape Navigator 3.0
- Microsoft's Internet Explorer 3.0

Navigator 3.0 (also called *Atlas*) is the next generation of Netscape browsers and is still in beta testing at the time of this writing. Internet Explorer 3.0 is a new arrival to the JavaScript world (previous versions of Explorer allowed only Microsoft's own extensions to the Web and HTML) and is currently an alpha release that supports a limited set of JavaScript functionality. Also, Explorer doesn't support the <FRAMESET> and <FRAME> tags, further restricting the presentation capabilities and making the display more closely approximate that of a non-<FRAME> browser (as in fig. 2.2).

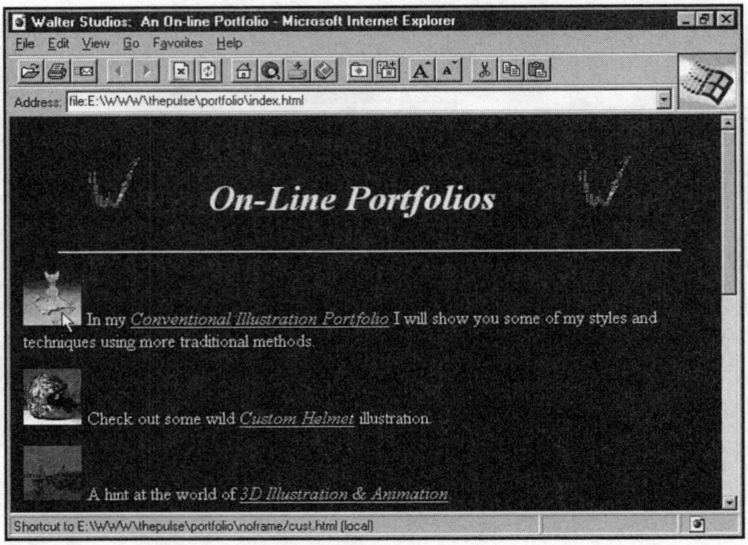

Figure 2.2
Viewing the same page through Internet Explorer 2.0, a non-JavaScript browser, produces an entirely different display. In fact, the only reason anything is displayed in this example is because the developer also designed a <NOFRAME> version of this page.

Alpha-beta Soup

In computer lingo, an *alpha* is a first test release of a program, well before it's considered "complete and ready" for the general public. Alphas are normally *very* buggy (error-prone) and may wreak havoc on your computer. After the programmer gets all the bugs out, the product becomes a *beta*, meaning that it *should* work correctly and the way the final (commercial or "public") release will.

Why even play with an alpha release? Alphas are sometimes the only chance other developers get to see and work with a program before it hits local computer store shelves. You use them to learn how a new technology will work, in hopes of being able to get going on your own support programs for the product so that, when the product finally ships, your programs will also be ready.

When using alphas, you need to understand that things may not work the way you expect them to—and how they work may well change from one alpha release to the next.

Navigator and Explorer aren't the only browsers in use on the Web (a visit to one of the popular online software sites will prove that). Other browsers often seen in cyberspace include

- Internet Explorer 2.0, the current Microsoft standard
- Mosaic, in a variety of forms—NCSA, Spry, Quarterdeck, and others

- America Online's Web interface, modeled after a browser formerly called InternetWorks
- CompuServe's Web interface, a Spry Mosaic derivative
- Lynx, a text-based browser that shows *only* text and is often used by people with slower Internet connections
- Arena, an HTML 3.0 browser provided by the World Wide Web Consortium
- MacWeb, a Macintosh browser
- HotJava, the Java-enabled browser from Sun Microsystems
- Other browsers that are derivatives of the preceding, many as "learning experiments" developed by Web programmers

Each of these browsers has its own pros and cons, but none support JavaScript. Figure 2.2 shows the page displayed in Figure 2.1 through one of these browsers (in this case, Internet Explorer 2.0). As you can see, the results are entirely different.

The moral of this story is, if you want to reach the largest possible base of Web surfers, you should develop and test your pages on several browsers, both JavaScript and non-JavaScript capable. Granted, it means that you literally need to duplicate your effort so the "browser challenged" can still enjoy your work, but the extra effort can be well worth it.

Platform-Related Limitations

Although JavaScript runs on all platforms for which Netscape Navigator exists (Windows, Macintosh, and UNIX), not all parts of JavaScript will run the same way (if at all). Two examples of this are as follows:

- Using *cookies* is a way to temporarily store additional information about a user with respect to a Web page, extending the customization capabilities of your site. Unfortunately, cookies work a little differently under Windows than they do on the Macintosh. (Cookies are covered in more detail in Chapter 16.)
- By using *random number generation*, you can create a card or dice game with JavaScript. One need of such a game is the ability to "pick" a card randomly from a deck, and a method is available that helps do this. However, this method works only on the UNIX platform. More information on this method (and how to work around it) is presented in Chapter 10, "Math Methods."

Other situations where the behavior of JavaScript differs between platforms will be mentioned as I come upon them.

Security-Related Limitations

Actually, a better description might be *restrictions* rather than *limitations*. The goal here is to protect data and prevent users from going where they're not wanted, not to curtail their natural surfing.

Network security is a popular catch phrase when it comes to the Net. We've all heard stories about hackers breaking a supposedly secure system and causing damage or stealing information. As the demand for more information (both in quantity and quality) increases on the Web, the potential for "security holes" will continue to pop up. Netscape, Sun, Microsoft, and others are all working to make the Internet as secure as possible (while at the same time trying not to stifle the flow of information), and JavaScript's development is no different.

JavaScript is designed to be "Web-safe," even safer than other, older methods of extending the Web (such as Perl scripting and CGI). To that end,

- JavaScript can't open, read, write, or save files on the user's computer. The only information it has access to is the information on the Web page on which it resides (or on other pages loaded at the same time, as in a frame).
- JavaScript can't open, read, write, or save files on the Web server. Although you can have JavaScript issue HTML commands (as shown in Chapter 3, "Basic Screen Output"), even HTML commands can't open files they aren't supposed to.
- JavaScript can't be used to create a "virus" that would damage anything on your computer. The worst that can happen is a poorly designed page would cause an error message to appear (and may require you to shut down the browser), but that's it.

In short, JavaScript exists within its own little world—the world of the Web page.

What You Need to Get Started

To enjoy the beauty (and creativity) of JavaScript-enabled Web pages, you need some basic hardware and software.

Hardware

Netscape recommends that you have one of the following system configurations to fully enjoy JavaScript:

- For 80×86 systems, a minimum of 8M of RAM. 12M to 16M is optimal, but you can manage on less. This is more a condition of the operating system (Windows 95, for example, prefers 12M or more, and Windows NT requires *at least* 12M) than of the browser itself. Macintosh users are encouraged to have at least 8M (again, primarily for the amount of overhead the operating system takes up).

- A monitor that can display 256 (or more) colors. Again, this is more a recommendation for the browser. Also, higher screen resolutions (800×600, 1,024×768, and so forth) allow more information to be displayed, but two "standards" (commonly used screen sizes) are found: 640×480 and 800×600.
- A proper hardware base, to surf the Internet at a fairly normal speed. The test systems for the examples in this book ranged from AMD586s to PowerPC 132s to an Intel P-166. None of the machines have less than 8M of memory, and two of them have more than 16M.
- Although using JavaScript reduces network overhead, I still recommend at least a 28.8kbps connection to the Net. You can surf at 14.4kbps, but you miss out on many of the new technologies (such as RealAudio, MPEG video, TrueSpeech, and QuickTime) out there.

Note: Although most new Web technologies will still work on connections slower than 28.8kbps, you'll have to wait much longer for the results. For example, a 14.4kpbs connection retrieves data at about 1K per second, meaning it would take 1,000 seconds (about 15 minutes) to download a 1M QuickTime movie (which, for those of you not familiar with QuickTime, is a *small* movie).

Software

A good, basic "JavaScript starter kit" to get you started is

- Netscape Navigator 2.0
- A simple text editor (such as NotePad, WordPad, TextPad, or EMACS)
- A flexible graphics program (such as PaintShop Pro)

To view JavaScript pages, all you really need (apart from an Internet connection) is a JavaScript-enabled browser (such as Navigator). To actually start *creating* your own pages, you'll need the other tools.

Now, there's no such thing as a "JavaScript editor." Although there are several good HTML editors (such as HotDog Pro, HoTMetaL, and WebEdit), none support JavaScript. You can always use one of them to create the initial look for your pages, but when you start writing JavaScript, it's a good idea to switch to a standard, plain ASCII (text) editor.

Also, to edit graphics, create animations, manipulate sounds, and do other multimedia Web stuff, a graphics program and sound editor would be excellent additions to your kit.

These programs (and many more) either come with your operating system or are available online. A good place to look for tools is **http://www.shareware.com/**, where you'll find a massive collection of software, including animators, sound editors, and so forth.

Summary

Although JavaScript is a powerful extension to the Web, it's not without its limitations. Currently, only Netscape Navigator and Internet Explorer support it—even then, only Navigator supports it fully. JavaScript is a secure language, and is prevented from directly interacting with anything on the user's computer outside of its Web page. Still, all that withstanding, JavaScript gives you added control over the presentation of information within the context of the World Wide Web.

Review Questions

The answers to the review questions are in Appendix D.

1. What makes JavaScript unique among current Web technologies?
2. What's a plug-in?
3. What browsers support JavaScript? What are some of the browsers that don't?
4. What's an *alpha release*? A *beta release*?
5. What's an example of a platform-related limitation of JavaScript?
6. How is JavaScript a "secure" environment?
7. What hardware do you need to run JavaScript?
8. What's a good set of software packages for a "JavaScript starter kit"?

Exercises

1. Install both Netscape Navigator 2.0 and Internet Explorer 2.0 on your system. Look for JavaScript sites on the Web and view them from both browsers. Observe the differences.
2. If you want, download a copy of Internet Explorer 3.0 (at Microsoft's Web site, **http://www.microsoft.com/**) and surf the Web with it. Notice how it handles (or doesn't) JavaScript-enabled sites.
3. Collect and install the software listed for the "JavaScript starter kit."

CHAPTER 3

Basic Screen Output

In the previous chapters, you were introduced to what JavaScript is, where it came from, and how it integrates into the Web's "scheme of things." You learned that JavaScript is interpreted by the browser, runs on several different platforms (with some limitations), has a collection of built-in objects, and can react to input from the user (through *events*). At this point, you should have enough of JavaScript's *background* and are itching to start *using* it. So let's start scripting by using JavaScript to display text within the browser.

The <SCRIPT> Tag

Within an HTML document, JavaScript is bracketed by a `<SCRIPT>...</SCRIPT>` tag pair. You can place `<SCRIPT>` tags either within the `<HEAD>` tag, the `<BODY>` tag, or both (you may incorporate multiple `<SCRIPT>` tags within the same document). Scripts within the `<HEAD>` tag are loaded before the rest of the page loads, making this an excellent place to put your JavaScript functions (to ensure that they are available for the other parts of your document). Placing scripts within the `<BODY>` tag makes it possible to dynamically create parts of your document (displaying, for example, the time of day).

The syntax of the `<SCRIPT>` tag is

```
<SCRIPT LANGUAGE="JavaScript">
// JavaScript code goes here
</SCRIPT>
```

As you can see, it consists of two parts:

- The `<SCRIPT>` tag proper, which alerts that browser's interpreter that a script is embedded in this tag.

- The LANGUAGE attribute, which identifies the scripting language used within the tag. Why do you need this? Well, Microsoft, in addition to supporting JavaScript, is currently developing a scripting language similar to Visual Basic, called VBScript.

> **Note:** Although Perl is also a scripting language, Perl scripts are totally different animals. Perl scripts can't be embedded within <SCRIPT> tags.

A third attribute—SRC—may become available to the <SCRIPT> tag in the future, although it currently isn't supported by any browser. SRC allows Web-page designers to call external script files (files on the server, not imbedded in the HTML page). These files should have the .JS extension, to show that they contain JavaScript code.

Creating Your First Script

Let's start with the first script. In keeping with programming tradition, let's start by saying "hello" to the Web world with the help of JavaScript (see listing 3.1).

Listing 3.1

```
<html>
<head>
<script language="JavaScript">
document.write("Welcome to the world of JavaScript!<br>");
</script>
</head>
<body>
</body>
</html>
```

But wait! There aren't any tags or text within the <body> tags. Shouldn't this page be blank?

On a browser that can't handle JavaScript, it *would* be blank, but as you can see in figure 3.1, the text in the document.write() function is displayed as though it were typed within the <BODY> tag. This is because document.write() tells the browser to place everything between the quotes on the page.

That wasn't so difficult, was it? Experiment with document.write() to get a feel for what you can do with it. As a suggestion, the <BR> tag in the output line should give you an idea that you can put other HTML tags within the displayed string. Try some others and see what happens.

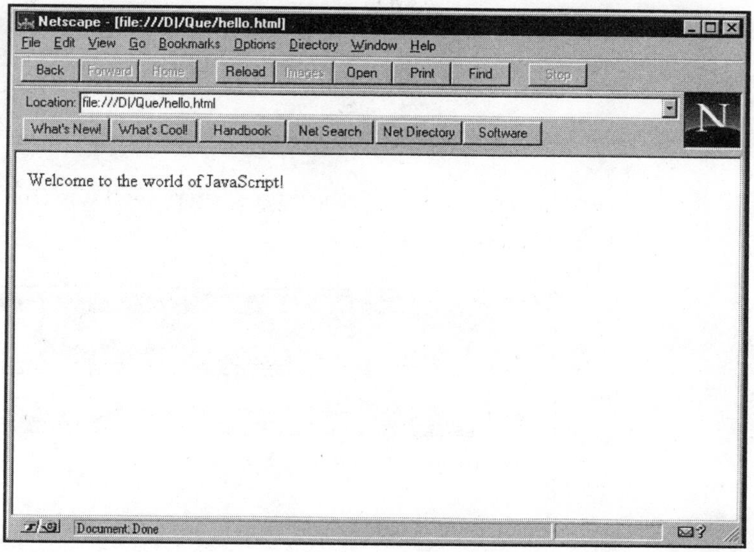

Figure 3.1
Saying "hello" to the Web world with JavaScript.

Not-So-Basic Output

Why would you want to use JavaScript when standard HTML takes a lot less space? For one thing, JavaScript allows you to construct text to display that includes values from variables that can be filled in by the user (see listing 3.2).

Listing 3.2

```
<html>
<head>
<script language="JavaScript">
var first = window.prompt("Please enter your name:","");
document.write("Welcome to the world of JavaScript, "
➥+ first + ".<br>");
</script>
</head>
</html>
```

When this page is first loaded, the `window.prompt()` command causes an input prompt dialog to appear, asking the user to type his or her name (see fig. 3.2).

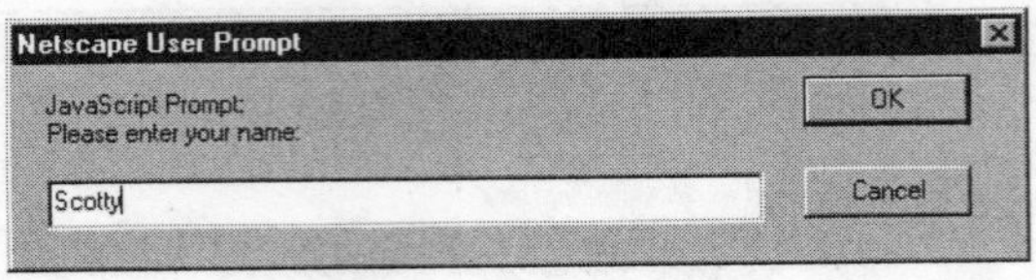

Figure 3.2
Using `window.prompt()` to get input from the user.

After the user clicks OK, the page is displayed with his or her name added to the text (see fig. 3.3).

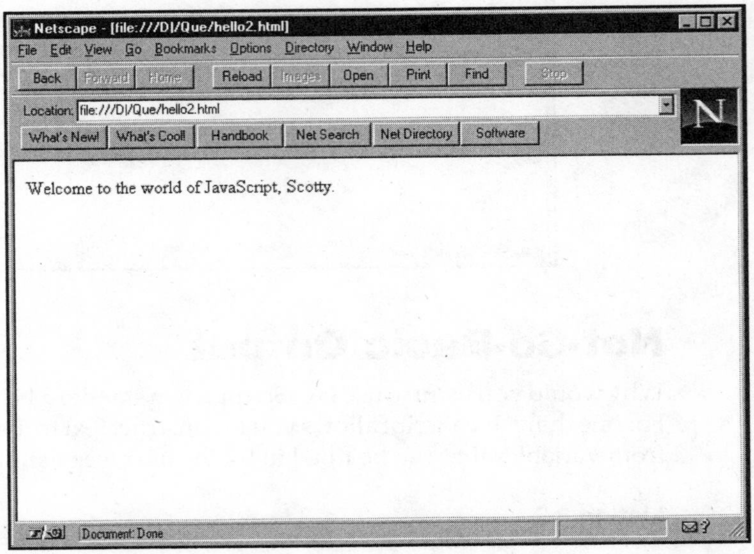

Figure 3.3
A page customized by the user's input.

By now, you should be beginning to see possibilities for JavaScript in your mind. You see interactive Web sites. You see dynamically created pages.

But not everyone uses a browser that supports JavaScript. As mentioned in Chapter 1, "Introducing JavaScript," only two browsers are designed to handle JavaScripts (Netscape Navigator 2.0 and Internet Explorer 3.0). So what does a page look like to a browser without JavaScript support (Internet Explorer 2.0, for example)? It looks like figure 3.4.

Not so pretty, is it? So how do you get around this? Simply place the script code within comment tags, as in listing 3.3.

Figure 3.4

If a browser doesn't support JavaScript, the program statements are interpreted as plain HTML text for formatting and display.

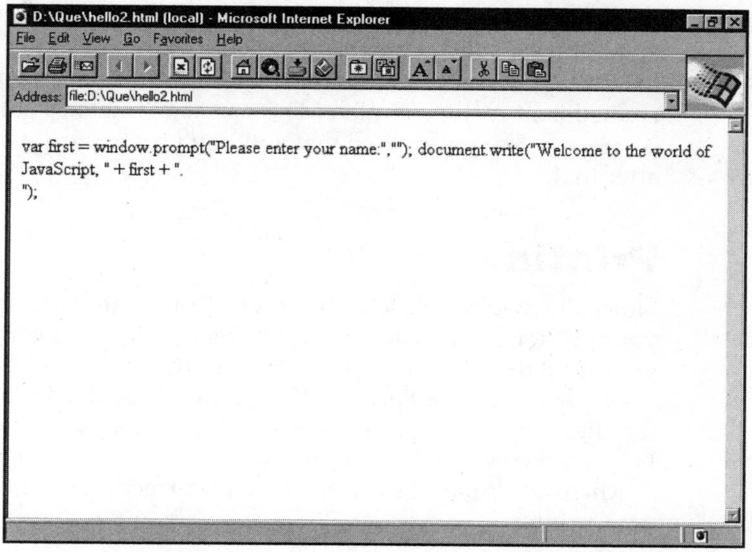

Listing 3.3

```
<html>
<head>
<script language="JavaScript">
<!--
var first=window.prompt("Please enter your name:","");
document.write("Welcome to the world of JavaScript, "
➥+ first + ".<br>");
//-->
</script>
</head>
</html>
```

When the other browsers read the comment tags, they should ignore all the text within the tags. JavaScript browsers also ignore the text (as far as the display side of the browser is concerned), but it's still downloaded, and then passed to the JavaScript interpreter for processing.

> **Note:** The ending comment tag line must start with `//` because this line also falls within the JavaScript interpreter's domain and the interpreter must also be told that it's a comment. Within JavaScript, comment lines start with `//`.

Also notice that a `<br>` tag immediately follows the text you want to display. Why is that there? Well, after the browser writes your data stream (the text you want to display), it doesn't close the stream. Until this stream is closed, the page you created isn't really complete. The `<br>` tag "finalizes" the page. You can also use `document.close()`, provided that you don't try to output anymore text to the screen after that.

Printing

Normally, you can click the browser's Print button to output the screen contents to your printer, or you can use the File menu's Save As command to save the code to your local drive. JavaScript is a bit different.

Navigator 2.0 can't print HTML output generated by JavaScript. If you try to save the file, rather than get the HTML as you may want to, you'll actually save the JavaScript code used to create a page.

Microsoft Internet Explorer 3.0 will correctly print JavaScript-generated text to your printer.

Summary

JavaScript is embedded within an HTML document using the `<SCRIPT>` tag. The tag currently takes one (required) attribute, `LANGUAGE`, which defines the scripting language that's used within the tag. `<SCRIPT>` tags can be placed anywhere within the document.

Displaying information to the user can be done by using the `document.write()` function. With it, both plain text and HTML tags can be displayed, as well as more complex configurations. To get information from the user, use `window.prompt()` to pop up a dialog box and ask for input.

Review Questions

The answers to the review questions are in Appendix D.

1. What HTML tag is used to identify JavaScript? What is its syntax?
2. Why does the `<SCRIPT>` tag need the `LANGUAGE` attribute?
3. What will the `SRC` attribute be used for?
4. What does `document.write()` do?
5. How can you get input from the user with JavaScript?
6. How can you hide your code from browsers that don't support JavaScript?
7. What have you learned about printing?

Exercises

1. Practice using the `document.write()` statement to make your own pages.
2. Try to use `window.prompt()` to build a more personal Web site.
3. Feeling more adventurous? Grab a copy of a browser that doesn't support JavaScript (such as Internet Explorer 2.0 or Mosaic) and experiment with creating a page that displays *something* (although it may be something different) on both JavaScript and non-JavaScript browsers.

CHAPTER 4

Understanding Events

I mention in Chapter 1 that JavaScript is an event-driven language. To understand that concept, let's look at events in general.

Events in Nature

Every day, as you wake up and head to work, school, or play, you bump into events along the way. These events affect how your days go. Events don't have to be huge or important to have an effect on you. A man running late for work leaves his coffee cup on the roof of his car as he gets in. He takes off down the interstate, and his coffee cup falls onto the highway and breaks. An hour later, you're on your way to the mall, and you run over the shards from the broken coffee cup. Your tire is punctured, and you have to call a tow truck to come repair your flat tire.

In this example, you had planned on going to the mall. But because of some events that you had little or no control over, your plans were changed. In the same way, when you program, you must take into account all the possible events that might occur while your application or script is running.

Events in JavaScript

JavaScript is an event-driven language. You use events (such as a mouse click or a button press) to control user interaction with your application. Conventional programs operate differently. A conventional program performs its code sequentially. Consider the following function:

> **Note:** A *function* is a collection of program statements that are grouped together because combined, they perform a particular task.

```
function print_out(){
   var n= "";
   while ( !(confirm("Want to quit?")) {
   document.write("Hello, Internet Community!");
   }
}
```

A program that wanted the user to confirm the printing of a phrase could use this function to gather the user's input. However, the program would be trapped in the `print_out()` function, waiting for a correct response. While there, you can't have any other operations going on. All other input and operations are put on hold until the user answers the question. Until the user gives the answer you expect, he will continue to be prompted.

A better approach would be to use one of the JavaScript event handlers to activate the following function:

```
function print_out(){
   document.write("Hello, Internet Community!");
}
```

JavaScript event handlers are represented as special attributes that modify the behavior of the HTML tag they're attached to. Event-handler attributes all start with `On` and identify the various events that can occur (for example, `OnLoad`, `OnClick`, and `OnMouseOver`). The value associated with the handler can be a sequence of JavaScript statements or a JavaScript function call.

In this version of the function, you haven't tied up the processing with one function. By using an event, users tell you when they're ready to perform the function.

JavaScript Event Handlers

JavaScript now has nine event handlers to interface your script with system activities and user responses or actions. These nine handlers can be divided into two categories: system events and mouse events.

System Events

System events don't require user interaction in order to be activated. For example, you can signal that a page has finished loading, that a page is about to be unloaded, or that a period of time has elapsed.

OnLoad

This event, activated after your HTML page (and all its parts) is *completely* loaded, is usually associated with the <BODY> or <FRAMESET> tag. When you're dealing with frames, it's often necessary to make sure that some panes have been loaded before others are updated (if, for instance, one frame contains a form whose fields are referenced by another frame). Because of the nature of the Net, there's no way to guarantee what document will load when, but you can be certain that `OnLoad` will be executed only after a frameset is finished loading.

For example, listing 4.1 presents a page that loads, displays the text within the <BODY> tag, and then opens an alert dialog box with a special message.

Listing 4.1

```
<html>
<head>
<script language="JavaScript">
<!-- hide from non-JavaScript browsers
function welcome(){
   window.alert("Welcome to JavaScript by Example!");
   window.alert("We hope you enjoy your visit with us today.");
}
// end hide -->
</script>
</head>
<body OnLoad="welcome()">
<h3>Chapter 4: OnLoad</h3>
<hr>
This text has already been written, and you may even have had a
chance to read it. But a window will soon open, welcoming you to
the page.
<p>
The OnLoad event activated the welcome() function after the entire
page had loaded.
</body>
</html>
```

OnUnload

The `OnUnload` event is useful for "cleaning up" after yourself. In the course of visiting your site, a user may have two or three windows opened by your scripts that need to be closed. By using the `OnUnload` handler, you can close all those open windows as the user leaves your site, you can wish them a good day, or both, as shown in listing 4.2.

Listing 4.2

```
<html>
<head>
<script language="JavaScript">
<!-- hide from non-JavaScript browsers
function welcome(){
   window.alert("Welcome to JavaScript by Example!");
   window.alert("We hope you enjoy your visit with us today.");
}
function goodbye(){
   window.alert("Thank you for stopping by. Please come again.");
}
// end hide -->
</script>
</head>
<body OnLoad="welcome()" OnUnload="goodbye()">
<h3>Chapter 4: OnLoad</h3>
<hr>
This text has already been written, and you may even have had a
chance to read it. But a window will soon open, welcoming you to
the page.
<p>
The OnLoad event activated the welcome() function after the entire
page had loaded.
</body>
</html>
```

In this code sample, the `OnLoad` event runs the `welcome()` function. When the visitor is ready to move to another page (by clicking a link or by using the browser's Forward or Back buttons), the `OnUnload` event displays the `goodbye()` function (see fig. 4.1). Later, you'll learn how to use the `OnLoad` and `OnUnload` events together to communicate between windows.

Figure 4.1

Results of the `OnUnload` script.

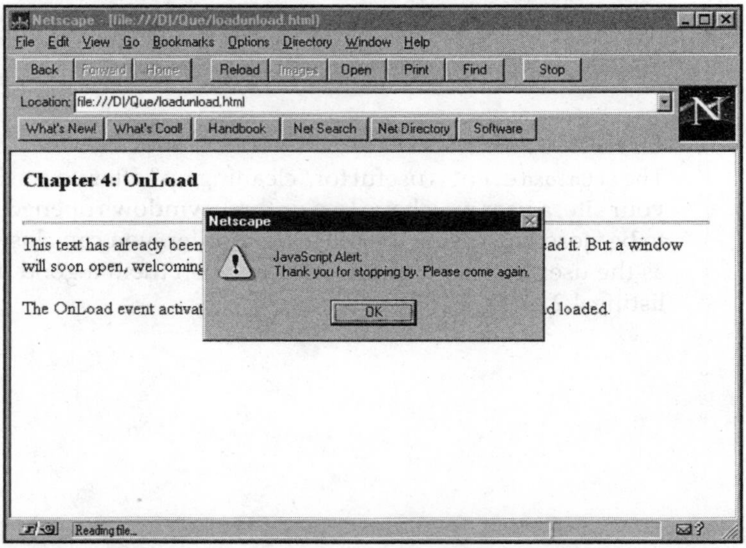

Mouse Events

Mouse events, as their name implies, require user (mouse) interaction in order to be triggered. Because you're building an interactive interface for your HTML pages, you'll be using these handlers most often.

OnClick

The most basic of the mouse events is the `OnClick` handler. This event is activated whenever you click an object that accepts such an event. Objects accepting an `OnClick` event are links, check boxes, and buttons (including submit, reset, and radio buttons).

Listing 4.3 gives an example of a simple form that responds to the user clicking one of the form components. Clicking a button, check box, or radio button on the form results in an alert dialog box being displayed (see fig. 4.2).

Listing 4.3

```
<html>
<head>
<script language="JavaScript">
<!-- hide from non-JavaScript browsers
// I-am_active is just a small function to demonstrate our point.
function i_am_active(){
   window.alert("An onClick event has been activated!");
}
// end hide -->
</script>
</head>

<body>
<h2>Chapter 4: onClick Events</h2>
<hr>
<a href="javascript:i_am_active()">Standard Link</a>
<form method="POST" enctype=application/x-www-form-urlencoded>
<input name="radio1" type="RADIO" OnClick="i_am_active()">Radio
Button<br>
<input name="checkbox1" type="CHECKBOX" OnClick="i_am_active()">
CheckBox<br>
<input name="button1" type="BUTTON" OnClick="i_am_active()"
value="Standard Button"><br>
<input type="RESET" OnClick="i_am_active()"><br>
<input type="SUBMIT" OnClick="i_am_active()"><br>
</form>
</body>
</html>
```

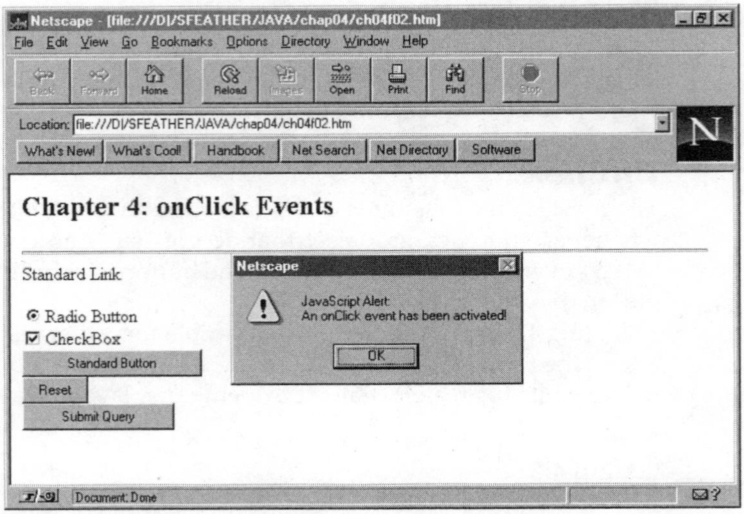

Figure 4.2
Results of the `OnClick` script.

Notice how `OnClick` is used in an object's input statement:

```
<input name="" type="BUTTON" OnClick="function()">
```

The event is placed directly into the `<input>` HTML tag.

OnFocus

Focus occurs when an object becomes the item in focus—or the "center of attention," so to speak. This happens when the user clicks or tabs to the particular object. If a user can enter data into a particular object (or change the selection in the case of list boxes), that object has the focus. The `OnFocus` event can be used only with `text`, `textarea`, `password`, and `select` objects.

> **Note:** `text`, `textarea`, and `password` objects are defined by the `<INPUT>` tag with the `TYPE` attribute set to one of those three objects. Select objects have their own tag (`<SELECT>`).

Listing 4.4 shows a simple form with first and last name fields. The `OnFocus` event is attached to the Last Name field and displays a dialog box when the user enters that field (see fig. 4.3).

Listing 4.4

```
<html>
<title></title>
<head>
```

```
<script language="JavaScript">
<!-- hide from non-JavaScript browsers
function am_focus(){
   window.alert("'Last Name' is in focus.");
}
// end hide -->
</script>
</head>
<body>
<h2>Chapter 4: OnFocus</h2>
<hr>
<form method="POST" enctype=application/x-www-form-urlencoded>
First Name: <input name="text1" type="TEXT">
Last Name: <input name="text2" type="TEXT" OnFocus="am_focus()">
</form>
</body>
</html>
```

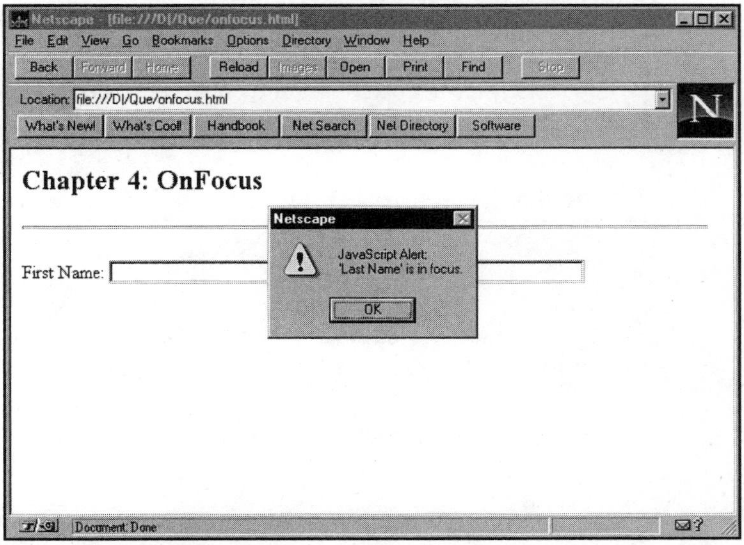

Figure 4.3

This alert box appears when the Last Name field (covered by the alert box) is in focus.

Notice the `OnFocus` handler in the `<input>` tag for `text2`. When that object gets the focus, it will activate the `am_focus()` function.

> **Caution:** Be careful when calling a function with `OnFocus`. It may just get caught in an endless loop, as this example did.

> I wanted to show the alert window when focus was given to the Last Name field. However, I failed to take into account that once on focus, it would stay there until removed. Focus couldn't be removed until the alert window was cleared, causing a loop. A setup such as this one on a page would force visitors to close and restart Navigator so they could continue surfing.
>
> The easiest way to prevent this is to avoid using any JavaScript statements in the `OnFocus` event that would cause the field to lose focus (such as opening a prompt window or alert dialog).

OnBlur

Blur occurs when an object is no longer in focus. This can be caused by switching to another window or application, or by clicking or tabbing to another object (see listing 4.5). As the reciprocal of the `OnFocus` event, the `OnBlur` event also applies only to the `text`, `textarea`, `password`, and `select` areas.

> **Note:** The `OnBlur` event doesn't really blur the object visually. It's just the terminology Netscape chose, and could be thought of as "OnUnFocus."

Listing 4.5

```
<html>
<title></title>
<head>
<script language="JavaScript">
<!-- hide from non-JavaScript browsers
function add_it(){
   document.form1.full.value = (document.form1.first.value + " "
   ➥ + document.form1.last.value);
}
// end hide -->
</script>
</head>
<body>
<h2>Chapter 4: OnBlur</h2>
<hr>
<form name="form1" method="POST"
enctype=application/x-www-form-urlencoded>
First Name: <input name="first" type="TEXT" OnBlur="add_it()"><br>
Last Name: <input name="last" type="TEXT" OnBlur="add_it()"><br>
<hr>
Full Name: <input name="full" type="TEXT">
</form>
</body>
</html>
```

In this example, you need to add the first and last names together to form the full name. Whenever focus is removed from the first or last object, the value of `full` changes.

OnChange

The `OnChange` event is activated whenever an object has lost focus *and* its value has been changed. This event applies only to `select`, `text`, `textarea`, and `password` objects. `OnChange` can be very useful when you want to calculate a running total of a number of values, as shown in listing 4.6. Moving from one field to the next (and changing the text in the fields) generates `OnChange` events, which fire the calculation function (see fig. 4.4).

Listing 4.6

```
<html>
<head>
<script language="JavaScript">
<!-- hide from non-JavaScript browsers
function calculate(){
   window.alert("Evaluating the data.");
   document.names.total.value = document.names.name1.value + " " +
   ➥document.names.name2.value + " " + document.names.name3.value
}
// end hide -->
</script>
</head>
<body>
<h3>Chapter 4: OnChange()</h3>
<form name="names" method="POST"
enctype=application/x-www-form-urlencoded>
First Name:<input name="name1" type="TEXT" size="10,1"
OnChange="calculate()"><br>
Second Name:<input name="name2" type="TEXT" size="10,1"
OnChange="calculate()"><br>
Last Name :<input name="name3" type="TEXT" size="10,1"
OnChange="calculate()"><br>
Total: <input name="total" type="TEXT" size="35,1">
</form>
</body>
</html>
```

Tip: `OnChange` is more economical than `OnBlur` when you're calculating totals in a form. To see what I mean, add the following line to the example for `OnBlur` anywhere in the `add_it()` function:

```
window.alert("I'm in the function again!");
```

> Now notice that every time you blur an object, you find yourself back in the function. That's because `OnBlur` always activates its associated function. `OnChange` activates only if the value has changed.

Figure 4.4

Whenever the text in one of the input fields is changed, `OnChange` causes `calculate()` to run and update the Total field.

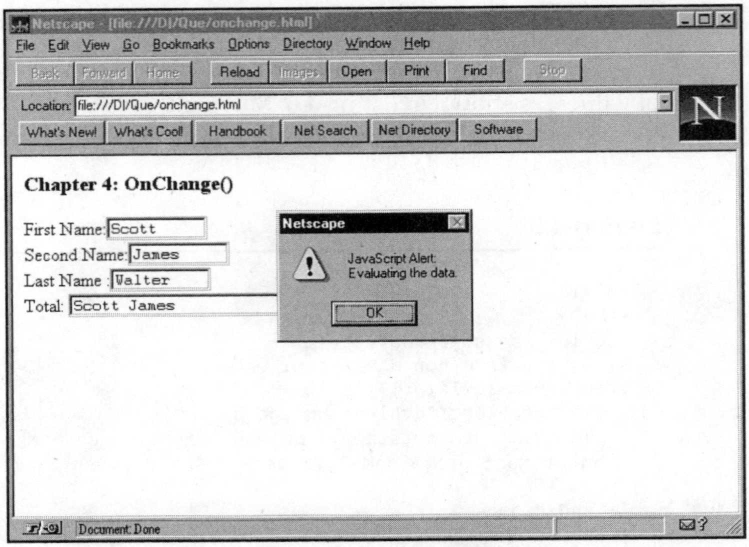

OnSelect

`OnSelect` applies only to `text`, `textarea`, and `password` objects, and is executed when the user *selects* (highlights) part of the text in one of those object types. The syntax is very similar to the `OnBlur` event:

```
<input name="myobject" Type="TEXT" OnSelect="function()">
```

OnSubmit

`OnSubmit` is used with the `form` object. Many times, data that has been entered into a form needs to be parsed, manipulated, or checked for errors before being transmitted to the server. `OnSubmit` allows the capturing and, if needed, the stopping of a form submission. This is accomplished by having the function called from the `OnSubmit` handler return true or false. If the handler function returns false, the form won't be submitted. Listing 4.7 is an example of how this can be done.

Listing 4.7

```
<html>
<head>
<script language="JavaScript">
<!-- hide from non-JavaScript browsers
function check(){
   if (document.num_form.num1.value.length == 5) {
      window.alert("Thank you for typing only 5 characters.");
      return true;
   } else {
      window.alert("Enter 5 characters please.");
      return false;
   }
}
// end hide -->
</script>
</head>
<body>
<h3>Chapter 4: OnSubmit</h3>
<hr>

<form name="num_form" method="POST"
enctype=application/x-www-form-urlencoded
OnSubmit="return check(this)">
Enter five characters: <input name="num1" type="TEXT" size="20,1">
<br>
<input type="SUBMIT">
</form>
</body>
</html>
```

By using a few methods that I'll describe later (in Chapter 11, "String Methods"), you can capture a form submission and check it for correctness. If it fails the check, the form isn't submitted.

OnMouseOver

The `OnMouseOver` event is very "soft," meaning that it doesn't require a mouse click to activate it. When the mouse pointer crosses over an object, the event is triggered. You can use the `OnMouseOver` event to explain links or buttons. Notice in listing 4.8 how the `OnMouseOver` event changes the text in the alert window shown in figure 4.5.

Listing 4.8

```
<html>
<head>
<script language="JavaScript">
<!-- hide from non-JavaScript browsers
```

continues

Listing 4.8 Continued

```
function explain1(){
   window.alert("This is a link to the White House.");
}
function explain2(){
   window.alert("This is a link to the QUE Home Page.");
}
function explain3(){
   window.alert("This is a link to the Author's Home Page.");
}
// end hide -->
</script>
</head>
<body>
<h3>Chapter 4: OnMouseOver</h3>
<hr>
<a href="http://www.mcp.com" OnMouseOver="explain2()">
Que Publishing</a><br><br>
<a href="http://www.whitehouse.gov" OnMouseOver="explain1()">
White House</a><br><br>
<a href="http://www.lobosoft.com" OnMouseOver="explain3()">
LoboSoft Software</a><br><br>
</body>
</html>
```

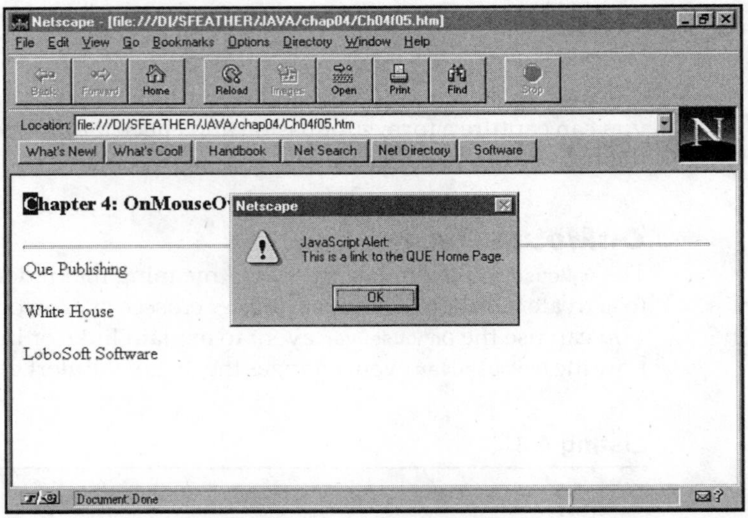

Figure 4.5

Depending on what link the user's mouse is over, the alert window displays a different string.

Summary

JavaScript is *event-driven,* meaning that it responds to things that happen or change in a Web page. Mouse clicks, button presses, and entering text in a field all constitute events, as do loading and unloading pages. Events are trapped in JavaScript through *event handlers,* functions or code segments that are activated by the appropriate event tag.

JavaScript has two types of events: system events and mouse events. System events happen without user intervention, whereas mouse events require the user to do something to cause them.

Review Questions

The answers to the review questions are in Appendix D.

1. What is an event?
2. How many events are now available to JavaScript programmers?
3. The `OnClick` handler can be applied to how many types of objects?
4. How do you know whether an object is in focus?
5. Where would you use an `OnUnload` event handler?
6. The `OnSubmit` handler can be used with which object type?
7. Which represents the more economical event handler—`OnBlur` or `OnChange`?
8. What danger can there be in using the `OnFocus` event handler improperly?
9. What could you use the `OnSubmit` event for?

Exercises

1. By using the `OnMouseOver` event and the example functions, have a function display text on-screen when you pass the mouse pointer over a button.
2. Find two uses for the `OnFocus` and `OnBlur` events.
3. Use the `OnMouseOver` event handler to build your own HTML page with explanations.

Part II

Programming Basics and JavaScript Constructs

CHAPTER 5

Programming Basics

This chapter introduces some basic programming skills. Even for the most experienced programmer, this chapter might give a new and interesting perspective on the basics. This chapter focuses attention on names, variables, and their places in programming.

Names: More than a Title

Everything in our life has a specific name and value to us. A name gives us a method of identifying an object. In our everyday lives, we call items by their "names." The parents of two girls would not go around calling their children Daughter Number One and Daughter Number Two. Instead, they would give each child a name, such as Jennifer or Amy. A name gives the person or object an identity.

Even in programming, names must be given to each object. As a programmer, you can use just about anything as a name. There are only a few restrictions on naming an object. The main restriction is the list of 43 reserved words, located in Appendix B. These words can't be used as names because JavaScript uses them internally. Other important restrictions are covered in the following sections.

No Spaces Allowed

You can't put a space in the middle of a name. A space in the name would cause the interpreter to read the name as two words, thus confusing the interpreter and causing errors.

No Hyphens Allowed

You also can't place a hyphen (-) in any part of a name. To you, it may represent a space between words. The computer, however, sees it as subtracting the first word from the second word. If the name was typed as *gross-adjusted*, the computer would subtract the value of *adjusted* from the value of *gross*. The best way to separate two words for a name is to uppercase the first letter of the second word or put an underscore between them:

```
addNumbers          gross_adjusted          FirstSecond
```

As you can see, the underscore and the uppercase letter stand out, making the name easier to read and understand.

> **Note:** The hyphen isn't the only punctuation character not allowed in a name. Periods, commas, quotation marks, questions marks…*none* of them can be in a name.

Must Start with a Letter

Although you can use digits within a name, it *must* start with a letter. For example,

```
time1
convert2HTML
```

are valid names, but

```
2ndLetter
```

is not.

Variables

Do you remember your locker in high school? At first it looked so big that you could fit all your books in it, plus a couple of other necessities. Then you went to gym class and found out that your gym locker was half the size of the first locker. There was just enough room to stuff a pair of gym shorts and shoes in it.

The gym locker was required to hold only your gym essentials; the regular locker was designed to hold your books and notebooks. Variables can be designed the same way. Variables are responsible for storing data. They're a part of every programming language and should be easy to understand, where no explanation is necessary. In your programs, variables can vary in value, depending on the kind of data they hold. Like objects, variables need to be named to differentiate each other. A variable holds data on which a program operates. The variable's name represents the value of data stored somewhere in computer memory when the program runs.

Naming Variables

As discussed earlier in this chapter, variables have the same basic naming restrictions, with only a few exceptions. Because variables can change in value, you need to understand what you want your program to accomplish. Some examples of names for variables are

```
x = 14          money = paid          Saturday = 7
```

As you can see, all you have to do to name a variable is to identify the value, insert an equal sign (=), and then decide on a name. It's very important to keep track of the names—otherwise, not only will you get confused, so will the computer. A very crucial part of a name is that it should be fairly descriptive of the variable's purpose.

> **Note:** Don't use the names of other programs or functions for any names in your programs. The computer will accept them only as functions. Once you create a function, JavaScript considers the function's name a reserved word.

Declaring Variables

Variables must either be declared as global or local. In the past, most of your programming probably used local variables, but both are useful. The only difference between the two in JavaScript is where they're placed in the code. You can declare variables before or at the same time you assign a value to them.

Local Variables

Local variables are defined inside the body of a function. Local variables are safer than global variables because they offer themselves only to the functions in which they're defined. Outside the function, the variables don't exist. An example of using local variables is as follows:

```
function add(val) {
   var a = val + 10;
   ...
}
function subtract(val) {
   var b = val - 10;
   ...
}
```

In this example, `a` is "seen" only by the `add()` function, and `b` is seen only by `subtract()`.

Global Variables

Global variables are defined outside all function bodies in a JavaScript file. This type of variable can be used all through the program. Extending the example of local variables, here is an example of global variables:

```
var total = 0;
function add(val) {
   var a = val + 10;
   ...
   total = total + a;
}
function subtract(val) {
   var b = val - 10;
   ...
   total = total - b;
}
```

The variable `total` is defined outside both the `add()` and `subtract()` functions, so it's accessible by both (as well as any other code in the file).

> **Note:** For a more detailed description of functions, see Chapter 7, "Understanding Objects."

Scope of Variables

A variable's *scope* refers to its visibility and life—meaning, what the variable has access to and for how long. The scope of local variables is very limited. Local variables are useful only within the function in which they're defined. Global variables, on the other hand, are very visible in the program. They have a part in the whole program, even if the function changes.

Figure 5.1 is an example of a scope. As you can see, the large circle has access to everything within. The smaller objects have access only within themselves.

Figure 5.1
The scope of the large circle in reference to the other objects.

Types of Values

When you declare a variable, a *type* (kind of variable) is created. There are four different variable types that JavaScript recognizes: numbers, logicals (Boolean), strings, and nulls. Exactly what type a variable is depends on the data you assign to that variable.

Numeric (Numbers)

This type of variable is quite easy to understand. A numeric value would be any number (positive or negative). For example, 53, 2.3875, or –23 would be considered numbers. Here are some examples:

```
Gross = 3000
```

or

```
x = 3
```

Logical (Boolean)

By the term *logical value*, I mean that JavaScript uses the literal words `true` and `false` to represent it. Throughout this book, this type of value is referred to as *Boolean*. The following is an example of the Boolean value:

```
{
form.display.value=Math.PI;
computed = true
}
```

Strings

A string value requires a set of quotation marks to identify it as a string. To declare a string value, all you have to do is type a double quotation mark (`"`), the word, and then the closing quotation mark. So the finished product would look something like this: `"Goodmorning"`, `"Gross"`, or `"First_Last"`. The following is how a string might look in JavaScript:

```
Document.form.button_name.value="new_label"
```

Note: Numbers can also be a string, but no arithmetic operations can be performed to such variable types. This concept will be discussed further in Chapter 6, "More Programming Basics."

Null Value

`null` is a special keyword denoting a null, or no value. The following is an example of a null value:

```
<input type="button" value='0'>
onClick="addChar(this.form.display,'0')>
```

Literals

The word *literal,* in the programming sense, means data that doesn't change. No matter what happens, this name will always remain the same. Another word for literal is *constant*.

In JavaScript, literals are represented the same way that variable values are represented. For example, 43, 7.98, and `"hello"` could be considered literals. Literals also can be divided into four different categories: integer, floating-point integer, Boolean, and string.

Integers

You can express integers in decimal, hexadecimal, or octal format. A decimal integer literal consists of digits without a leading zero. An octal integer literal contains a leading zero and includes only the digits 0–7. A hexadecimal integer literal has a leading `0x`. The remaining integers include digits (0–9) and the letters a–f and A–F.

Floating-Point Integers

A floating-point integer (or *decimal*) must have one of the following parts: a decimal integer, a decimal point, a fraction, or an exponent. (By the term *exponent*, I mean `e` or `E` followed by an integer.) Some examples of floating-point integers follow:

2.5641   –4.1E12

*.8e12   *6E-12

An example of a floating exponent is

```
{
    form.display.value=Math.E;
    computed = true
}
```

Boolean Literals

A Boolean literal has two literal values: `true` and `false`.

String Literals

A string literal contains zero or more characters enclosed in double (`"`) or single (`'`) quotation marks (it doesn't matter which type of quotation mark is used). For example, the following would be considered string literals:

```
"1234"            'good'
'Bad'             "hello"
```

There are also special characters allowed in JavaScript string literals. They are as follows:

- `\b` indicates a backspace
- `\f` indicates a form feed
- `\n` indicates a new-line character
- `\r` indicates a carriage return
- `\t` indicates a tab character

Here's an example of how these are used:

```
var str = "Here's one line\nAnd the next line";
```

This creates a string with a new line embedded within it.

Summary

Variables are how JavaScript programs store information for manipulation. They're identified by their *names*, which are words that represent them in the JavaScript program. JavaScript has certain restrictions on the creation of variable (and function) names, and divides variables into four basic types: numeric, logical, string, and null. Variables can be global or local, depending on where they're defined within the program.

Review Questions

The answers to the review questions can be found in Appendix D.

1. Name three characters that aren't permitted in a variable's name.
2. Where do you declare a global variable? a local variable?
3. How many data types does JavaScript support?
4. Give an example of a special character you can use within a string.

Exercises

1. Practice naming variables descriptively (to store such items as an address, phone number, and invoice total).
2. Practice declaring variables and giving them a value at the same time.

CHAPTER 6

More Programming Basics

It's time to brush up on your high school algebra, because a great deal of JavaScript involves mathematical equations. If you're feeling a little rusty with your math, don't panic. This chapter looks at some basic math principles, such as expressions and operators, and then tours through some of the "special" words that JavaScript uses to extend its abilities beyond just adding and subtracting.

Expressions: When Does 1+5=15?

An *expression* is a set of literals, variables, and operators that evaluates to single value. The value can be a number, a string, or a Boolean value. For example, `23+57` is an expression that evaluates to 80, whereas `5>32` is an expression (a *Boolean* expression) that evaluates to false (5 is not greater than 32).

> **Note:** A *Boolean value* is something that can have only one of two possible values—"true" or "false." This kind of value was named after George Boole, an 18th century British mathematician who developed a method of using algebra to represent logic as equations (*Boolean algebra*).
>
> In JavaScript, virtually any variable (or expression) can be looked at in a "Boolean" way, according to the following rules:
>
> - If a value (or expression) is numeric and equals zero, it is considered "false."
> - If a value (or expression) is a string and is "empty" (no characters) or equals "null," it's considered "false." (Check out Chapter 11, "String Methods," for more information on null values.)
> - If neither of the preceding conditions is met, the value (or expression) is considered "true."

Expressions can also assign a value to a variable, as in `y=4`, which assigns 4 to y; `b=a`, which assigns the value of a to b; or `result=153+44`, which assigns 197 to `result`. The last example is one of an expression that evaluates both to a value (197 on the right side of the equal sign) and then assigns that value to the variable `result` on the left.

> **Note:** The variable `result` is an example of the kinds of *variable names* (words or strings you can use for variables) that JavaScript supports. You aren't limited to single characters. You can use words, provided that they aren't *reserved words* (discussed later in this chapter), they don't begin with a digit (but they can have digits in them, as in `result2`), and they don't have any spaces (such as `ThisIsAGoodButLongVariable` instead of `This Is Not A Variable`). Chapter 5, "Programming Basics," explains more about JavaScript naming conventions.

JavaScript has three kinds of expressions:

- *Arithmetic* expressions, which evaluate to a number (as in the preceding examples).
- *String* expressions, which evaluate to a sequence of characters (or *string*). Strings in JavaScript are represented as characters enclosed in either double or single quotation marks ("Scotty" and 'Jason' are both strings).
- *Logical* (or Boolean) expressions, which evaluate to true or false. JavaScript uses the special (*reserved*) words `true` and `false` (no quotation marks) to represent logical values.

Operators: Basic Arithmetic

Basic arithmetic involves the manipulation of operands by operators. *Operators* are special symbols that control how an expression is to be evaluated (+, –, /, and * are all operators). *Operands* are pretty much anything else in an expression (variables, constants, other expressions).

JavaScript uses two types of operators: binary and unary. A *binary* operator requires two operands—one before the operator and one after the operator—as follows:

```
operand1 operator operand2
```

Examples of binary operators would be

```
4 + 7
x / y
```

Unary operators require only a single operand, either before or after the operator, like so:

```
operator operand
```

or

```
operand operator
```

The following two examples are unary operators:

```
x++
-3
```

To see exactly what types of operators JavaScript has (and to learn what that funny ++ thing does), move on to the next section.

Arithmetic Operators

Arithmetic operators create arithmetic expressions. They expect numerical values for their operands and return a single numerical value. There are eight arithmetic operators: +, –, *, /, %, ––, ++, and –. The first five are binary (requiring two operands, as explained in the preceding section), the remaining three unary (one operand). Let's look at each in turn.

Standard Arithmetic Operators

The standard arithmetic operators are addition (+), subtraction (–), multiplication (*), and division (/). These operators work the same as in regular math problems, as shown in table 6.1.

Table 6.1 Arithmetic Operators

Operator	*Example Expression*
+	`3 + 5`
–	`19 - 5`
*	`34.95 * salesTax`
/	`100 / 4`

As you can see, variables (as in `salesTax`) work just as well with arithmetic operators as numbers (called *constants*) do. This is true, as long as the variables themselves are numeric.

Modulus (%)

The *modulus operator* returns the remainder of the operands, as though you were doing integer division and not computing a decimal point. For example,

```
22 % 5
```

evaluates to 2. 5 goes into 22 a total of 4 times evenly. 5 times 4 is 20, with 2 (the modulus) remaining.

Increment (++)

If you remember from earlier, an operator that consisted of two plus signs was used to demonstrate unary operators. The ++ is a special operator called the *increment operator*, and it's a programmer shorthand way of adding 1 to an operand (programmers are always adding 1 to things, as in counting the number of names in a list). In other words,

```
operand++
```

is a short way of writing

```
operand = operand + 1
```

The increment operator can be written `operand++` or `++operand`. Which side of the operand it's on controls *when* it adds one to the operand (with respect to the rest of the expression). If it's used *after* the operand, it returns the value of the operand *before* incrementing it. For example, if `x` is 3, the statement

```
y = x++
```

first sets `y` to 3, and then increments `x` to 4. If, however, the increment operator is placed *before* the operand, it returns the value of the operand *after* incrementing. Using the preceding example, the statement

```
y = ++x
```

would first increment `x` to 4, and then set `y` to 4 (the new value of `x`).

> **Note:** The increment operator is practical only when working with variables. `23++` is a no-no, because you can't change the value of a constant.

Decrement (--)

Just as the increment operator adds 1 to an operand, the *decrement operator* subtracts one from it, and is shorthand for writing

```
operand = operand - 1
```

Like its counterpart, the decrement operator can be written `var--` or `--var`, its position controlling *when* the subtraction occurs. If the decrement operator is placed after the operand, it returns the value before decrementing. For example, if `x` is 3, the statement

```
y = x--
```

sets y to 3, and then decrements x to 2. Conversely, if the decrement is placed before the operand, it returns the value after decrementing. Again, using the preceding example, the statement

```
y = --x
```

decrements x to 2, and then sets y to 2 (the new value of y).

Also, as with the increment operator, the decrement operator works only with variables (not constants).

Unary Negation (–)

The *unary negation* operator negates its operand. For example,

```
x = -x
```

negates the value of x. If x is 4, it becomes –4.

Comparison Operators

A comparison operator compares its operands and returns a Boolean (true/false) value. These operands may be number values or string values. The six comparison operators are as follows:

- *Equal (==).* If operands are equal, returns true.
- *Not equal (!=).* If operands are not equal, returns true.
- *Greater than (>).* If left operand is greater than right operand, returns true.
- *Greater than or equal to (>=).* If left operand is greater than or equal to right operand, returns true.
- *Less than (<).* If left operand is less than right operand, returns true.
- *Less than or equal to (<=).* If left operand is less than or equal to right operand, returns true.

> **Note:** Strings are compared by trying to *alphabetize* the two strings. A string is less than (<) another string if it comes before it alphabetically. Likewise, a string that's greater than (>) another is one that comes after it alphabetically. Strings are equal (=) only if they're exactly the same—including any punctuation and capitalization. For example, "Matt" and "MATT" are *not* equal.

String Operators

String values can also be added together (or *concatenated*). For example,

```
"good" + " night"
```

returns the string

```
good night
```

> **Note:** Notice the space before the *n* of "night" within the quotation marks. Concatenation tacks strings together without adding any spaces unless you've added spaces within the quotation marks. If the preceding example had been `"good" + "night"`, the result would have been `goodnight`.

You can use numbers in strings to combine them. For example, the expression

```
1 + 5
```

would return a value of `6`. But the expression

```
"1" + "5"
```

would return a value of 15. The difference be tween the two is that one is a numerical expression and the other a string expression.

> **Note:** Quotation marks identify string expressions and tell JavaScript *not* to evaluate anything inside them. In JavaScript, you can use either single quotes (`''`) or double quotes (`""`) to identify strings.

Logical Operators

Another set of operators that return Boolean values are the *logical operators*, of which there are three:

- AND (`&&`). A binary (two-operand) operator that returns `true` only if both operands are true, and `false` otherwise.
- OR (`||`). A binary operator that returns `true` if either or both operands are true, and `false` otherwise.
- NOT (`!`). A unary operator that returns true if its operand is `false`, and vice versa.

> **Note:** Logical operators perform *short-circuit evaluation*, meaning that in a complex (multiple-operator) expression, such as
>
> ```
> expression && whateverElseYouWantToGoHere
> ```
>
> JavaScript stops and doesn't evaluate anything else on the line if ***`expression`*** is false. Likewise,

```
expression || whateverElseYouWantToGoHere
```

JavaScript stops evaluating the line and returns `true` if *`expression`* is true. This means that any "side effects" that the rest of the line may cause won't happen, so careful ordering of the expressions is necessary to either avoid or ensure that parts are evaluated.

Bitwise Operators

Computers "think" in *binary* (base 2, where something is either "on" (1) or "off" (0)). Internally, numbers that we recognize as 3, 5, and 15 are stored in the computer as 11, 101, and 1111, respectively. Sometimes we want to directly manipulate a number at the *bit* (*b*inary dig*it*) level. To do this, we need another collection of operators for *bitwise* manipulation.

For example, colors in HTML (like the background color of a document) are often stored as a 6-digit *hexadecimal* (base 16) number—2 digits for each of the primary colors (red, green, and blue). Because it has 2 hex digits, each primary can have a value between 00 and FF (or 0 and 255). If you want to create a new color that's a combination of two other colors, you could create the color by "adding" them together—but that wouldn't work properly if the sum of the two red components (or green, or blue) exceeded 255. However, by using bitwise operators, we can do this easily.

Note: Red, green, and blue are *additive primaries*, so-called because the other colors of the spectrum are created by adding these three colors together in various amounts (as is done by combining different colored light beams, such as the light transmitted by your computer monitor). This is in contrast to the *subtractive primaries*—cyan, magenta, and yellow. In this case, color isn't created by the transmission of light, but the reflection of light not absorbed by a pigment (like paint).

Before solving this example, you need to look at the operators. There are four bitwise logical operators:

- AND (`&`). Returns 1 if both operands are 1, and 0 otherwise.
- OR (`|`). Returns 1 if either or both operands are 1, and 0 if both operands are 0.
- XOR (`^`) or *exclusive-or*. Returns 1 if only one of the operators is 1 (not both), and 0 otherwise.
- NOT (`~`). A unary operator that returns 1 if its operand is 0, and 0 if it's 1.

They work by manipulating their operands as follows:

- Converting their operands to 32-bit integers, expressed in base 2 as a series of zeros and ones.
- Pairing each bit of the first operand with the corresponding bit in the second.
- Applying the operator to each pair of bits in turn, the result of the operator becoming the bit in the same position in the overall result.

So if you use 25 (11001) and 10 (1010) as operands,

- `25 & 10` evaluates to 8 (`11001 & 1010 = 1000`)
- `25 | 10` evaluates to 27 (`11001 | 1010 = 11011`)
- `25 ^ 10` evaluates to 19 (`11001 ^ 1010 = 10011`)
- `~25` evaluates to `-26`

> **Note:** While *bitwise-and* and *bitwise-or* use the same characters as their logical counterparts, the bitwise operators only use one character (the logical operators use two). A common mistake when building JavaScript expressions is to use the wrong number of characters—and thus the wrong type of operator. For example,
>
> ```
> 5 | 3
> ```
>
> evaluates to 7, whereas
>
> ```
> 5 || 3
> ```
>
> evaluates to true.

Also, there are three bitwise *shift* operators, which "shift" the bits of the first operand by the number of places specified by the second:

- Left shift (<<)
- Right shift (>>)
- Zero-fill right shift (>>>)

There are two right-shift operators because the left-most bit of a number is its *sign bit.* If the bit is set (1), the number's negative; if not (0), it's positive. The right-shift operator will "extend" the sign bit by copying it repeatedly as you shift right (preserving the sign bit for negative numbers).

The zero-fill shift pushes zeros in on the left side of the number (the same way zeros are pushed in on the right side when doing a left shift). For example,

- 5<<2 evaluates to 20 (101 shifted left 2 is 10100).
- 5>>2 evaluates to 1 (101 shifted right 2 is 1).
- -5>>2 evaluates to –2 (preserving the sign).
- -5>>>2 evaluates to 1073741822 (the sign bit becomes part of the number).
- 5>>>2 evaluates to 1 (for positive numbers, >> and >>> are the same).

Now, back to the example. I want to be able to "mix" colors, yet make sure that I don't use more than 255 "units" of red, green, or blue. I can do this easily by using the and (&) operator:

```
newColor = color1 & color2;
```

Assignment Operators

JavaScript supports a "shorthand" method for writing standard arithmetic and bitwise operations (you've already met the increment and decrement operators, which are shorthand ways of adding or subtracting 1). Suppose that you had an operation that said x = x + y. The shorthand way to write this would be x += y. You would write what it's equal to, insert the operator (+, –, *, \, or %), and then insert the other variable. The shorthand for the rest of the arithmetic and bitwise operations is as follows:

- x -= y means x = x - y
- x *= y means x = x * y
- x \= y means x = x \ y
- x %= y means x = x % y
- x <<= y means x = x << y
- x >>= y means x = x >> y
- x >>>= y means x = x >>> y
- x &= y means x = x & y
- x ^= y means x = x ^ y
- x ¦= y means x = x ¦ y

Operator Precedence

When you're presented with an expression such as

5 + 4 * (3 / 2 % 12)

there must be a set of rules defining which operator to evaluate first. Without such rules, starting in different places will yield different results. In JavaScript, operators have a certain *order of precedence*, or what operators are evaluated first, and in what order. The order of precedence, from highest (first) to lowest (last), is as follows:

- Call and member (`()` and `[]`)

> **Calling All Members...**
>
> *Call* operators refer to parentheses, which may be used within an expression to override the default order of precedence. They have the highest precedence, meaning that while
>
> ```
> 5 * 4 + 3
> ```
>
> would evaluate to 23 (multiplication has a higher precedence than addition),
>
> ```
> 5 * (4 + 3)
> ```
>
> would evaluate to 35 (the parentheses are evaluated first).
>
> *Member* operators (the square brackets) are for accessing parts of arrays. For more on arrays, see Chapter 9, "Building Arrays."

- Negation, increment, and decrement (!, ~, -, ++, and --)
- Multiplication and division (*, /, and %)
- Addition and subtraction (+ and -)
- Shift (<<, >>, and >>>)
- Relational (<, <=, >, and >=)
- Equality (== and !=)
- Bitwise-and (&)
- Bitwise-xor (^)
- Bitwise-or (¦)
- Logical-and (&&)
- Logical-or (¦¦)
- Conditional (?:)
- Assignment (=, +=, -=, *=, \=, %=, <<=, >>=, >>>=, &=, ^=, and ¦=)
- Comma (,)

> **Note:** The comma operator allows you to put more than one JavaScript statement together into one large logical JavaScript statement. It's not commonly used, except when initializing multiple variables in a `for` statement (covered later in this chapter).

Statements

If all JavaScript could do was evaluate expressions like the ones we've seen so far, its use would be somewhat limited. Like other programming languages, JavaScript extends the basic functionality of expressions with statements. A *statement* is a sequence of keywords, operators, operands, and/or expressions, terminated by a semicolon (;).

> **Note:** In JavaScript, certain words can't be used as variables, functions, methods, or object names. These "special" words are called *keywords* or *reserved words* (because they're reserved for JavaScript's specific use). There are 53 reserved words (some are currently used in JavaScript, while others are reserved for future use):

```
abstract      float         public
boolean       for           return
break         function      short
byte          goto          static
case          if            super
catch         implements    switch
char          import        synchronized
class         in            this
const         instanceof    throw
continue      int           throws
default       interface     transient
do            long          true
double        native        try
else          new           var
extends       null          void
false         package       while
final         private       with
finally       protected
```

> Appendix B, "Reserved Words," also lists these special words.

The individual pieces of a statement are separated by *white space* (a space, a tab, or a blank line), so JavaScript can tell them apart. Statements may even extend over multiple physical lines, as in

```
x = 3.14159 *
    radius * radius;
```

or more than one statement may be put on the same line:

```
y = 3 + 4;  x = width * height;
```

> **Note:** Strings are an important exception to the white space rule. JavaScript doesn't interpret anything enclosed in quotation marks, so any white space within a quoted string becomes part of the string (producing possibly an unacceptable result).
>
> If a string becomes too long to easily manage in your text editor, a good trick is to break the string into substrings, concatenated with the + operator. You can then place the individual substrings on separate lines without affecting the output. See the section earlier in the chapter about string operators.

All JavaScript statements can be grouped into one of four categories: *comments*, *conditional*, *loop*, and *object manipulation*.

Declaring Variables with *var*

The `var` statement declares that the word immediately after it is a *variable*, which you can set to whatever value you want. For example,

```
var i;
```

would declare `i` to be a variable. Optionally, you can initialize the variable at the same time you declare it:

```
var i = 10;
```

This would declare `i` and set its initial value to 10. You can also create (and initialize) more than one variable at a time:

```
var i, j = 5, x, myAnswer;
```

As explained in Chapter 5, "Programming Basics," variables can be virtually any word or collection of words, *except*

- They can't be one of the *reserved words* listed earlier, although they may contain reserved words (`newVariable`).
- They must begin with a letter (A to Z), although they can include numbers after the initial character (`item10`).
- They may consist of more than one word but can't contain any spaces. You can use the underscore (_) character to separate words (`my_variable`), or you can pack the words together (`myvariable`), although an option that's easier to read would be to capitalize successive words (`myVariable`).

A variable that's declared in the current function has the scope of that function; if it's declared outside a function, the scope is the current document.

Note: *Scope* defines the existence of a variable (that is, what JavaScript code can "see" the variable). For example,

```
function myFirstFunction() {
   var i = 5;
   document.write(i);
}
function mySecondFunction() {
   document.write(i);
}
```

Calling the second function would print out nothing, because `i` is given a value only within the first function. When JavaScript encounters `i` in the second function, it creates a new variable and initializes it (sets its value) to an empty string. Likewise,

```
var i = 15;
function myFirstFunction() {
   var i = 5;
   document.write(i);
}
function mySecondFunction() {
   document.write(i);
}
```

would result in 15 being printed when the second function is called, because the `i` JavaScript "sees" from within `mySecondFunction()` is the *global* variable. Calling `myFirstFunction()` would print out 5, because the `i` "seen" in that function is *local* to it.

Comments

Sometimes it's necessary to "jot notes" inside your JavaScript to help you remember what the code does (when you start writing a lot of code, it's easy to forget). You may remember that you can embed a *comment* in an HTML document by placing the comment between `<!--` and `-->` tags, which effectively makes the browser ignore everything between those tags.

JavaScript has its own comment statements. For comments that extend over more than one line, you can use `/*` to start the comment and `*/` to end it, as in

```
/* everything inside here is treated as a comment
   x = x + 5;
   even the previous statement will be ignored */
```

Or, if you want to add a comment to the end of a statement, you can use `//`, as in

```
total = total + subtotal;   // add them up
```

where everything on the line after the `//` will be ignored.

Conditional Statements

Conditional statements let you control the sequence in which JavaScript executes statements, based on a *condition* (the truthfulness or falseness of an expression). Normally, JavaScript executes statements *sequentially*, one right after the other. With a conditional statement, you can change the order of execution.

The JavaScript conditional statement uses the keywords `if` and `else`, and has the following syntax:

```
if (condition) {
   // do something if "condition" is true
} else {
   // do something if "condition" is false
}
```

`condition` represents a valid expression. Alternatively, you can omit the `else` block, if you want to do something only if a condition is met (but don't care if it isn't), as in

```
if (value > 5) {
   // do something, because value is greater than 5
}
```

> **Note:** You'll see braces (`{}`) used often in JavaScript. They define a "block" of statements that are to be treated (executed) as a unit. With braces, you can execute more than one statement within an `if` statement. For example,
>
> ```
> if (value > 5)
>    y = 4;
>    z = 3;
> ```
>
> would always set `z` to 3, because that statement is "outside" the `if` expression (the extra white space to line up the statements means nothing to JavaScript). However,
>
> ```
> if (value > 5) {
>    y = 4;
>    z = 3;
> }
> ```
>
> would set `z` to 3 *only* if `value` were greater than 5.

Loop Statements

Often in JavaScript, you want to repeat a collection of statements more than once (as in counting the values in an array). Loop statements allow you to do this without having to duplicate the statements repeatedly. There are two loop statements—`for` and `while`.

for

If you wanted to print out the numbers from 1 to 5, one per line, you could do this in HTML:

```
<body>
1
2
3
4
5
</body>
```

Or you could do this in JavaScript:

```
<script language="JavaScript">
document.write("1<br>");
document.write("2<br>");
document.write("3<br>");
document.write("4<br>");
document.write("5<br>");
</script>
```

But using a `for` loop makes statement more compact (and flexible):

```
<script language="JavaScript">
for (i = 1; i <= 5; i++) {
   document.write("" + i + "<BR>");
}
</script>
```

This isn't necessarily much savings when you're only counting from 1 to 5, but if you're creating a table with a large number of elements (for example, 50), a `for` loop can make things *much* easier.

Now that you've seen what a `for` statement can do, let's look closer at its parts. The overall syntax of the `for` statement is

```
for (initialization ; condition ; increment) {
   statements
}
```

It's made up of the following parts:

- *`initialization`* An expression that's commonly used to initialize a *counter variable* (the variable you use to control the number of times the loop is executed). In the preceding example, this is `i = 1`.
- *`condition`* A Boolean expression that's evaluated on each pass through the loop, before the body of the loop is executed. As long as the expression is true, the loop will execute.
- *`increment`* An expression used to update (by incrementing or decrementing) the counter variable.
- *`statements`* One or more JavaScript statements. This is the *loop body*, and is executed once each time through the loop.

> **Note:** Any of the preceding four parts of the `for` statement may be omitted (left blank). For example, if you don't have a counter to initialize, the following statement is valid:
>
> ```
> for ( ; condition ; increment ) {
>    // whatever ...
> }
> ```
>
> Likewise, *`condition`* or *`increment`* can also be left blank—you just need to remember that the semicolons *must* still be there.
>
> If the *`condition`* expression is blank, it's assumed to be true, meaning that the loop won't terminate (an *endless loop*) unless you use the `break` statement (discussed later). This can be a bad thing (it will "hang" your code—cause the browser to continue to execute the loop body forever), or it can be beneficial (if you want to loop until a variable is set to a particular value, but you don't know how many *iterations*—trips through the loop—it will take).

Knowing all of this, let's look at the example again:

```
for (i = 1; i <= 5; i++) {
   document.write("" + i + "<BR>");
}
```

If I were to describe what this loop does in plain English (a programming technique called *pseudocoding*), it would be as follows:

Set `i` *to 1.*
If `i` *is less than 5, execute the* `document.write()` *statement. Otherwise, stop processing the loop.*
Increment `i`*.*
Go back to step 2.

while

A `for` statement is good for loops that have a start (initialized value) and a known ending (by incrementing until a condition is reached). If you just want to keep doing something but don't know how many iterations it will take, a `while` statement is a better choice. The syntax is

```
while (condition) {
   statements
}
```

This means "while *`condition`* is true, execute *`statements`*." You could take the earlier `for` loop example and rewrite it as a `while` loop this way:

```
var i = 1;
while (i <= 5) {
   document.write("" + i " "<BR>");
   i++;
}
```

Notice that, with `while` loops, you need to do your own initializing *outside* the loop. Also, the increment section (from the `for` loop) has to be handled inside the body of the loop.

You can also have a `while` statement where the condition is always true:

```
while (1) {
   // endless loop
}
```

This will keep looping forever—unless you "break" the loop. Although this sounds like something you'd *never* want to do, sometimes you want to keep looping until one condition (or more) is met—and those conditions can't easily be written into one simple expression. How you control when to break such a loop is discussed next.

break and continue

Even inside the body of a `for` or `while` loop, you can control what statements to execute (as with `if` statements). Two other JavaScript statements give you additional control over how (or if) the loop continues to execute—`break` and `continue`.

The `break` statement is a "stop looping *now*" instruction that cancels a `while` or `for` loop immediately, sending the JavaScript interpreter to the next statement outside the body of the loop. It's a one-word statement that comes in very handy for stopping loops that have conditions that are always true (like the endless loops mentioned earlier):

```
break;
```

In the following example, although the loop is supposed to execute forever, the `break` statement terminates it when `y` is 3:

```
var y =  0;
while (1)  {
    if (y == 3)
       break;
    y++;
}document.write(y);
```

The `continue` statement, on the other hand, skips over all the rest of the statements in the loop body and goes to the next iteration of the loop. For example, the following `for` loop is set to execute five times:

```
for (i=1, total=0 ; i<=5 ; i++) {
   if (i > 2)
      continue;
   total += 5;
}
document.write("total = " + total);
```

However, the `if` statement says that if `i` is larger than 2, the rest of the statements (adding 5 to the total) should be skipped. This means that the final line will print a value of 10 (the last two iterations through the loop wouldn't result in any addition).

> **Note:** This is also an example of using the comma (`,`). In this loop, I wanted to initialize the counter variable and the total variable. I could have done
>
> ```
> var total = 0;
> for (i=1 ; i<=5 ; i++) {
> ...
> ```
>
> which would have worked the same way. The comma allows you to do more than one initialization, which helps visually keep the pieces of the loop together (I'm visually showing that, before I start looping, I want both variables initialized).
>
> You can initialize more than two variables this way as well. Just separate each initialization with commas.

In a `for` loop (as the example shows), the `continue` statement takes you to the increment statement, then to the condition, and (if the condition is still `true`) back into the body of the loop.

In a `while` loop, the `continue` statement would go back to the condition. Any increment statement would be in the body of the loop and (depending on where it is in respect to the `continue`) it could be skipped. If you're using a `continue` inside a `while` loop, you need to make sure that you're not skipping your increment or termination test; otherwise, you have another endless loop.

Object-Manipulation Statements

JavaScript is an *object-based* language (as explained in Chapter 1, "Introducing JavaScript"). The next two chapters look more closely at JavaScript objects; for now, remember that an object is a "thing" that has components associated with it that store various values. These components are called *properties*. Sometimes you'll want to perform some operation on all the properties of an object (say, for example, to list out what those properties are). It's also entirely possible (and somewhat common) not to know what properties an object has. Fortunately, JavaScript supplies two statements that allow easy manipulation of objects: `for...in` and `with`. Also, there's a special operator for objects (`new`) and a special keyword (`this`).

The *new* Operator

When you create a variable, you create an *instance* of that variable. The same holds true for objects, except that objects are more than simple variables and need a special operator to create their instances. This is the `new` operator, and it works as follows:

```
newVar = new objectType(optionalParameters);
```

`newVar` is the created object variable, `objectType` is the kind of built-in JavaScript object you're creating, and `optionalParameters` are any parameters the particular object needs to be created correctly. For example,

```
newDate = new Date();
```

creates a new `Date` object called `newDate`. After that, `newDate` can be treated as a `Date` object, complete with all the properties and methods associated with the `Date` object:

```
document.write("" + (newVar.getMonth() + 1) + "-" + d.getDate());
```

> **Note:** The `Date` object is covered in Chapter 12, "Date Methods."

The *this* Keyword

JavaScript objects are made up of *properties* and *methods* (covered in the chapters in Part III, "Methods, Properties, and Cookies"). Many of the built-in objects (such as `Document` and `Window`) also contain other objects, which may contain other objects...and so on. It's sometimes difficult to keep track of exactly where you are in the object tree, even when you want to deal with a current object (such as the document you're in). Fortunately, JavaScript provides a shortcut method of referencing the current object—`this`. It's a special keyword that translates to "the current object," regardless of the object type. For example, to access the `cookie` property in the current document, you could use

```
document.cookie
```

Or, using `this`, you could use

```
this.cookie
```

which makes it clear that you mean "this document's cookie," not some other document's cookie (for more information on cookies, see Chapter 16).

> **Note:** What the keyword `this` represents depends greatly on where it's used within the document. Another common use of `this` is inside the event handlers of an HTML anchor tag, in which case `this` refers to the anchor, not the document. So in
>
> ```
> <a href="http://www.winternet.com/~sjwalter/"
>     onmouseover="message(this.href);">
> ```
>
> `this` represents the anchor, and the `href` property is **http://www.winternet.com/~sjwalter/**.
>
> For more information on events and handlers, check out Chapter 4, "Understanding Events."

for...in

A `for...in` statement repeats a variable over all the properties of object. This is a special kind of loop statement that (instead of a counter or increment) works across *all* of an object's properties. The correct syntax would be

```
for (propertyName in object) {
     statements
}
```

where *`object`* is the object you're working with, and *`propertyName`* is the name of a property of the object. With each pass through the loop, *`propertyName`* is set to a different object property. The loop ends when it has visited all the properties of an object.

One common example of using a `for...in` statement is to list all the properties of a particular object. For example, listing 6.1 is a simple HTML file that lists all the properties of the `Document` object.

Listing 6.1

```
<html>
<body bgcolor=ffffff>
<h3>Properties of "Document"</h3>
<hr>
<script language="JavaScript">
for (propertyName in document) {
   document.write(propertyName + "<BR>");
}
</script>
</body>
</html>
```

You can use this technique (fig. 6.1 shows the output) to view properties of JavaScript objects, or objects of your own creation.

> **Tip:** Because JavaScript is a new language, it's constantly changing as new versions of the browsers that support it appear. Often, new functionality is built in that doesn't necessarily make its way to the documentation for some time. The `for...in` loop is a good way to check to see what objects can do (that is, what new properties have popped up), as well as check to see whether you're setting the correct properties if you're modifying them.

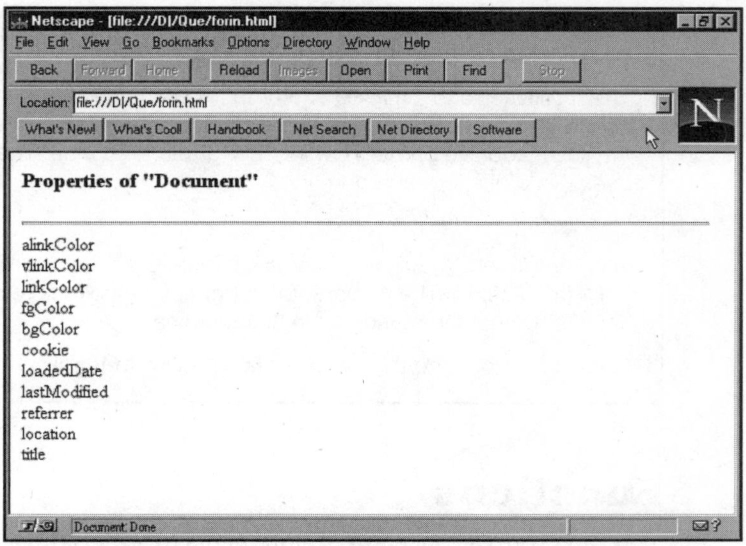

Figure 6.1

The value that's returned in `property` in listing 6.1 is a string. You can reference the actual value of the property itself by using named-array indexing, as in `document [property]`. More on name arrays is covered in the upcoming chapters.

with

If you know which properties you want to manipulate and want to do something to several properties of a single object, you can save yourself some typing by using a `with` statement. The `with` statement says that "for the body of this statement, any variable references are assumed to be properties of *`object`*." For example,

```
with (document) {
```

would set `document` as the default object inside the `with` block. This means that rather than have to type

```
document.fgColor = "#000000";
document.bgColor = "#FFFFFF";
```

you could use

```
with (document) {
   fgColor = "#000000";
   bgColor = "#FFFFFF";
}
```

And because you could replace `document` with an object reference, you could use the above block to change the color of *any* document.

> **Hexi and the Amazing Technicolor Dream Code**
>
> The "`#000000`" and "`#FFFFFF`" references are hexadecimal representations of colors. As mentioned earlier in this chapter, colors are stored as a combination of the three additive primary colors: red, green, and blue. The hex representation uses two digits for each primary,
>
> *#rrggbb*
>
> where *rr* is red, *gg* is green, and *bb* is blue. Color values range from `00` (no color) to `FF` (total color). The `#` character in front of the color is necessary to tell JavaScript that the number is in hexadecimal.
>
> Common colors and their values are listed in Appendix C.

Functions

You can group a collection of statements together into a *function*, or a sequence of statements that perform a specific purpose. Functions are identified by the `function` keyword, a word called the *function name*, and pair of parentheses (`()`) that enclose one or more parameters. All the statements within the function are enclosed in braces:

```
function message() {
   // function statements go here
}
```

The parentheses are *always* necessary, even when the function has no parameters (as in the example above). *Parameters* are values that you can pass to the function to be used or operated on, and may be constants, variables, or even expressions.

You call a function by specifying its name and parameters as a simple statement,

```
message();
```

which would call the `message()` function (which has no parameters, as represented by the empty parentheses). Alternatively, you can have the function return a value to another variable. To do this, you use the special statement `return`. For example, if you had a function,

```
function cubed(value) {
   return value * value * value;
}
```

you could use it as

```
result = cubed(3);
```

which would set `result` to 9. Also, you can use `return` to return from the function immediately (much in the way that `break` stops the execution of a loop):

```
function doSomething(value) {
   if(value == 3)
      return 0;
   return value + 2;
}
```

If `doSomething(3)` were called, the value returned would be 0 (the rest of the function would be skipped).

Summary

JavaScript extends its capabilities beyond simple math operations by using *statements,* which are a series of operators, operands, and other expressions that evaluate to a particular end result.

Operators manipulate variables and constants (called *operands*) in various ways. With them you can add, shift, subtract, or compare operands.

All JavaScript statements are terminated (ended) with a semicolon (`;`). You can place more than one statement on a physical line, or a single statement may extend over multiple lines. The statements supported by JavaScript are grouped into four categories: comments, conditional, loop, and object manipulation. Statements can also be grouped together into *functions,* or sequences of statements that perform a particular task.

Review Questions

The answers to the review questions are in Appendix D.

1. What are the three kinds of expressions?
2. What is an operator? an operand?
3. What is a Boolean?
4. What are *unary* operators? *binary* operators?
5. Name some of the different types of operators. Give an example of each.
6. Give an example of a "shorthand" operator.
7. How do comparison operators handle strings?
8. What is operator precedence? Give an example of how it works.
9. What is a statement? a reserved word?
10. What are the four types of statements in JavaScript? Give an example of each.

Exercises

1. Write a loop to display the numbers from 1 to 10. Show how to do this by using both the `for` and the `while` loop structure.

2. Left- and right-shifting have analogous operations in simple math (addition, subtraction, multiplication, and division). Write an example to demonstrate this.

3. Write a function that will enumerate (list) all the properties of *any* object that it's given.

Understanding Objects

Object-oriented design is the methodology of treating software as a collection of "things" or "black boxes" (*objects*) that each, independently, do a specific task and, when plugged together, can perform larger tasks. The focus of object-oriented development is not on the individual lines of code, but on the overall project at hand.

This chapter will briefly touch on JavaScript. You may think it strange to have a chapter dedicated to object-oriented concepts when some of it may not currently apply to JavaScript. Why would I do this? JavaScript is a very new language that's object-*based* in nature, meaning that it's a special type of object-oriented language, with ready-made objects already built in. Although this isn't the perfect picture of object orientation, concepts behind object-oriented design are very applicable to any JavaScript scripts you build.

What Are Objects?

As you may gather from the name, *objects* are the basic building blocks of an object-oriented language. Everywhere you look, you see objects. This book is an object; the chair or couch you're sitting in is an object; the coffee you had for breakfast and the cup it was served in are objects. This may sound imprecise, but the concept of an "object" is imprecise—objects are *things*, plain and simple.

In the non-programming / computer world, each item has two attributes—a *state* and a *function*—associated with it. For example, every pair of scissors has a handle, two blades, and a screw (to create a pivot point, which can be opened or closed). These are the states that, when combined, serve the function of cutting.

The objects you use in object-oriented programming are designed like objects you find in the real world. Each software object uses variables to hold its state and methods to perform its functions. Objects are nothing more than packages of data.

Because just picking up a software object at the local convenience store is difficult, let's use an old Model T as an example of an object. A software object that represented your Model T would have all the same characteristics that your real-world car has, using variables to express color, size, location, and, if moving, speed.

> **Note:** Rather than use the terms *state* and *function*, I'll instead refer to these as *variable* and *method* throughout the rest of this discussion.

Your software object would also have methods to represent the actions your Model T could perform. It would have methods to speed up, slow down, or turn. Figure 7.1 illustrates some of the misconceptions of objects. While you're adding to the objects in figure 7.1 that make up the car, you're also implicitly eliminating items the car isn't. The car doesn't water lawns (there's no sprinkler attached to the car). The car doesn't fly (it doesn't have wings).

Figure 7.1

The "real world" comparison of objects and what it illustrates.

One use of methods is to hide the true values of the variables. When you see a car drive past, do you ask yourself what gear it's in? No—you may wonder how fast it's moving, but rarely in terms of a gear ratio. In the same way, the driver of the vehicle doesn't just say, "I want to go 55 mph," and have it happen. The car has methods to assist him in getting the car up to the desired speed (he presses the gas pedal to accelerate and the brake pedal to slow down). The vehicle's methods act as an interface between the driver and the "nuts and bolts" of the vehicle.

> **Note:** The hiding of variable values behind methods is called *encapsulation*.

Hiding the variables has various benefits:

- *The basic state of hiding the information so that others don't have access to it without your permission.* By setting up methods to help users change a variable's values, you shield them from an object's inner workings. This also makes things easier for users (who, for example, don't have to know *how* to paint a dot on-screen, just that your method will do it).
- *The ease with which objects can be exchanged.* Rather than write code that mentions an item or object specifically, you can use general code and pass the objects to the code. For example, a piece of code that adds 500 to an object through its `add()` method could easily perform the same operation with an object of another type—provided that it had the same method.

> **Note:** JavaScript permits the declaration of new objects *on the fly*, which means that you, as the programmer, don't have to plan ahead on what objects you'll use.

How Do Objects Communicate?

Objects use *messages* to communicate. Envision these messages as green memo sheets. When you want to leave a message for an employee, you might write it down. Then you might hand deliver the note yourself, but that may not be the most economical method of transport. You most likely would give it to your secretary, who in turn would pass it on, and so forth until it reached the specified employee. Figure 7.2 shows how objects work through messaging.

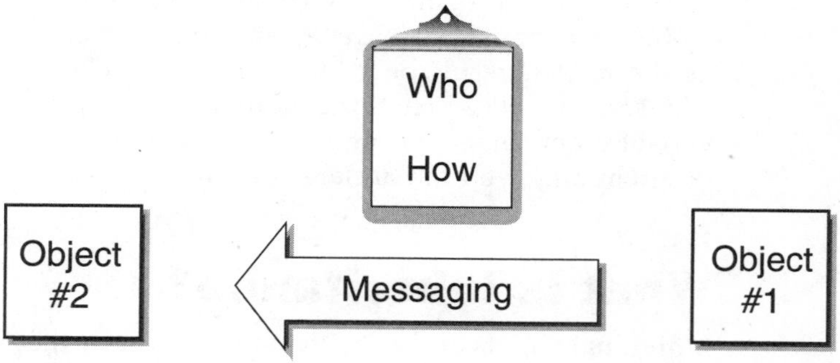

Figure 7.2
Using messaging through objects in everyday actions.

When the other employee receives the note, she'll respond to the contents. Her response will be influenced by various factors, or *variables*, such as length of employment, attitude toward you, or the time of day. How she responds is handled by her *methods*.

In the relationships between software objects in JavaScript, you also find messages in use. Each message has three parts at a minimum. When you look at the message between you and your employee, you find these three parts:

- The *name* of the recipient (employee)
- The *method* to perform (content of the note)
- *Parameters* in which to perform the method (special instructions)

The greatest benefit of using messages to communicate is efficiency. You need only one communication method to send a message to each and every employee—all you would need to do is change the recipient's name.

Object Classes

In the outside world, you find that many items or objects are of the same type. All trees have certain characteristics, as do all cars, bicycles, and even people.

You could say that your Model T is an *instance* of a *class* of objects called cars. You know that all cars have wheels. You know that all cars have a steering device.

If you wanted to build a car, you would grab a blueprint of the design. It would be easier and more efficient to read the blueprint than it would be to disassemble an already built car to see how it was built.

In object-oriented programming, you find many objects that have methods or variables that are similar in nature.

Objects and classes are mentioned quite often in everyday conversation. When you see someone on television trying to persuade you to buy this fine 1966 Rambler for only $1,999, what do you think? Do you *class*ify him as a salesman or—worse—as a used-car salesman? Why do you classify him as that? You classified him based on his characteristics and recognizable methods. He was selling. He was selling used cars. As a result, he fits the "profile" of a used-car salesman.

A software class is nothing more than a template or blueprint that defines the variables and methods common to objects of a certain type. In object-oriented programming, you can declare your own classes of objects.

What Is Inheritance?

Individual objects are normally defined by how they relate to a certain class. You might expect the used-car salesman to be wearing a plaid suit, if your own idea of the salesman class puts each one in a plaid suit. Many times our view of a class is wrong. And when it's wrong, you tend to discriminate against a particular class of objects.

It's difficult to declare a class based on already existing objects. By definition, inheritance flows down, not up. Classes don't inherit the traits of its objects, but objects inherit the traits of their classes.

Now, it's possible to have subclasses. Let's declare a class called *used-car salesman*. This example class has the following characteristics:

- Used-car salesman
- Human
- Sells only used automobiles

As another example, figure 7.3 illustrates the class (squares) and the subclasses of squares.

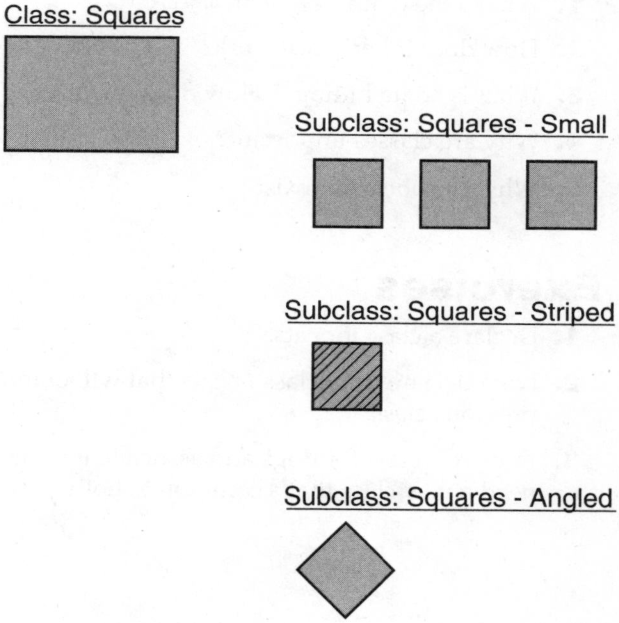

Figure 7.3

Subclasses of squares and how they are seen by others.

Now, having declared the preceding class, you find an object that's female and sells used cars. Is this object a used-car salesman? The answer is yes.

Okay, now you find an object that's male, sells used automobiles, and who wears plaid suits. Is this object a used-car salesman? Yes. Does this mean that the first object must wear plaid suits to be in the same class? No. You have found an instance of a subclass within the class used-car salesman. It inherits the properties of a used-car salesman (human, sells used cars, and so forth) *and* has new properties of its own (male, plaid suits). Another name for a class like this is a *derived class* or *child class*.

Summary

Object-oriented programming deals with the use of *objects* ("things that do particular tasks") and the process of combining them together to complete a complex task. Objects consist of *variables* (storage places for the object's state information) and *functions* (operations that use the variable data to perform tasks).

Review Questions

The answers to the review questions can be found in Appendix D.

1. What's the definition of an *object*?
2. How does inheritance work?
3. What is "data hiding"? How does it work?
4. Why are classes important?
5. Why do subclasses exist?

Exercises

1. Declare a class for cats.
2. Now declare a subclass of cats that will eliminate at least half of the previous class.
3. Declare a class for dogs and associate it to the class for cats. (*Hint:* You may need a new class that's common to both.)

CHAPTER 8

JavaScript Objects

As discussed in Chapter 7, "Understanding Objects," JavaScript is an object-based language (a special type of object-oriented language, where a collection of standard objects is built directly into the language). In this chapter, you'll learn how JavaScript relates to HTML tags as well as the built-in objects that can control Navigator itself.

In an object-oriented environment, it's good to lay out how each object layer relates to other objects around it, and JavaScript is no different.

The top level of objects in JavaScript consists of those objects belonging to Navigator. Directly below that level are the window objects. Each window has a tree of levels branching from it. These trees consist of location, history, and document. At each level are other objects, and under the document tree is yet another branch. At this level are three array objects—namely forms, anchors, and links. Figure 8.1 shows the JavaScript object hierarchy.

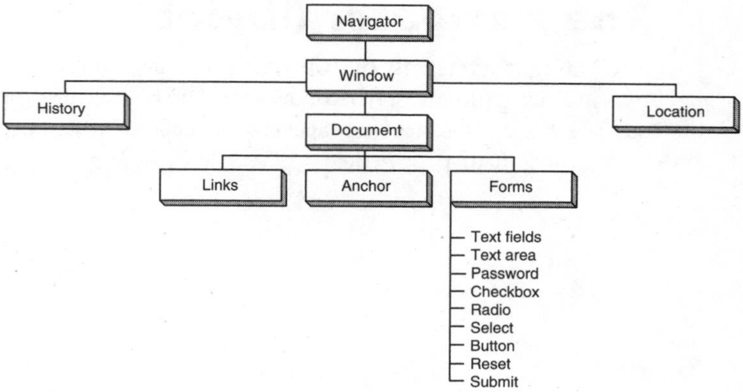

Figure 8.1

The JavaScript hierarchy of objects. Notice how all objects stem from (are children of) the base object.

The Object-Oriented Nature of HTML

JavaScript considers HTML an object-oriented language, where the various HTML tags correspond to different types of JavaScript objects. Let's break down the following mini-HTML page, and see it through the eyes of JavaScript:

```
<html>
<body>
<head>
<title>This is a Title</title>
</head>
<body>
<a href="http://www.myhome.com">My Home</a>
<form>
<input type="button" name="Button1">
</form>
</body>
<html>
```

From this simple HTML page, you've automatically gathered the following JavaScript objects:

- `document.title = "This is a Title"` (from the `<TITLE>` tag)
- `document.form` (the form on the page)
- `document.form.Button1` (the button on the form)

And this is just a sampling of nearly a dozen other objects JavaScript automatically creates directly from HTML. What you're seeing is that nearly every HTML element can be used as an object. Not only can you read the values of these objects, but you can also set the values for many of them on the fly. Keep in mind as you lay out your HTML page that you're actually defining objects and their values for JavaScript.

The *navigator* Object

The Navigator has only one object, `navigator`, which provides information about the Navigator application (the browser). The `navigator` object has four properties that supply the values: `appName`, `appVersion`, `appCodeName`, and `userAgent`. Figure 8.2 illustrates these four properties.

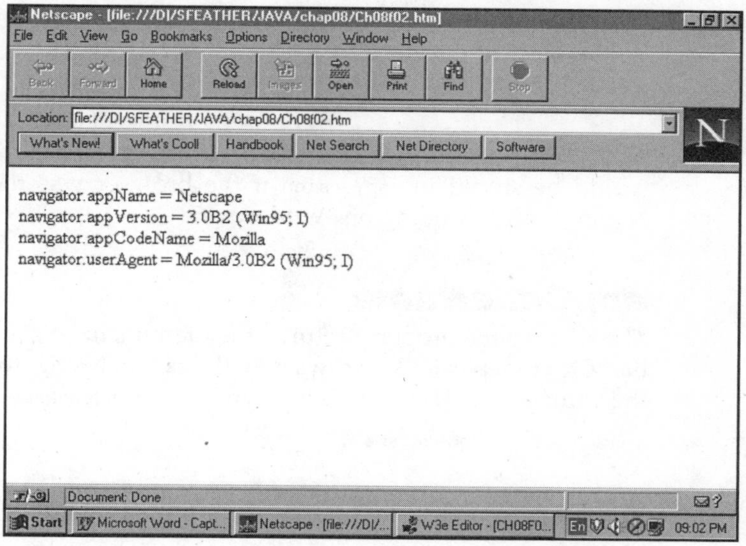

Figure 8.2

The Navigator properties `appName`, `appVersion`, `appCodeName`, and `userAgent` provide access from JavaScript to information about the browser with which the user is surfing.

appName

The `appName` property returns the name of the user's browser. In this example, it should return `Netscape`. The correct syntax is

```
navigator.appName
```

appVersion

The `appVersion` property of the `navigator` object returns not only the version of the browser, but also the operating system it was built for. It may return a variety of results, including Win32 (Windows NT/95), Win16 (Windows 3.x), UNIX, or Macintosh. This can be very useful for tracking the types of systems being used to contact your site. This property also returns the country codes that particular browser supports. The proper syntax is as follows:

```
navigator.appVersion
```

The value stored in `appVersion` is of the form

```
releaseNumber (platform; country)
```

where

- *`releaseNumber`* is the version number of the browser (such as `2.0` or `3.0b4`)
- *`platform`* is the platform on which the browser is running (such as `Win16`, `Win95`, or `Mac`)

- *country* is either I for the international release, or U for the domestic (U.S.) release of the browser

For example,

```
2.0 (Win95; I)
```

would be stored in appVersion if the browser was the international release of Navigator 2.0, running on Windows 95.

appCodeName

The appCodeName property returns the manufacturer's in-house development code name for that particular browser. In the case of Navigator 2.0, this property returns the value of Mozilla. The correct syntax for appCodeName is as follows:

```
navigator.appCodeName
```

userAgent

The userAgent property, used in every HTTP header for identification purposes, is the combination of the appCodeName and appVersion properties. HTTP (Web) servers use this information to identify the abilities of the browser. The correct syntax is

```
Navigator.userAgent
```

Using the previous appVersion example, the value of userAgent would be

```
Mozilla/2.0 (Win95; I)
```

The *location* Object

The location object helps identify the current document and consists of a complete URL. The six properties of the location objects each represent a different piece of the total URL. A complete URL looks like this:

```
protocol//hostname:port/pathname
```

where

- *protocol* defines the transport protocol.
- *hostname* defines the name of the host computer.
- *:port* specifies the port for the address. This is specified only if a non-default port is being used (otherwise, it and the colon are omitted).
- *pathname* is the path and file name.

An URL may also end with one of the following two additional components:

- `?search` defines a query string, normally submitted to a CGI script for processing.
- `#hash` identifies an anchor in the document. If a hash value is given, the document is loaded with the anchor tag (rather than the top of the page) specified at the top of the browser window. This is often used for subindexing into a large document.

Also, JavaScript provides two more properties that are combinations of different components:

- `host` is the combination of *`hostname`* and *`port`*.
- `href` is the entire URL (all components).

The individual components are discussed in more detail in the following sections. For now, each component in an URL has a matching `location` object property of the same name (for example, the *`hostname`* component is accessed via the `hostname` property), as shown in figure 8.3.

Figure 8.3

Location properties URL defined.

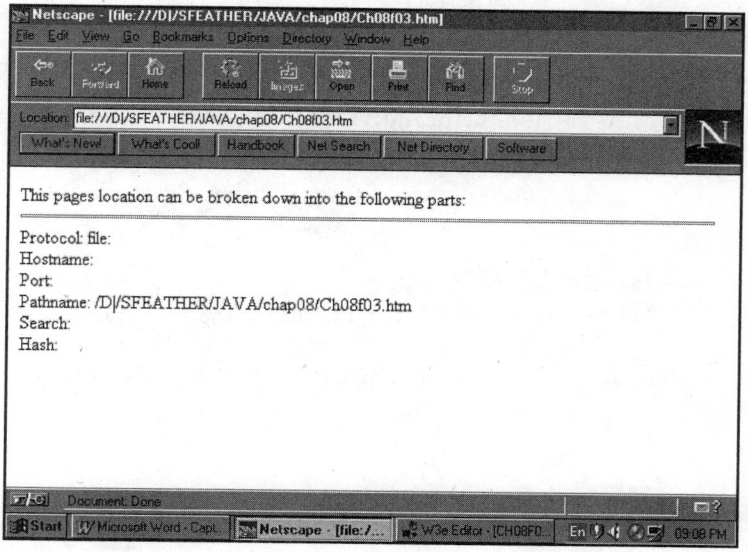

protocol

The `protocol` property may return any number of results, depending on the method of communication you have with the server. What follows is a short list of the more popular protocols used on the Internet:

- http: (HyperText Transfer Protocol)
- news: (Network News Transfer Protocol)
- gopher: (Gopher search protocol)
- ftp: (File Transfer Protocol)

You'll use http most often in your scripts, because it's the protocol for the Web. HTTP, news, Gopher, and FTP are all protocols and URL types. There are also several additional "protocols" that aren't really protocols at all, but are provided for added flexibility:

- javascript:, which allows calling JavaScript functions as though they were an URL
- about:, which accesses the browser's "about" information
- file:, which identifies a file on a local disk drive
- mailto:, which activates the browser's mail interface for sending e-mail

As you look at the individual components that make up the `location` object, you'll examine the pieces of the following URL:

http://www.mcp.com/que/index.html

hostname

The `hostname` can be, but isn't limited to, the top-level domain of a site (org, com, gov, edu) and the secondary domain. It may also include the machine name (www, news, main) of the site. By using the preceding example URL, `hostname` would have the value `www.mcp.com`.

port

When you think of a port, you probably think of the area behind your computer where you plug in your mouse or modem. That is a different type of port. Each protocol has been given a default port on which to make its connections (for example, the Web uses port 80 by default). Occasionally, it's necessary to change the default port to another. The `port` property returns the number of the port the browser is currently communicating on.

Again referring to the example (**http://www.mcp.com/que/index.html**), no port is specified, so `port` is set to the default value (80 for http).

pathname

The `pathname` represents the path or location on the server's drives to the current page. A slash separates each directory.

Referring to the example URL, `pathname` would hold `que/index.html`, identifying the file index.html in the que directory.

search

The `search` property returns any query commands that may be in the current URL. Query data is separated from the rest of the URL by a question mark (`?`), and is normally created by the browser when submitting a form to the server (for CGI processing, for example). As such, they aren't often manipulated from within JavaScript.

hash

The `hash` property returns any anchor tags that may have been passed in the URL. Hash values are separated from the rest of the URL by a pound sign (`#`).

For example, if the file index.html had an anchor defined somewhere within it called `newbooks`,

```
<a name="newbooks">New Que Books</a>
```

the URL http://www.mcp.com/que/index.html#newbooks would specify that the document be loaded with the `newbooks` anchor being at the top of the browser window instead of the top of the document.

Forms Objects

You'll most likely recognize forms objects as elements of the `<form>` tag. Therefore, the object must be defined within the `<form>` and `</form>` tags. As mentioned earlier, many of the HTML tags are recognized as objects within Navigator. This means they also can be treated as objects. As objects, you can access their values and, on a few of them, actually change the values.

Buttons

Buttons have been used for everything from loading new pages to actually sending a user snide remarks. Because of their simple design and function, they appear to be the current interface object of choice.

The `button` object has two properties—`name` and `value`. The `value` specifies the label placed on the button's face.

> **Tip:** You can change the label on a button from a script. Use the statement
>
> `Document.form.button_name.value="new_label"`

Only one event handler applies to the `button` object—`OnClick`.

Check Boxes

Check boxes are popping up more and more every day. Before JavaScript hit the streets, it was difficult to parse the value of a check box. Because JavaScript treats the box as an object, you can capture the value of a check box with ease:

```
if (formname.CheckBoxName.value =="on"){
  perform(function)}
```

It's just as simple to set the value of the box:

```
formname.CheckBoxName.value = "on"
```

Hidden Objects

Hidden objects are powerful tools. You can use them to transport information behind the scenes. Until the 2.01 security patch was released in Netscape Navigator, these little fellows were used to "steal" e-mail addresses from unsuspecting Web visitors. Although that "feature" (the steal) has been removed, the basic idea still exists. Even if you're using a form only to send a "mailto:" out, you can hide a great deal of information in one of these objects. Notice the snippet below:

```
<form method="post" action="mailto:somebody@somewhere.com"
   onSubmit="this.platform.value=navigator.appVersion;return true;">
...
<input type="hidden" name="platform">
...
</form>
```

This snippet adds the visitor's browser version and platform to an outbound e-mail message when the form is submitted. By using a parsing utility on the server side, you can capture that information and place it in your database. Why? If you're a hardware reseller, maybe you'd like statistics on how many of your visitors are Mac, Windows, or UNIX users. This would give you a bit of insight on what type of hardware you need to be advertising on your pages.

Radio Buttons

Radio buttons are an interesting item. They're actually an array of buttons. As an array, all buttons in a group share the same `name` property. You can access the data in this array, whether the button has been set or not.

> **Note:** The buttons are placed into the array opposite the way they are called.

The last radio button defined is actually

```
formname.radio[0]
```

and not

```
formname.radio[x]
```

For more information on arrays, see Chapter 9, "Building Arrays."

The *reset* Object

The `reset` object, although not used as prevalently as some of the other form objects, still has a very important function and use. As soon as the `OnClick` event (of any button on the form) is in progress, this object may be set from within a script, without the user ever clicking the reset button. Why would you ever want to do that? If you're verifying the input of a form and the format of an entry is wrong, you can reset the entire form.

To call a reset from within your script, use the following code:

```
formname.resetname.click()
```

This will simulate the clicking of a reset button and clear all the values on a form.

> **Note:** You can't use the `OnClick` event of the reset button itself to cancel the reset process. Once the reset button is clicked, the form is cleared.

The *select* Object

The JavaScript `select` object accesses the information in an HTML `<SELECT>` tag. Through its `options` property (another array), you can identify what option (or options, in the case of multiple selections) the user has selected, as the following code fragment demonstrates:

```
function listSelect(obj) {
  for(var i=0; i<obj.length; i++) {
    document.write("" + obj.options[i].name + " is ");
    if(!obj.options[i].selected) {
      document.write("not ");
    }
    document.write("selected<br>");
  }
}
```

This would display *name* `is selected` or *name* `is not selected`, depending on the state of each option.

It's also possible to set the default selection from your script. This would be useful if, by analyzing the visitor's previous choices on other forms, you have a fairly good idea of the selection he might make. For example, if in a "tell-me-your-hobbies" form the visitor clicks an "I like to fish" box, you'll be able to set the default magazine in a selection of magazines to *Field and Stream*. Figure 8.4 shows an example of the `select` object.

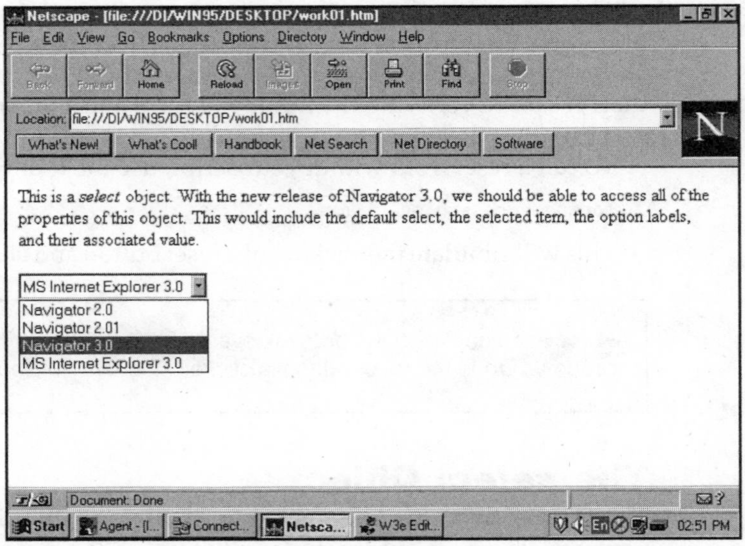

Figure 8.4

Accessing the `select` object.

The *submit* Object

The `submit` object is a powerful link to the outside world, and is associated with a form's submit button. It's the key for interfacing JavaScript to other CGI resources. When the submit button is clicked, an `OnSubmit` event is generated. Through the

`OnSubmit` event, you can verify the information in a form and (if necessary) cancel the submission. (For a detailed example of `OnSubmit` in action, see Chapter 4, "Understanding Events.")

The *text* Object

Consider the `text` object to be one of your best resources. Whereas many of the other objects permit only Boolean answers, such as yes or no, the `text` object allows more flexible input. A `text` object is declared just as you've been doing with the `<input>` tag. Gathering a value from a `text` object is quite simple:

```
<input name="txtObj" type="text" value="Bloodhound">
...
<script language="JavaScript">
   document.write("The value is '" + txtObj.value + "'");
</script>
...
```

This would display the following:

```
The value is 'Bloodhound'
```

Not only are `text` objects great for accepting input, they can be used for showing output. To display the results of a function or statement, you usually need to rewrite the entire HTML page or load your information into a new window or frame. With a `text` object, you merely change the object's value to update the current screen. You'll be using this feature quite a bit in Chapter 10, "Math Methods," when creating the output display of a mini-calculator to demonstrate how the various math methods operate.

> **Note:** For more information on the `text` object and its relatives (`textarea` and `password`), see Chapter 14, "Miscellaneous Methods and Functions."

Essentially, you use the following format for changing the value:

```
textObject.value="whatever_the_new_text_is"
```

Normally, the screen is updated immediately after the value changes. Depending on the loops you use in your code and other system-intensive calls, however, it may be a few seconds before the results are displayed.

Four event handlers apply to the `text` object: `OnBlur`, `OnChange`, `OnFocus`, and `OnSelect`. Figure 8.5 shows how to access a text object in JavaScript.

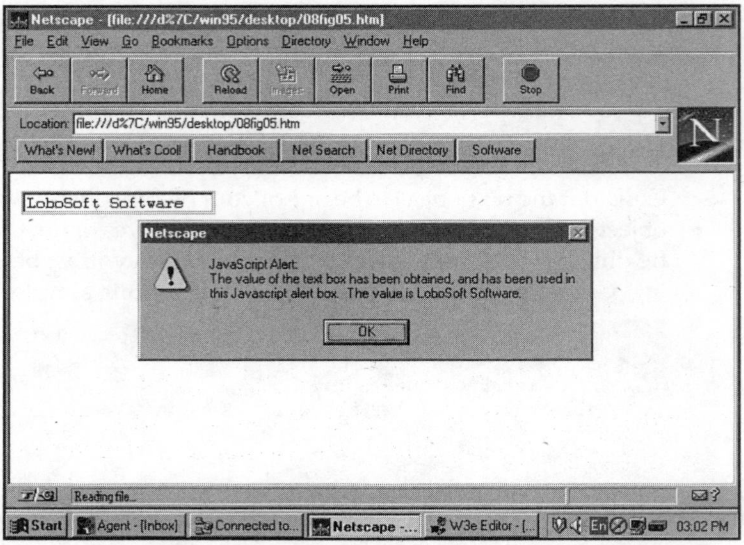

Figure 8.5
Example of accessing a text object.

The *textarea* Object

Used most often in comment forms, the `textarea` object has one advantage over the text object. Although you can define the `text` object with multiple lines, those lines are seen only one at a time. The `textarea` object, on the other hand, allows you to define it with multiple rows and columns.

As with the `text` object, the value of the text area can also be updated dynamically.

Summary

JavaScript objects provide a means to access many of a document's HTML tags, such as the document title or the components that make up a form. Also, the `navigator` object provides you with information about the user's browser configuration, allowing you to adjust how you display your information.

Accessing form components from within JavaScript makes it possible to tailor a form's selections to the user's preferences, test the validity of a form's data, or build entirely new pages based on the choices a user makes.

Review Questions

Answers to the review questions can be found in Appendix D.

1. What are the properties of the `navigator` object?
2. What are some of the objects that are part of a form?
3. How can you store information in a form without displaying it to the user?
4. What's one use for the `submit` object (and the `onSubmit` event)?

Exercises

1. Design a page that greets users and tells them about their browsers. (*Hint:* Use the `navigator` object.)
2. Using a `select` object, design an "URL JumpStation" that presents users with a selection of URLs to pick from and a button to take them there.
3. Design a feedback form that requests the user's name and e-mail address, and then uses form validation to ensure that the fields are filled out and that the given e-mail address is valid ("*name@domain*"). If the form isn't valid, inform the user, clear the form, and start again (without submitting it).
4. Design a form that lets the user design a custom page, consisting of a user-selected background color, title, and message.

Building Arrays

If you have several variables that hold the same information (such as several strings of text to display), rather than use a unique variable for each element, you can group them in an array. An *array* is a structure that can hold multiple pieces of data that's all the same type (strings, integers, floats, or objects). JavaScript arrays are *associative* in nature, which means that you associate a particular location with certain information, or data. This chapter examines the different types of JavaScript arrays and their various uses.

Built-In Arrays

As you discovered in Chapter 8, "JavaScript Objects," many HTML tags create "objects" that can be accessed and manipulated through JavaScript (as in the `<INPUT>` objects created in a form). It's also possible to treat some of the upper-level objects (such as the built-in window, location, and frames objects, which are covered elsewhere) as arrays of smaller objects. Figure 9.1 is an example of a built-in array.

The built-in arrays store various information, such as lists of history URLs, frames, anchors, links, and form options. The next sections look at several of these more commonly referenced arrays.

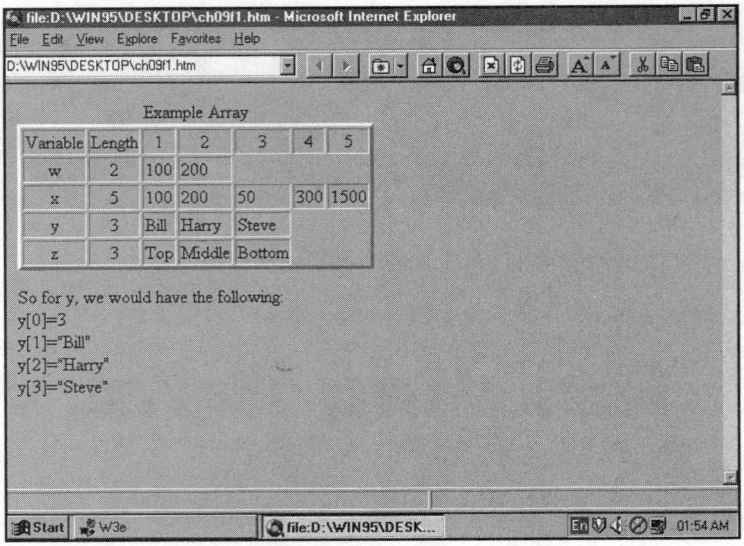

Figure 9.1
An example of a two-dimensional JavaScript array.

Forms Array

Any forms defined in an HTML document are placed into an array that's a *property* (part) of the `document` object. For example, given the following HTML fragment that creates two forms,

```
<html>
<body>
<form name="myForm">
</form>
<form name="yourForm">
</form>
</body>
</html>
```

you can access each form through the `forms[]` array:

```
document.forms[0] // the first form
document.forms[1] // the second form
```

The `length` property of the `forms[]` array will reflect the number of forms in the document (in the example, `forms.length` is equal to 2).

To make things easier to read (and remember), you can reference a form by name (if you specify the `NAME` attribute in the `<FORM>` tag). In the previous fragment, the forms were named `myForm` and `yourForm`, meaning that you could access them as follows:

```
document.myForm // the first form
document.yourForm // the second form
```

You're probably saying, "I always name my forms. How will this help me?" Suppose that you have several different forms on a page. With one click of a button, you want to submit all those forms. Consider the following pseudocode:

If (something is true) then submit all forms
submit form baby
submit form cars
submit form taxes
submit form houses
submit form clothes

Well, that would work well enough. But if you had more forms than that—or if you added another form and forgot to change your JavaScript code—it could get a bit messy. What about doing it this way:

If (something is true) then submit all forms
for x = 1 to forms.length
submit form[x]
next

So the cleaner way to handle multiple forms, of course, is the second way. This technique of using a `for()` loop to step through all the elements of an array can be used on any type of array in JavaScript.

Anchors Array

The next type of array to discuss is the anchors array. Although the forms array is used more often, the anchors array is unique. *Anchors* are the links within an HTML page (specified by the <A> tag), and one of the few ways of accessing the anchors from within JavaScript is through the array. Why? It really isn't the norm to name each anchor individually. The anchors are placed automatically into the array as they're declared in the HTML page. For example, the following HTML fragment creates a simple page:

```
<html>
<body>
<a href="http://www.mcp.com">
<a href="http://home.netscape.com">
<a href="http://www.microsoft.com">
</body>
</html>
```

This results in the `anchors[]` array being loaded with the URLs of the links. You could verify this with a JavaScript fragment that printed out these values:

```
document.write("There are " + anchors.length + " anchors.<br>");
for(var i=0; i<anchors.length; i++) {
   document.write("Anchor " + i+1 + ": "
   ➥+ anchors[i].value + "<br>");
}
```

which would display the following:

```
There are 3 anchors.
Anchor 1: http://www.mcp.com/
Anchor 2: http://home.netscape.com/
Anchor 3: http://www.microsoft.com/
```

> **Note:** The values in the anchors array are read-only and can't be altered.

Notice that the length of the array has a value of 3, which tells you how many elements are in the array. When you format the `Anchors x` part of the display string, you must add 1 to the counter variable, because JavaScript arrays begin at index 0.

Figure 9.2 is an example of manipulating the array of anchors.

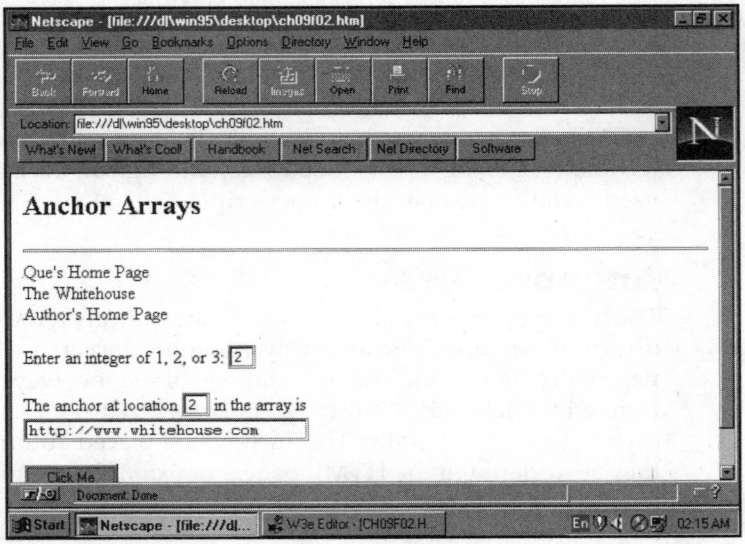

Figure 9.2
Example of an array of anchors.

Custom Arrays

Because of the close relationship between arrays and the object structure of JavaScript, you can easily build your own arrays. As with all object types, you must first declare the new object.

Initializing for Data

Because you're creating a new object, you must first declare it and then initialize its values. The following code snippet, courtesy of the engineers at Netscape, is an initialization function for a simple array:

```
function initArray(){
this.length = initArray.arguments.length
for (var i=0; i < this.length; i++)
this[i] = initArray.arguments[i]
}
```

Now, you use the function as follows:

```
var newArray = new initArray("Tom","Bill","Jimmy","Richard")
```

Notice the `new` statement in the preceding line. Rather than merely input a value to a location, you're actually creating a new location for that data. You've just created an array with the following properties:

```
newArray.length = 4
newArray[0] = Tom
newArray[1] = Bill
newArray[2] = Jimmy
newArray[3] = Richard
```

Now you're probably saying that this is great if you want to build the array and fill it with data at the same time. But what if you want the visitor to fill the array? Can you declare an array and not fill it with information until later? Yes, you can. Rather than pass arguments that represent data, let's change the function around a bit:

```
function initArray(){
this.length = initArray.arguments.length
for (var i=0; i < this.length; i++)
this[i] = ""
}
```

This function now accepts a number argument, which represents the size of your array. If you want an array with 10 locations, pass the function the argument of 10:

```
var myArray = new initArray(10)
```

This function can be used to dynamically create an array that's exactly the size you desire.

You now have an array called `myArray` with the following properties:

```
myArray.length=10
myArray[0] = ""
myArray[1] = ""
myArray[2] = ""
myArray[...] = ""
myArray[9] = ""
```

Filling the Empty Array with Data

Now that you've built an array with no values, you can begin to fill in those locations. You do this by calling your data, as in

```
myArray[2] = "Now it's full"
```

which would load `Now it's full` into the third element in the array.

You recall the information from the array just as you would the value from any other object. If you wanted to know the value of the third name in the array, you would access it via

```
var name3 = myArray[2]
```

which, assuming the previous code fragments, would set `name3` to `Now it's full`.

Also, as with built-in arrays, using a loop allows you to move through the entire array and perform operations on each element:

```
for(var i=0; i<myArray.length; i++ {
   document.write("" + myArray[i] + "<BR>");
}
```

Creating the Presidential Array

Well, the best way to explain a concept is to have a working example, which listing 9.1 shows.

Listing 9.1

```
<html>
<head>
<script language="JavaScript">
// The initArray is used for initializing an array. It
// defines the array's size, and then fills it with data.
function initArray(){
// As with all custom arrays, we need to define the size of
// the array. We do this by setting the length property of the
// array to the integer value of the array's size. In our
// case, the size of the array is 42.
this.length = 42
// Now that we have defined the size of the array, we need
// to fill each location with data.
this[0] = "George Washington"
this[1] = "John Adams"
this[2] = "Thomas Jefferson"
this[3] = "James Madison"
this[4] = "James Monroe"
this[5] = "John Quincy Adams"
this[6] = "Andrew Jackson"
this[7] = "Martin Van Buren"
this[8] = "William Henry Harrison"
```

```
this[9] = "John Tyler"
this[10] = "James K. Polk"
this[11] = "Zachary Taylor"
this[12] = "Millard Fillmore"
this[13] = "Franklin Pierce"
this[14] = "James Buchanan"
this[15] = "Abraham Lincoln"
this[16] = "Andrew Johnson"
this[17] = "Ulysses S. Grant"
this[18] = "Rutherford B. Hayes"
this[19] = "James A. Garfield"
this[20] = "Chester A. Arthur"
this[21] = "Grover Cleveland"
this[22] = "Benjamin Harrison"
this[23] = "Grover Cleveland"
this[24] = "William McKinley"
this[25] = "Theodore Roosevelt"
this[26] = "William H. Taft"
this[27] = "Woodrow Wilson"
this[28] = "Warren G. Harding"
this[29] = "Calvin Coolidge"
this[30] = "Herbert Hoover"
this[31] = "Franklin D. Roosevelt"
this[32] = "Harry S. Truman"
this[33] = "Dwight D. Eisenhower"
this[34] = "John F. Kennedy"
this[35] = "Lyndon B. Johnson"
this[36] = "Richard M. Nixon"
this[37] = "Gerald R. Ford"
this[38] = "Jimmy Carter"
this[39] = "Ronald Reagan"
this[40] = "George Bush"
this[41] = "Bill Clinton"
}
// After finishing the function that will initialize an
// array, we now need to actually create an array. We will
// call our array presidents. To create the new array, we
// just apply the initArray() function against our variable,
// and, using the new statement, this will work.
var presidents = new initArray()

</script>
</head>
<body>
<br>
<h3> Chapter 9: Presidential Array</h3>
<hr>
<form name="list" method="POST">
<!-- Having finished creating the array, and filling it with -->
<!-- data, we now build the interface. Using a form, we -->
<!-- gather an integer from the visitor: -->
```

continues

Listing 9.1 Continued

```
Enter an integer between 1 and 42: <input name="number" type="TEXT"
size=3,1 value="42"><br>
Our script will dynamically change the value of the pres object.
The President:<input name="pres" type="TEXT" size=30,1
value="-None-"><br><br>
<hr>
<!-- When the OnClick event handler for the BUTTON is -->
<!-- activated, it does two things. First, it determines the -->
<!-- name of the president associated with the integer -->
<!-- passed to it. Second, it applies that value to the pres -->
<!-- object. -->
<input type="BUTTON" value="Hit Me" OnClick="document.list.pres.value=
presidents[document.list.number.value-1]">

</form>
</body>
</html>
```

Figure 9.3 shows this program and how it would look on-screen.

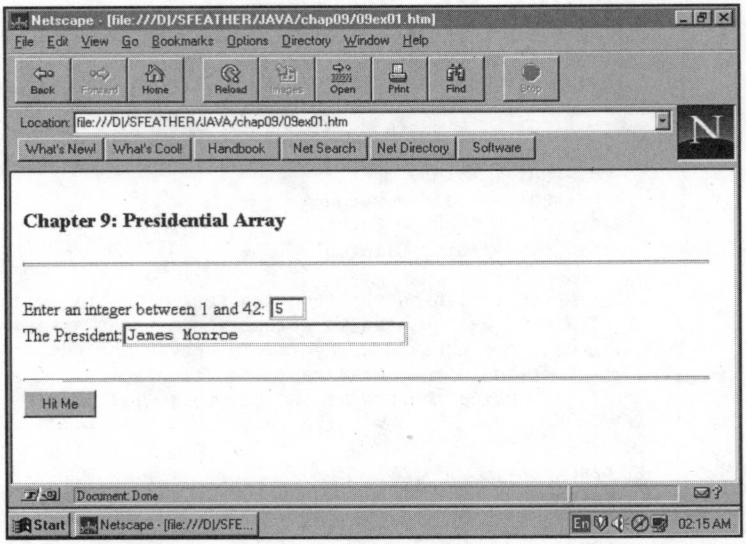

Figure 9.3

Creating an array of the names of the presidents and using a form to select from the array.

You had the default value (specified by the `VALUE` attribute) of the `pres` object equal to `-None-` to start. What happens if you enter an integer value outside the suggested range (1 to 42)? Because the array has a size of only 42 elements, if you try to look at a location that doesn't exist (for example, the 50th element), you're trying to view a value that hasn't been defined, and JavaScript returns a result of <undefined>.

Summary

Arrays are a powerful way to group together collections of similar data (such as an array of strings). An array object has a `length` property, which identifies the number of elements, and a number of elements, access by indexing (as in `array[3]`). Array indexing always starts at 0 (the first element).

In JavaScript, arrays can either be built-in (like the `anchors[]` and `forms[]` arrays), or user-created. User-created arrays can be *static* (all the information is loaded into the array from within JavaScript and all the data is fixed) or *dynamic* (the data in the array can be changed based on the user's actions). This gives JavaScript rudimentary database capabilities that open up the possibilites for customizing the information you display to a user.

Review Questions

Answers to the review questions can be found in Appendix D.

1. Is it possible to edit the values in the anchors array?
2. What array property defines the size of the array?
3. What result is returned if a location greater than the array's size is queried?
4. What are examples of built-in JavaScript arrays?

Exercises

1. Build your own array to hold the 50 states.
2. Create a simple "shopping database," with several products (for example, diskettes, computers, monitors, and the like) that the user can browse through and add to a "shopping cart" (another array storing selected items).

Part III

Methods, Properties, and Cookies

CHAPTER 10

Math Methods

Although the ability to dynamically create HTML pages seems to be the most popular reason for the growing interest in JavaScript, you also need to learn about the math methods included with JavaScript. The math methods allow you to perform simple calculations without ever recontacting the server.

> **Note:** You access the math methods through JavaScript's `Math` object. For example, to execute the `round()` method, you would type
>
> ```
> roundedValue = Math.round(unRoundedValue);
> ```

Currently, there are 17 math methods (see table 10.1). You'll find this study of the math methods divided into two categories: standard and trigonometric.

Table 10.1 The Math Methods

Standard Mathematics Methods	*Trigonometric Methods*
`abs()`	`sin()`
`ceil()`	`cos()`
`exp()`	`tan()`
`log()`	`asin()`
`floor()`	`acos()`
`max()`	`atan()`

continues

Table 10.1 Continued

Standard Mathematics Methods	*Trigonometric Methods*
`min()`	
`pow()`	
`random()`	
`round()`	
`sqrt()`	

Standard Mathematics Methods

The methods in the following sections reflect concepts from algebra and calculus. Trigonometric functions are covered in a separate section within this chapter.

abs()

In mathematics, sometimes it's useful to know the exact, or absolute, value of a number. By *absolute*, I mean that if the number were placed on a number line, its absolute value would be its distance from zero. This is accomplished by making the number positive if it's negative, or leaving it alone if positive (the absolute value of 23 is 23, whereas the absolute value of –523 is 523).

JavaScript has a built-in method for determining the absolute value of a number. Look at the HTML tag for the `activate` button in the following code, which generates the form in figure 10.1. Do you see the `OnClick` event handler (which is in boldface so you can find it more quickly)? Rather than complicate the examples with the use of unnecessary functions, I've put the JavaScript statements directly into the HTML tags.

```
<form method="POST" enctype=application/x-www-form-urlencoded>
Enter a number here:<br>
<input name="number" type="INT" value="0"><br>
The absolute value of your number is:<br>
<input name="answer" type="INT" value="0"><br>
<input name="activate" value="Calculate" type="BUTTON"
OnClick="form.answer.value=Math.abs(form.number.value)">
</form>
```

> **Tip:** Putting JavaScript commands directly into the HTML tags eliminates many of the compatibility problems with older browsers. This is also the one place in a document where you don't bracket JavaScript with a `<SCRIPT>` tag.

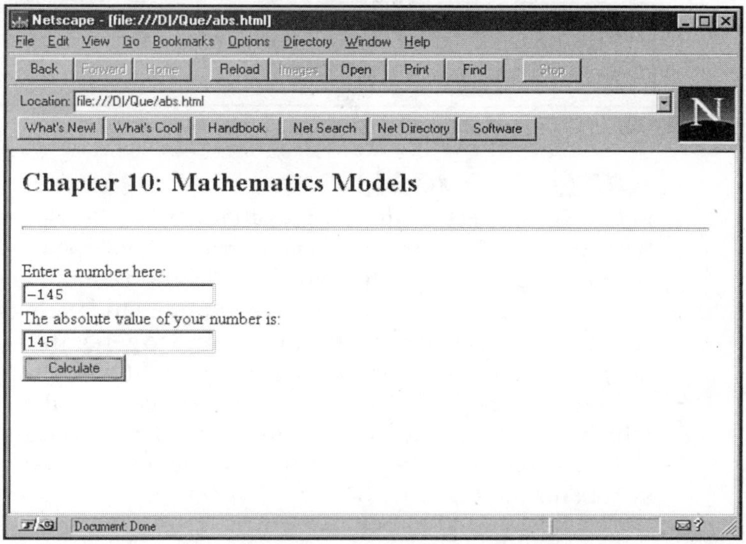

Figure 10.1 The absolute value of a number is simply that number, stripped of its sign (made positive).

ceil()

If you're reading this book indoors, look above you. Whether you're on the first floor or the top floor, you see a ceiling. JavaScript has a ceiling method that returns the lowest value integer greater than or equal to the current number. For example, if your number were 2.456, the `ceil()` of that number would be 3. Hey, that sounds like rounding! Although rounding is very similar, the strict rules of rounding return the next lower integer, if the decimal portion of a number is less than .50. The `ceil()` method always returns the larger integer.

> **Note:** Remember that negative numbers are "below" zero. This means that, for example, –2 is larger than –2.5 (not the other way around), so the `ceil()` of –2.5 would be –2, not –3. It's not uncommon for people to use `ceil()` with negative numbers and wonder why the value being returned is "wrong."

You can take the code fragment used with the `abs()` method earlier and change it to show off the `ceil()` method:

```
<form method="POST" enctype=application/x-www-form-urlencoded>
Enter a number here:<br>
<input name="number" type="INT" value="0"><br>
The ceil of your number is:<br>
<input name="answer" type="INT" value="0"><br>
<input name="activate" value="Calculate" type="BUTTON"
OnClick="form.answer.value=Math.ceil(form.number.value)">
</form>
```

> **Tip:** This method is useful for business applications, when you always want to round up to the next whole dollar.

exp() and *log()*

Before computers made complex math calculations a breeze, man had to do it all with pencil and paper. *Logarithms* were developed to help deal with the more complex equations (such as volume of a grain container or projecting the birth rate within a community). Even with computers today, logarithms are often found in equations that relate to *nature* (the attempt to generate 3-D images of real objects can get heavily logarithmic), hence *natural logarithms.*

The `exp()` method represents a number (called *Euler's constant*, represented by *e*, which is approximately equal to 2.71828) raised to the *number* power, or e^{number}. Euler's constant is the understood value for the base of natural logarithms. The syntax for the `exp()` method is

```
Math.exp(number)
```

The `log()` method, on the other hand, returns the other value. You can use it to work in the other direction. `log()` returns the natural logarithm of a number, which would be the *`number`* parameter in the `exp()` method. In other words, you've already seen that `exp()` raises *e* to the *number* power:

```
e_to_number = Math.exp(number);
```

If you take the result and give it to `log()`, you get your original number back:

```
number = Math.log(e_to_number);
```

The code in listing 10.1 accepts a number and shows the result of passing the entered number through `exp()` and `log()` in several different ways. The results are then passed back through their companion methods (the output from `exp()` becomes the input to `log()` and vice versa), proving that you can arrive back where you started (see fig. 10.2). This example will help you understand the relationship between the two methods.

Listing 10.1

```
<html>
<head></head>
<script language="JavaScript">
function natural(form)
{
   form.E1.value = Math.exp(form.number.value);
   form.L1.value = Math.log(form.E1.value);
```

```
    form.L2.value = Math.log(form.number.value);
    form.E2.value = Math.exp(form.L2.value);
}
</script>
<body bgcolor=#ffffff>
<h3>exp() and log() Example</h3>
<hr>
<form method="POST">
<center>
<table>
   <tr>
      <td colspan=3 align=center>
         Enter a number here:
         <input name="number" type="INT" value="0">
         <br><br>
         <input name="activate" value="Calculate" type="BUTTON"
         OnClick="natural(form)">
         <input name="reset" value="Clear" type="RESET">
         <br><br>
      </td>
   </tr>
   <tr>
      <td align=center>
         applying <b>exp()</b> to your<br>
         number returns:<br>
         <input name="E1" type="INT" value="0">
      </td>
      <td width=50></td>
      <td align=center>
         applying <b>log()</b> to your<br>
         number returns:<br>
         <input name="L2" type="INT" value="0">
      </td>
   </tr>
   <tr>
      <td align=center>
         and, applying <b>log()</b> to </i>that</i><br>
         number returns:<br>
         <input name="L1" type="INT" value="0">
      </td>
      <td width=50></td>
      <td align=center>
         and, applying <b>exp()</b> to </i>that</i><br>
         number returns:<br>
         <input name="E2" type="INT" value="0">
      </td>
   </tr>
</table>
</center>
</form>
</body>
</html>
```

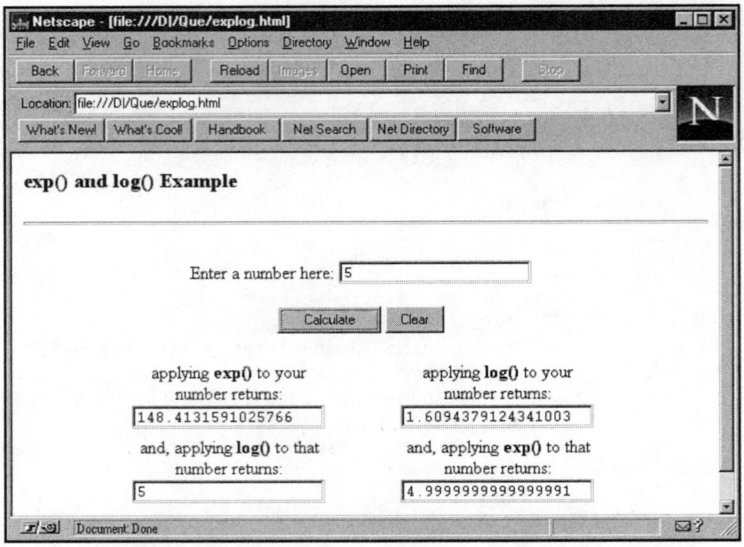

Figure 10.2

Take a number, pass it to `exp()`, and then take the returned result and pass that to `log()` to get the original number back (and vice versa).

floor()

Just as JavaScript provides a method to round up, you also get a method to always round down—the `floor()` method. It's the opposite of the `ceil()` method mentioned earlier, and an example of its use is shown in listing 10.2.

Listing 10.2

```
<form method="POST" enctype=application/x-www-form-urlencoded>
Enter a number here:<br>
<input name="number" type="INT" value="0"><br>
The floor of your number is: <br>
<input name="answer" type="INT" value="0"><br>
<input name="activate" value="Calculate" type="BUTTON"
OnClick="form.answer.value=Math.floor(form.number.value)">
</form>
```

> **Note:** Remember, as with `ceil()`, negative numbers are "upside down." The `floor()` of –2.5 is –3, not –2.

max()

Quite often in even the simplest of scripts, you'll find yourself wanting to compare to values and use only one of them. The `max()` method returns the larger of two values passed to it. This can be very useful in sort utilities, where you want to put a collection of numbers into ascending or descending order.

The form in listing 10.3 determines which of two entered numbers is greater when the user clicks the Calculate button.

Listing 10.3

```
<form method="POST" enctype=application/x-www-form-urlencoded>
Of your two numbers (<input name="number1" type="INT" value="0">
and <input name="number2" type="INT" value="0">),<br>
<input name="answer" type="INT" value="0"> is the greater of the
two.<br>
<input name="activate" value="Calculate" type="BUTTON"
OnClick="form.answer.value=Math.max(form.number1.value,
➥form.number2.value)">
</form>
```

min()

The correlative method to `max()` is `min()`. Just as `max()` returned the greater of two values, `min()` returns the lesser of two values compared. By using the same form fragment that you did with `max()`, you can test `min()`, as shown in listing 10.4.

Listing 10.4

```
<form method="POST" enctype=application/x-www-form-urlencoded>
Of your two numbers (<input name="number1" type="INT" value="0">
and <input name="number2" type="INT" value="0">),<br>
<input name="answer" type="INT" value="0"> is the lesser of the
two.<br>
<input name="activate" value="Calculate" type="BUTTON"
OnClick="form.answer.value=Math.min(form.number1.value,
➥form.number2.value)">
</form>
```

Figure 10.3 shows the output of listing 10.4.

pow()

Need to figure out the surface area of a square? Need to know the volume of a cube? The `pow()` method returns the value of the first argument (the *`base`*) raised to the power of the second argument (the *`exponent`*):

```
result = Math.pow(base, exponent);
```

So your square's surface area would be represented like this:

```
surfaceArea = Math.pow(side,2);
```

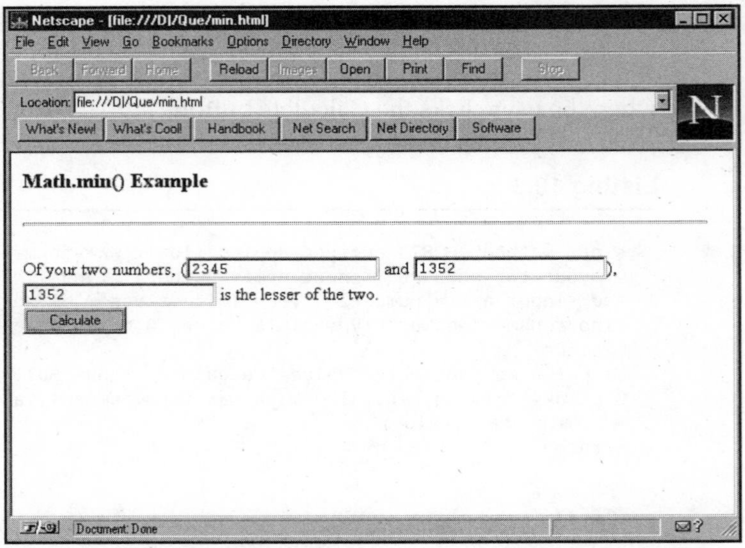

Figure 10.3

Example of `min()`, which returns the lesser of two numbers. Its counterpart, `max()`, returns the larger of two numbers.

Now to figure out the volume of that cube I mentioned, use this:

```
volume = Math.pow(side,3);
```

The volume is quickly calculated for you. Using the `pow()` method is faster and simpler to use than typing

```
volume = eval(side * side * side);

<form method="POST" enctype=application/x-www-form-urlencoded>
Your first number (<input name="number1" type="INT" value="0">)
raised to the <input name="number2" type="INT" value="0"><br>
equals <input name="answer" type="INT" value="0">.<br>
<input name="activate" value="Calculate" type="BUTTON"
OnClick="form.answer.value=Math.pow(form.number1.value,
➥form.number2.value)">
</form>
```

random()

For games of blackjack and dice, you'll need many random numbers generated (to "pick" a card from a deck, or "roll" the dice by picking a number from 1 to 6). In its early implementation (shown in listing 10.5), the `random()` method is about as close as you'll get—for now. This method produces a pseudo-random number. However, the returned value will be between 0 and 1—not very useful for most applications. But it's a start.

Caution: The `random()` method is implemented only in UNIX versions of Navigator. Using it from another version (Macintosh or Windows) may crash your system and most certainly will generate an error message.

Listing 10.5

```
<form method="POST" enctype=application/x-www-form-urlencoded>
Your random number is:<br>
<input name="answer" type="INT" value="0"><br>
<input name="activate" value="Calculate" type="BUTTON"
OnClick="form.answer.value=Math.random()">
<font color="red"> WARNING!! Do not click this button unless you
run UNIX</font>
</form>
```

Tip: Because of the limited implementation of the `random()` method, a better solution (that *does* work across all platforms) is to "roll your own" `random()` function. One possible function is

```
function random(iMax)
{
    var now=new Date();
    var time=now.getTime();
    return (time/10) % iMax;
}
```

This returns an integer number between 0 and (iMax–1). This uses the `Date` method (discussed in Chapter 12, "Date Methods") to get the time of day, which it manipulates. Because the time of day is always changing, this `random()` function will return a different value each time it's called.

round()

When I discussed the `ceil()` and `floor()` methods earlier, I noted that they're very similar to the `round()` method. The `round()` method does just as its name implies. If you pass it a value of 3.499999, it will return a value of 3. If you pass it 3.5, it will return a value of 4. Listing 10.6 shows an example of `round()`.

Listing 10.6

```
<form method="POST" enctype=application/x-www-form-urlencoded>
Enter a number here:<br>
<input name="number" type="INT" value="0"><br>
```

```
Your number rounded of is:<br>
<input name="answer" type="INT" value="0"><br>
<input name="activate" value="Calculate" type="BUTTON"
OnClick="form.answer.value=Math.round(form.number.value)">
</form>
```

sqrt()

Also included in the JavaScript bag of math methods is `sqrt()`. When you pass it a value, `sqrt()` returns the square root of that value, as shown in the following code:

```
<form method="POST" enctype=application/x-www-form-urlencoded>
Enter a number here:<br>
<input name="number" type="INT" value="0"><br>
The square root of your number is:<br>
<input name="answer" type="INT" value="0"><br>
<input name="activate" value="Calculate" type="BUTTON"
OnClick="form.answer.value=Math.sqrt(form.number.value)">
</form>
```

> **Note:** The value passed to `sqrt()` must be positive. If you pass a negative value, the returned value would be 0 because the square root of a negative number is an *imaginary number*, something that JavaScript doesn't support.

Trigonometric Methods

The methods in the following sections come from the world of trigonometry. Without delving too deeply into a lesson on trigonometry, I'll try to explain the concepts as simply as possible.

Trigonometry deals with the properties and the relations between different facets of geometry (such as sides of shapes and angles). All triangles have three sides and three angles by definition.

Figure 10.4 shows one side that's longer than all the rest. This side is called the *hypotenuse* (hyp). That leaves two sides, which I'll define as the *adjacent* (adj) and the *opposite* (opp) sides, with respect to the angle of the lower left corner of the triangle (θ). (I'll be referring to the triangle in figure 10.4 for the rest of the examples.)

If you picked two sides and divided one by the other (opposite divided by hypotenuse, or *opp/hyp* using fig. 10.4), you would have a *relationship* that expresses a *facet* of the angle θ. Although there are six different two-side relationships you can create from the triangle's three sides, it was arbitrarily decided that only three of them would be defined. Table 10.2 shows these three relationships, their trigonometric function name, and the corresponding JavaScript `Math` object method.

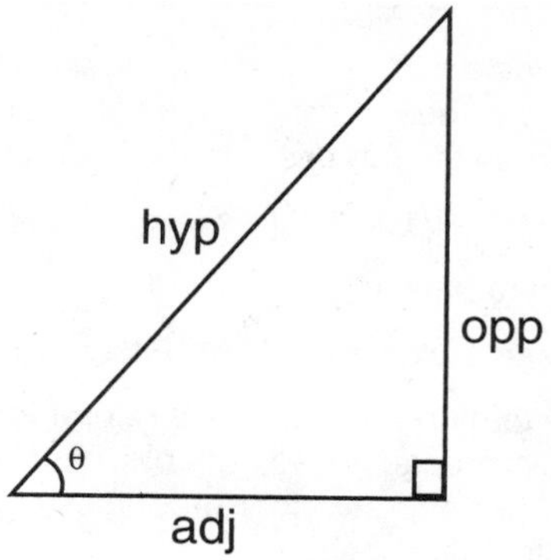

Figure 10.4
The triangle serves as the basis for all trigonometric relationships.

Table 10.2 The Trigonometric Functions

Relationship Between Sides	*Trigonometric Function*	*JavaScript Method*
opp / hyp	sine θ	`Math.sin(`*rad*`)`
adj / hyp	cosine θ	`Math.cos(`*rad*`)`
opp / adj	tangent θ	`Math.tan(`*rad*`)`

These JavaScript methods accept the size of an angle (in *radians*) as an argument, and return a numeric value within a specific range, as shown in figure 10.5.

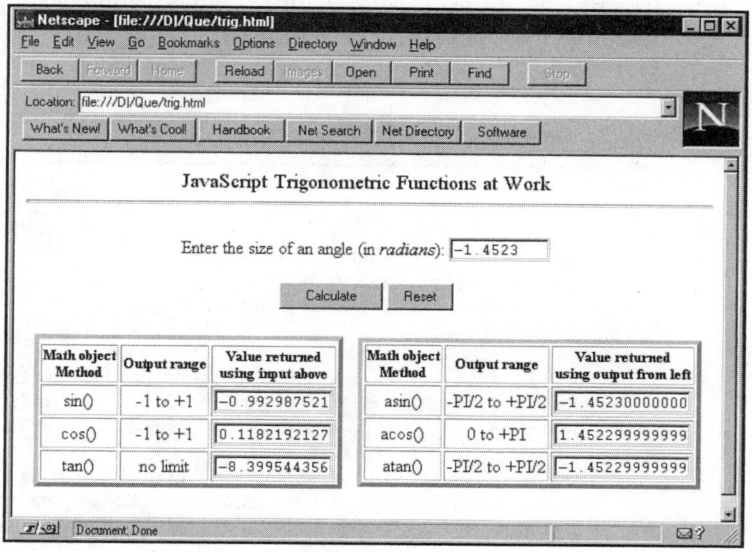

Figure 10.5
The three functions on the left use the radian input value as their parameter; those on the right take the result from their opposite (such as `asin()` from `sin()`) and return the angle. The discrepancies between the arc function results and the original angle are due to computer rounding error.

> **Note:** *Radians* are a system of measuring angles, different but related to *degrees*, based on π (the ratio of a circle's diameter to its circumference). You can convert from degrees to radians with the following formula:
>
> ```
> radians = Math.PI * degrees / 180;
> ```
>
> and from radians to degrees with
>
> ```
> degrees = radians * 180 / Math.PI;
> ```
>
> In these formulas, `Math.PI` is a reference to the `PI` property of the `Math` object, which is a precalculated variable that holds the value of π (approximately 3.14159). `PI` and the other properties of the `Math` object will be covered in more detail later in this chapter.

The three additional methods in figure 10.5 are the remaining three trigonometric functions: `asin()`, `acos()`, and `atan()`. They reverse the effects of `sin()`, `cos()`, and `tan()`, and return the *angle* that has the given sine, cosine, or tangent. For example, the cosine of π radians is –1, while the arccosine of –1 would be the angle whose cosine is –1, or π radians.

> **Note:** The `sin()/asin()`, `cos()/acos()`, and `tan()/atan()` pairs are related to each other much the same way that `exp()` and `log()` are related (as shown earlier). One undoes or reverses the other.

Before you look more closely at the individual trigonometric methods, you may be wondering how I formatted figure 10.5, with two tables side by side. Listing 10.7 presents the entire HTML document which, while a simple example of using the math methods, also presents a nice formatting trick as a bonus: embedding tables within tables.

Listing 10.7

```
<html>
<head>
<title>JavaScript Trigonometry</title>
<script language="JavaScript">
<!-- hide from non-JavaScript browsers
function calc(form)
{
   form.sine.value      = Math.sin(form.radians.value);
   form.cosine.value    = Math.cos(form.radians.value);
   form.tangent.value   = Math.tan(form.radians.value);

   form.asine.value     = Math.asin(form.sine.value);
   form.acosine.value   = Math.acos(form.cosine.value);
   form.atangent.value  = Math.atan(form.tangent.value);
```

```
}
// end hide -->
</script>
</head>
<body bgcolor=ffffff>
<center>
<font size=4>JavaScript Trigonometric Functions at Work</font>
<hr>
<form name="trig" method="POST">

Enter the size of an angle (in <i>radians</i>):
<input name="radians" type=TEXT size="10,1">

<p>

<input name="activate" value="Calculate" type="BUTTON"
OnClick="calc(form)">
<input name="reset" value="Reset" type=RESET>

<p>

<table>
<td><table border=4><tr>
   <tr>
      <th><font size=-1>Math object<br>Method</font></th>
      <th><font size=-1>Output range</font></th>
      <th><font size=-1>Value returned<br>using input above</font>
      </th>
   </tr>
   <tr>
      <td align=center>sin()</td>
      <td align=center>-1 to +1</td>
      <td><input name="sine" type=TEXT size="12,1"></td>
   </tr>
   <tr>
      <td align=center>cos()</td>
      <td align=center>-1 to +1</td>
      <td><input name="cosine" type=TEXT size="12,1"></td>
   </tr>
   <tr>
      <td align=center>tan()</td>
      <td align=center>no limit</td>
      <td><input name="tangent" type=TEXT size="12,1"></td>
   </tr>
</table></td>
<td><table></table></td>
<td><table border=4>
   <tr>
      <th><font size=-1>Math object<br>Method</font></th>
      <th><font size=-1>Output range</font></th>
      <th>
         <font size=-1>Value returned<br>
          using output from left</font>
```

continues

Listing 10.7 Continued

```
         </th>
      </tr>
      <tr>
         <td align=center>asin()</td>
         <td align=center>-PI/2 to +PI/2</td>
         <td><input name="asine" type=TEXT size="14,1"></td>
      </tr>
      <tr>
         <td align=center>acos()</td>
         <td align=center>0 to +PI</td>
         <td><input name="acosine" type=TEXT size="14,1"></td>
      </tr>
      <tr>
         <td align=center>atan()</td>
         <td align=center>-PI/2 to +PI/2</td>
         <td><input name="atangent" type=TEXT size="14,1"></td>
      </tr>
   </table></td>
   </tr></table>
   </form>
   </center>
   </body>
   </html>
```

sin()

The sine of an angle is the result of dividing the length of the opposite side by the hypotenuse. By using figure 10.4 as your reference,

```
sine = opp / hyp;
```

By using the `sin()` method and the measure of the angle in radians,

```
sine = Math.sin(radian);
```

The value returned by `sin()` always falls in the range of –1 to +1.

cos()

The cosine of an angle is the result of dividing the length of the adjacent side by the hypotenuse. By using figure 10.4 as your reference,

```
cosine = adj / hyp;
```

By using the `cos()` method and the measure of the angle in radians,

```
cosine = Math.cos(radian);
```

The value returned by `cos()` always falls in the range of –1 to +1.

tan()

The tangent of an angle is the result of dividing the length of the opposite side by the adjacent side. By using figure 10.4 as your reference,

```
tangent = opp / adj;
```

By using the `tan()` method and the measure of the angle in radians,

```
tangent = Math.tan(radian);
```

Although the other trig methods have limits on the values they can return, the `tan()` method has no such limit.

asin()

Arcsine "undoes" sine, returning the angle (in radians) that has the sine passed to it. In other words, if

```
sine = Math.sin(radians);
```

then

```
radians = Math.asin(sine);
```

The radian value returned by `asin()` is in the range of $-\pi/2$ to $+\pi/2$, or $-90°$ to $+90°$.

acos()

Arccosine "undoes" cosine, returning the angle (in radians) that has the cosine passed to it. In other words, if

```
cosine = Math.cos(radians);
```

then

```
radians = Math.acos(cosine);
```

The radian value returned by `acos()` is in the range of 0 (zero) to π, or $0°$ to $180°$.

atan()

Arctangent "undoes" tangent, returning the angle (in radians) that has the tangent passed to it. In other words, if

```
tangent = Math.tan(radians);
```

then

```
radians = Math.atan(tangent);
```

The radian value returned by `atan()` is in the range of $-\pi/2$ to $+\pi/2$, or $-90°$ to $+90°$.

Math Properties

As you've already seen in the earlier sections of this chapter, many different *constants* (numbers) are commonly used (you've already been introduced to *e* and π). Rather than require you to keep a math textbook or calculator handy, the JavaScript `Math` object also has eight constants predefined as properties, as listed in table 10.3.

Table 10.3 *Math* Method Properties

Property	*Meaning*	*Approximate Value*
`E`	Euler's constant *e*	2.71828
`LN2`	Natural log of 2	0.693
`LN10`	Natural log of 10	2.302
`LOG2E`	Base 2 log of *e*	1.442
`LOG10E`	Base 10 log of *e*	0.434
`PI`	Ratio of a circle's circumference to its diameter	3.14159
`SQRT1_2`	Square root of 1/2	0.707
`SQRT2`	Square root of 2	1.414

You reference any of them by typing

```
value = Math.property;
```

where `property` is the desired property (as in the `Math.PI` example used in the "Trigonometric Methods" section earlier in this chapter).

> **Note:** These `Math` object properties are constants for use in other equations and, as a result, are read-only. You can't change their values.

Summary

The `Math` object provides a collection of methods that allow more advanced mathematical manipulation than simply adding, subtracting, multiplying, or dividing. With the `Math` object, you can round, truncate, work with natural logarithms, and perform trigonometric calculations. Also, the `Math` object has several predefined constants as properties, giving you easy access to common mathematical constants.

Review Questions

The answers to the review questions are in Appendix D.

1. What is the range of numbers valid for use by the `sqrt()` method? (*Hint:* Is the sign of the number important?)
2. What is the return value of the `log()` method if the argument is a negative number? (*Hint:* Remember the relationship between `log()` and `exp()`. Can `exp()` ever produce a negative answer?)
3. What can the `floor()` method be used for?
4. Can the `random()` method be used on a Windows NT system?
5. Explain the differences between the `round()`, `ceil()`, and `floor()` methods.
6. Name the output ranges for the six trigonometry methods.
7. Why does `Math.sin(Math.asin(`*`radians`*`))` return the value that it does?

Exercises

1. Write a function that will take three numbers and return the larger and smaller of the set.
2. By using `abs()` and `sqrt()`, process a negative number to get the square root of its positive reciprocal.
3. Using what you wrote in Exercise 2, create a simple square root calculator form that properly handles positive and negative numbers. Remember, the square root of a negative number is an *imaginary number* and is represented by the square root of its absolute value and the letter *i* (as in `sqrt(-4) = 2i`).
4. Using the JavaScript trigonometry methods, build an equation to return the value of `(sin(D) / tan(D))`, where `D` is an angle measured in *degrees* instead of radians.
5. Build a function that accepts degrees instead of radians as its argument.
6. Build a statement that returns the degrees of an angle, if the sine of that angle is known.

CHAPTER 11

String Methods

In this chapter, you learn how to use the methods associated with string objects. Although the math methods discussed in Chapter 10 are quite important to a script, unless you use string objects and their functions, a visitor to your Web site would never know that the math calculations even exist. The string objects and their methods allow you to display the results of your other calculations. In this chapter, you learn the methods, their syntax, and their mirror HyperText Markup Language (HTML) tags.

The *length* Property of the String Object

Strings have only one property, `length`. This property's value represents the respective number of characters that the string contains. To obtain this value, you use the following syntax:

```
stringName.length
```

Consider the following example:

```
var findLength = "This is to test the length property."
var haveLength = findLength.length
document.writeln(findLength + "<br>")
document.writeln(haveLength)
```

This example produces the following output:

```
This is to test the length property.
36
```

The first line results from `writeln()`'s string value. For the second line, because the example's `length` property is numeric, `haveLength` is also treated as a numeric variable.

Methods of the String Object

JavaScript offers 19 string methods that give you great control over how JavaScript displays your information. (As with any new language, the number of available string methods may change in the future.) The following are the current string methods and the functional category to which they belong:

Name	*Functional Group*
`anchor()`	Navigational
`big()`	Size
`blink()`	Attribute
`bold()`	Attribute
`charAt()`	Manipulation
`fixed()`	Size
`fontcolor()`	Attribute
`fontsize()`	Size
`indexOf()`	Manipulation
`italics()`	Attribute
`lastIndexOf()`	Manipulation
`link()`	Navigational
`small()`	Size
`strike()`	Attribute
`sub()`	Position
`substring()`	Manipulation
`sup()`	Position
`toLowerCase()`	Case
`toUpperCase()`	Case

The following sections discuss each method alphabetically within its functional group.

Attribute Methods

The attribute methods for strings specify the way that normal text appears on-screen as viewed by the user. After all, no one wants to look at endless text (boring!), even if the text provides important and interesting information. The attribute methods provide the ideal way to spice up a page to make it attractive, pleasing, and well-frequented by users.

> **Note:** Yes, many users out there still surf the Web with text-based browsers, such as Lynx. But because Lynx doesn't support JavaScript, these users need to be addressed in the parts of your document you design for the non-JavaScript community.

Each attribute method corresponds to an HTML tag (such as `bold()` and `italics()`, which equate to the `<B>` and `<I>` tags) or attribute (such as `fontsize()` and `fontcolor()`, which equate to the `SIZE` and `COLOR` attributes of the `<FONT>` tag).

> **Note:** Although you can still use the HTML tags and attributes, having access to these attributes from within JavaScript permits you to dynamically change the appearance of your pages (without having to create multiple pages, each showing a different combination of attributes).
>
> In many cases, using JavaScript will result in more typing (the HTML tags are often shorter), but
>
> - With JavaScript, you don't need to remember whether a particular tag has a closing tag associated with it (for example, does `<B>` have a `</B>`?).
> - JavaScript allows you to change how text is displayed without having to rewrite the page itself.

blink()

As its name implies, the `blink()` method causes the text to *blink* (alternate between visible and invisible at the rate of one "blink" per second). This method is a good way to catch the user's eye. It's equivalent to the HTML `<BLINK>` tag.

The method's syntax is as follows:

```
string.blink();
```

The following is an example of `blink()`:

```
function blinky() {
   var blinkString = "blinks";
   document.writeln("A portion of this sentence " +
   ➥blinkString.blink());
}
```

> **Note:** Be careful how often you use the `blink()` method. Many Web surfers consider blinking text an irritation and enough impetus to steer clear of any Web

site that uses it. If you have something *extra special* that you want to draw the user's attention to, consider blink. But, out of respect for other surfers, you may want to consider using other attribute combinations (text size or color) to emphasize things.

bold()

The `blink()` method catches your visitor's eye, but the `bold()` method expresses power and importance. You can use `bold()` to emphasize important sections or words. By increasing the font's size (using the `big()` or `fontsize()` methods) and making it bold, you can actually place more emphasis on that text than blinking would—and also make your text easier on your visitor's eyes (`blink()` tends to strain the viewer's eyes after a while). `bold()` is equivalent to the HTML `<B>...</B>` tag pair.

The syntax for `bold()` follows:

```
string.bold();
```

The following is an example of `bold()`:

```
var boldString = "is Bold";
document.writeln("A portion of this sentence " + boldString.bold());
```

fontcolor()

One of the greatest features of the Web is its capability to produce color-rich documents. The `fontcolor()` method allows you to change the color of individual strings, or to change the color on each reload or event. Again, this method has an equivalent HTML tag—`<FONT COLOR=color>`.

The syntax for `fontcolor()` is

```
string.fontcolor(color);
```

where *`color`* is any valid representation of a color scheme. *`color`* can be a literal name or a "triplet" of three two-digit hexadecimal numbers representing the red-green-blue (RGB) values. For example, examine the following code (see the file colors.htm or chap11ex.htm on the companion CD, as both contain this code section):

```
var redString = "Red";
var blueString = "Blue";
var greenString = "Green";
var brownString = "Brown";
document.writeln("<H1><CENTER>");
// Makes the text large so it can be seen.
document.writeln(redString.fontcolor("red")+"<BR>");
document.writeln(blueString.fontcolor("blue")+"<BR>");
```

```
document.writeln(greenString.fontcolor("green")+"<BR>");
document.writeln(brownString.fontcolor("brown")+"<BR>");
document.writeln("</CENTER></H1>");
```

This code produces the output shown in figure 11.1.

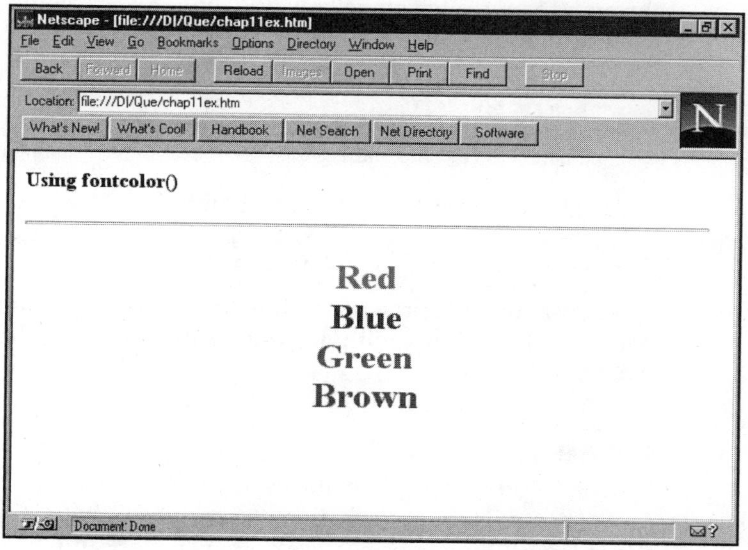

Figure 11.1
With `fontcolor()`, you can specify the color of a text string without having to resort to `<FONT COLOR=>...</FONT>` tags.

italics()

When you want to emphasize slightly (or draw attraction slyly) to a word, phrase, title, or link, use the `italics()` method. By italicizing a portion of text, you distinguish it from the rest of the text, although not as sharply as you can with `blink()` and `bold()`. For example, you can italicize all your links to distinguish them from the rest of the text (especially if the site includes text of same size and color) and avoid confusing the user. When you use `italics()` to highlight your links, the highlighting is subtle enough not to annoy your site's visitors as they read your text, but clear enough to indicate which portions of the text they can click to invoke an action. The `italics()` method is equivalent to the `<I>...</I>` HTML tag pair.

The syntax for `italics()` is as follows:

```
string.italics();
```

The following is an example of `italics()`:

```
var italicString = "is Italicized";
document.writeln("A portion of this sentence " +
➥italicString.italics()+"!!!");
```

strike()

When presenting revised information, you sometimes not only want to show your revisions but also to highlight specifically the information that you revised. Likewise, on the Web you might create a page in which you prompt answers from the visitor and then highlight incorrect answers by "crossing them out" with a line through them (called *strikethrough*). The `strike()` method is the perfect choice for such situations, as in the following example:

```
var wrong = "Augusta";
var correct = "Atlanta";
document.write("The capital of Georgia is " + wrong.strike() + ".<br>");
document.write("The capital of Georgia is " + correct.bold() + ".<br>");
```

This code produces the following output:

```
The capital of Georgia is Augusta.
The capital of Georgia is Atlanta.
```

Many new word processors contain HTML conversion utilities. The <STRIKE> tag permits compatibility with documents that may have been produced by different word processors.

Case Methods

When accepting input from the user, you have no control over how the text is typed (as far as case is concerned). Some users type with the Caps Lock key permanently down (everything in uppercase); others never capitalize anything. If you take any of the data and want to compare it against certain values, you would have to account for all possible combinations of upper- and lowercase characters. JavaScript sees case in strings as important—for example, *Scotty* is not the same as *scotty*, *SCOTTY*, or *sCoTtY* (and so on). For example,

```
if(name == "Scotty" || name == "SCOTTY" || name == "scotty" ...
```

can produce code that is very long, complex, and difficult (if not impossible) to maintain. To give you a bit more control over text, the JavaScript string object supports two methods to convert uppercase to lowercase, and vice versa.

toLowerCase()

The `toLowerCase()` method translates every individual character in a particular string to its lowercase state. This method can be useful if you're planning to pass form information to another JavaScript function, a CGI script, or a Java applet for comparison purposes.

Notice how the following example handles the possibility that the user might enter his or her choice in either lower- or uppercase form:

```
function compare(this.form.choice) {
   if ((choice.value == "a") || (choice.value == "A"))
      perform(1);
   if ((choice.value == "b") || (choice.value == "B"))
      perform(2);
   if ((choice.value == "c") || (choice.value == "C"))
      perform(3);
}
```

This example must duplicate each comparison, which forces you to write nearly twice as much scripting as is really necessary. Now consider the following example:

```
function compare (this.form.choice) {
   var string = choice.value.toLowerCase();

   if (string == "a")
      perform(1);
   if (string == "b")
      perform(2);
   if (string == "c")
      perform(3);
}
```

By using the `toLowerCase()` method, you not only reduce your development time, you also reduce the amount of memory that you need to store the script. The smaller script also loads much more quickly than the larger one.

toUpperCase()

The reciprocal of the `toLowerCase()` method is the `toUpperCase()` method. You use it the same way as you use the `toLowerCase()` method. You often want to reformat a form's data to enable a CGI script to read it or to improve the form's appearance.

Manipulation Methods

The manipulation methods provide various ways to search for and extract characters from within a text string. You can use these methods to format and manipulate string variables input by users. Four methods—`charAt()`, `indexOf()`, `lastIndexOf()`, and `substring()`—allow you to manipulate a string. Two—`charAt()` and `substring()`—extract one or more characters from a string. The remaining two—`indexOf()` and `lastIndexOf()`—return numeric values for the location of the specified search value's first character.

charAt()

`charAt()` returns one character from a specified string. This method is useful in a situation in which places in a string sequence hold specific significance. The method's syntax is as follows:

```
string.charAt(index);
```

index is a number between zero and one less than the string's length (which you can find by using the `length` property). Consider the following example:

```
var lookWhatIHave = "This Shows All the Characters I Have.";
document.writeln("The first character is numbered 0: " +
➥lookWhatIHave.charAt(0)+"<br>");
document.writeln("Here is a capital S: " +
➥lookWhatIHave.charAt(5) + "<br>");
document.writeln("Here is a small s: " +
➥lookWhatIHave.charAt(3) + "<br>");
document.writeln("Here is another small s: " +
➥lookWhatIHave.charAt(9) + "<br>");
```

This code returns the following output:

```
The first character is numbered 0: T
Here is a capital S: S
Here is a small s: s
Here is another small s: s
```

> **Note:** The reason `charAt()` returns a value between 0 and the string's length less one comes from the programming world, where the first character in a string is at an "offset" of 0 from the beginning of the string. Therefore, the last character is at an "offset" of `length - 1`.

To understand how you might use this method's functionality in real life, suppose that you have a page in which users can place orders with your company, and that you offer special discounts to business customers. To compute a customer's total invoice, you must know whether you're dealing with a business customer.

To make sure that you know when you're dealing with a business customer, you can give each customer an ID that he or she must enter and have validated when placing an order. You can build into this ID an indication of whether it belongs to a business customer. Suppose that each customer ID consists of five digits, the first two digits being the year that the customer opened an account with you, the next indicating whether the ID belongs to a business customer, and the last two being a sequential number. With this scheme, 54B03 would tell you that

- You're dealing with a long-standing customer.
- He or she is a business customer.
- Sequentially, he or she was the third customer to apply in 1954.

Although you can gather these facts from the ID 54B03 if you understand how the IDs are assigned, a computer script can read the string only as a whole and can't discern information from individual pieces—unless you use `charAt()`. By using `charAt()`, you can extract just the middle character and use `if...then` statements to assign a value to a variable, `discount`, that you use to calculate an invoice total:

```
if (customerID.charAt(2) == "B") {
   var discount = .05;
} else {
   var discount = 0;
}
```

Suppose that you instead want to provide discounts based on the length of the customer's relationship rather than a business orientation. You can do this as well. However, extracting the first digit, then extracting the second digit, and finally recombining them to get the year is neither expedient nor fun. Instead, you should use the `substring()` method.

substring()

Just as `charAt()` returns one character, `substring()` returns a sequence of characters from a larger string. This method is useful in situations similar to the example given in the preceding section. The `substring()` method's syntax is as follows:

```
string.substring(indexA, indexB)
```

`indexA` and *`indexB`* both are numeric values between zero and the string's `length` property.

> **Note:** Current documentation states that indexes should be from zero to one less than the `length` property. However, the final character can't be retrieved with such index lengths, because `length-1` references that character and `substring()` returns a string before but not including the upper index. Therefore, to retrieve the last character, you must set one of the indexes to equal the `length` property. This means that, to make sure that you retrieve the last character of a string (if you want to), *`indexB`* should be set equal to `length`, not `length - 1`.

If *`indexA`* and *`indexB`* are both the same, `substring()` returns the NULL character. If *`indexB`* is less than *`indexA`*, the returned string is still the "forward" string, from left to right, starting at the lower index and continuing until the higher index. In the following example, the third and fourth calls to `substring()` return the same thing:

```
var lookWhatIHave = "This Shows All the Characters I have.";
document.writeln("The first word is obtained from substring(0,4): "
➥+ lookWhatIHave.substring(0,4) + "<br>");
document.writeln("Here is index of same number (5,5): "
➥+ lookWhatIHave.substring(5,5) + "<br>");
document.writeln("This substring is not a word, as you see: "
➥+ lookWhatIHave.substring(7,25) + "<br>");
document.writeln("Here is that same substring 'backward': "
➥+ lookWhatIHave.substring(25,7) + "<br>");
document.writeln("Here is the string from 7 until the end: "
➥+ lookWhatIHave.substring(7,200) + "<br>");
```

> **Note:** Entering values (for one index) above the string's `length` property returns the remainder of the string from the first index forward.
>
> Although it's possible to use values above the string's `length` property, doing so isn't recommended programming or scripting procedure. Granted, it's an easy way to guarantee that you always retrieve the rest of the string, but it's not considered "clean" programming practice. Also, this is technically undocumented behavior, meaning that at some time in the future the way an index beyond the string length is handled may change (or generate an error).

Here's the output from the preceding example:

```
The first word is obtained from substring(0,4): This
Here is index of same number (5,5):
This substring is not a word, as you see: ows All the Charac
Here is that same substring 'backward': ows All the Charac
Here is the string from 7 until the end: ows All the Characters I Have.
```

> **Note:** The fourth line of output in the previous example demonstrates what happens when *`indexB`* is smaller than *`indexA`*. The string that's returned is as though the positions of *`indexB`* and *`indexA`* were reversed in the `substring()` call. This does *not* physically reverse the string—it just reverses the indexes.

`charAt()` and `substring()` work fine if the string is known beforehand and can be counted to obtain the desired extraction of characters, as in

```
var knownString = "This is an example of a known string.";
```

where the string exists in its entirety before using any string methods. In an unknown string (such as a string that the user has input), the script must determine dynamically where to begin (and, in the case of `substring()`, where to stop) extracting. To allow the script to determine this, JavaScript provides the `indexOf()` and `lastIndexOf()` methods.

indexOf()

When displaying an unknown string, such as user input, you face problems manipulating that string. However, you can manage such strings by using `indexOf()`. The `indexOf()` method returns a numeric value corresponding to the location of a search value that the method was instructed to locate within a larger string. `indexOf()` searches the given string from left to right. You can use the returned numeral in the `charAt()` and `substring()` methods as one of their indexes.

The `indexOf()` method's syntax is as follows:

```
string.indexOf(searchValue, [fromIndex]);
```

`string` is the larger string in which `indexOf()` will locate the specified `searchValue`. `searchValue` is the character, or string of characters, for which you're searching in `string`.

`fromIndex` is an optional index value representing the position from which to begin the search. `fromIndex` has restrictions similar to the indexes of `charAt()` and `substring()` (`0` to `length-1`). `fromIndex` can't be larger than one less than `length`, because nothing is left to search at that point. If you don't specify `fromIndex`, the method assumes the default of zero and searches the entire string.

`indexOf()` returns the offset (from the beginning of the string) of the first character of `searchValue`'s first occurrence. Even if `fromIndex` is specified, the returned value is still relative to the beginning of the string (earlier potential occurrences of `searchValue` are ignored).

> **Note:** Remember that the place values (or *indexes*) in a string or sentence always start from zero (the first character at 0, the second at 1, and so forth).

Consider the following code example:

```
var lookWhatIHave = "This Shows All the characters I have to show.";
document.writeln("The first 's' is located at position number: "
➥+ lookWhatIHave.indexOf("s") + "<br>");
document.writeln("The first 's' after position 4 is at position: "
➥+ lookWhatIHave.indexOf("s",4) + "<br>");
document.writeln("The first 'C' is located at position: "
➥+ lookWhatIHave.indexOf("C") + "<br>");
document.writeln("The first 'v' after 36 is located at position: "
➥+ lookWhatIHave.indexOf("v", 36) + "<br>");
document.writeln("The first 'sh' is located at position: "
➥+ lookWhatIHave.indexOf("sh") + "<br>");
```

This example returns the following output:

```
The first 's' is located at position number: 3
The first 's' after position 4 is at position: 9
The first 'C' is located at position: -1
The first 'v' after 15 is located at position: -1
The first 'sh' is located at position: 40
```

In examining the code and the resulting output, notice the following:

- On the second line of the example, `indexOf()` starts searching at the beginning of the string (position 0).
- On the third line, `indexOf()` starts searching at the exact position that it's given (in this case, skipping over the first occurrence of *s* in the string).
- On the fourth line, upper- and lowercase letters are seen as different characters. There's a lowercase *c* in the string, but no uppercase *C*, so the return value is –1.

- On the fifth line, if a search is started *after* the last occurrence of `searchValue`, the returned value is –1.
- As the last line shows, more than one character can compose `searchValue`. The returned index is where the `searchValue` string starts.

lastIndexOf()

Occasionally, such as when you're separating one long string into smaller segments, knowing the location of the *last* occurrence of a search value in a given string is beneficial. The `lastIndexOf()` method is exactly the same as `indexOf()` except that it searches the given string from right to left. `lastIndexOf()` still returns the position of the first character of the given string rather than the position of the last letter.

Consider the following example:

```
var lookWhatIHave = "This Shows All the characters I have to show.";
document.writeln("The last 's' is located at position number: "
➥+ lookWhatIHave.lastIndexOf("s") + "<br>");
document.writeln("The last 'v' after 15 is located at position: "
➥+ lookWhatIHave.lastIndexOf("v", 15) + "<br>");
document.writeln("The last 'sh' is located at position: "
➥+ lookWhatIHave.lastIndexOf("sh") + "<br>");
```

This code returns the following output:

```
The last 's' is located at position number: 40
The last 'v' after 15 is located at position: -1
The last 'sh' is located at position: 40
```

Notice that –1 is still the return value for an unfound `searchValue`, and that the first and last occurrences of *sh* are the same location. Also, even though you're starting at the end of a string and searching backward, you're still comparing the string to `searchValue` in a "forward" direction.

Examine the following code (before looking at the output) and determine its result:

```
var doYouKnow = "JavaScript is not a very fun scripting language,
➥and I do not like programming in it!!";
var place = 0;
var result = "";
while (doYouKnow.indexOf("not", place) != -1) {
   result += doYouKnow.substring(place, doYouKnow.indexOf("not", place));
   place +=  doYouKnow.indexOf("not", place) + 4;
}
result += doYouKnow.substring( doYouKnow.lastIndexOf("not")+4,
➥doYouKnow.length);
document.writeln("The final string is:<br>");
document.writeln(result + "<br>");
```

Here's the output:

```
The final string is:
JavaScript is a very fun scripting language, and I do like programming in
it!!
```

Navigational Methods

If you've tried your hand at creating your own Web pages, you've encountered anchors and links. An *anchor* is like putting a bookmark at a particular place in a page (so that you can return to it easily); a *link* is a reference to another page (or an anchor on the same or a different page).

For example, if you had defined an anchor in one document,

```
<a name="anchorHere">This text is anchored</A>
```

and you had defined a link in another document,

```
<a href="document1.html#anchorHere">Go to the anchor</A>
```

clicking the `Go to the anchor` text will load the first page and position the top of your browser window at the text `This text is anchored`. This makes it possible to section up a large document into subsections that can be jumped to directly, without having to scroll through the entire file.

JavaScript gives you control over anchors and links (and the text associated with them) through the `anchor()` and `link()` methods.

anchor()

An *anchor* is a hypertext target. You use an anchor to navigate through a long HTML page quickly. To reference an anchor, you use a link (discussed in the next section).

You can use the `anchor()` method to replace a standard HTML anchor in your code. The syntax itself is quite simple and matches the same format that you've used for previous methods:

```
string.anchor(anchorName);
```

Consider the following example:

```
var indexString = "Index";
document.writeln(indexString.anchor("anchorName"));
```

This code segment creates the same output as the following HTML statement:

```
<a name="anchorName">Index</a>
```

This statement displays the text `Index` on-screen; `anchorName` is the anchor's actual name. Anchors such as this one are commonly used by links to jump to the anchor's exact position on the page.

link()

`link()` complements the `anchor()` method by launching the hypertext jump to the target. You can use the `link()` method to replace a standard HTML href (a *hypertext reference,* identified by the `HREF` attribute) in your code. The syntax itself is quite simple and matches the same format that you've used for previous methods:

```
linkText.link(href)
```

`linkText` is the text on-screen for the user. The *`href`* attribute doesn't need to be an anchor, but can instead be a valid Uniform Resource Locator (URL) reference.

The following example demonstrates how to use `link()` to create a link to the anchor demonstrated in the preceding section:

```
var indexString = "Index"
document.writeln(indexString.link("#" + "anchorName") + "<BR>")
```

This code segment creates the same output as the following HTML statement:

```
<a href="#"+"anchorName">Index</a>
```

This statement displays the text `Index` on-screen formatted as a link (commonly by underlining); `anchorName` is the anchor's actual name and where in the document the top of the browser's client window will be set when the link is clicked.

> **Caution:** Be sure to include the pound symbol (#) in your references to internal anchors. To include the pound symbol, you must use quotation marks within the `writeln()` function and use the plus sign to combine the complete reference, as shown in the preceding examples.
>
> If you omit the pound symbol, the link target is thought to be a file rather than an anchor. Clicking the link will cause the browser to try to load the file by that name (`anchorName` in the example), which, because the file doesn't exist, will generate a `Not found` error message.

Position Methods

If you're trying to present scientific data on your Web site (and many researchers are using the Web for just that purpose), you'll often find yourself needing to *subscript* or *superscript* information (for exponents, array subindexes, footnotes, and so on). Although there are HTML tags that support this (<SUB> and <SUP>), JavaScript replaces these with its own methods—`sub()` and `sup()`.

sub()

Subscript text is prevalent in chemistry. H_20, CO_2, and H_2O_2 all represent chemical compositions. The example in listing 11.1 allows users to enter the number of atoms or a particular element, and then shows the molecular structure. Although the outcome might not be chemically feasible, the example does demonstrate the use of the `sub()` method. Focus on the function `demonstrate()` (the rest of the program uses methods you've already seen) and how it produces the scripted text. (On the companion CD, you can find this script as sub.htm.)

Listing 11.1

```
<html>
<title>Chapter 11 - sub()</title>
<head>
<script language="JavaScript">

function create(){
     var temp="O"+document.chemicals.oxygen.value.sub()+"C"
     ➥+document.chemicals.carbon.value.sub()+"H"
     ➥+document.chemicals.hydrogen.value.sub();
      temp += "N"+document.chemicals.nitrogen.value.sub();
     document.chemicals.result.value=temp;
}

function demonstrate(){
     var temp="O"+document.chemicals.oxygen.value.sub()+"C"
     ➥+document.chemicals.carbon.value.sub()+"H"
     ➥+document.chemicals.hydrogen.value.sub();
      temp += "N"+document.chemicals.nitrogen.value.sub();
     document.chemicals.result.value=temp;
     document.open();
     document.writeln("A view of the HTML code we generated: "
     ➥+document.chemicals.result.value);
     document.close();
}
</script>
</head>

<body>
<h1>Chapter 11 - Demonstration of the sub() Method</h1>
Ok, now we are ready to write some <em>subscript</em> text.<br>
The directions are real easy. Just enter a numeric value from one to nine
in each of the boxes below.<br>
After all the boxes are filled, the value of the <b>temp</b> variable
will be shown in the Results box.<br>
The results may surprise you!<br>
<table border=2>
<form name="chemicals" method="POST" enctype=application/x-www-form-
urlencoded>
```

continues

Listing 11.1 Continued

```
<tr><td>Oxygen</td><td><input name="oxygen" type="TEXT"  size=2,1
OnChange="create()" value=""></td></tr>
<tr><td>Carbon</td><td><input name="carbon" type="TEXT"  size=2,1
OnChange="create()" value=""></td></tr>
<tr><td>Hydrogen</td><td><input name="hydrogen" type="TEXT"  size=2,1
OnChange="create()" value=""></td></tr>
<tr><td>Nitrogen</td><td><input name="nitrogen" type="TEXT"  size=2,1
OnChange="create()" value=""></td></tr>
<tr><td>Resultant Compound</td><td><input name="result" type="TEXT"
size=60,3 value="- Chemical Compound -"></td></tr>
<tr><td><input name="submit" type="BUTTON" value="True Results"
OnClick="demonstrate() "></td><td><input type="RESET" value="Reset">
</td></tr>
</form>
</table>
</script>
</body>
</html>
```

sup()

Whereas subscript text most often appears in chemical formulas, superscript text can be found in mathematical equations. The example program shown in listing 11.2 lets you enter as many as three variable coefficients and exponents as well as a numeral. The program then does some basic testing on the exponents to format the output better, although it doesn't perform such tests on the coefficients. The program demonstrates the use of the `sup()` method in displaying the results of such equations. Focus your attention on the `demonstrate()` function, which uses the `sup()` method. (On the companion CD, you can find this code in the file sup.htm.)

Listing 11.2

```
<html>
<title>Chapter 11 - sup()</title>
<head>
<script language="JavaScript">

function create(){
     var temp=document.mathformula.CoefficientX.value+"x"
     ➥+document.mathformula.ExponentX.value.sup()+" + ";
      temp+=document.mathformula.CoefficientY.value+"y"
      ➥+document.mathformula.ExponentY.value.sup() + " + ";
      temp+=document.mathformula.CoefficientZ.value+"z"
      ➥+document.mathformula.ExponentZ.value.sup() + " + ";
      temp +=document.mathformula.Constant.value;
     document.mathformula.result.value=temp;
}
```

```
function demonstrate(){
     var temp="";
     if (document.mathformula.ExponentX.value ==1)
          temp+=document.mathformula.CoefficientX.value+" + ";
     else if (document.mathformula.ExponentX.value != 0)
     temp+=document.mathformula.CoefficientX.value+"x"
     ➥+document.mathformula.ExponentX.value.sup()+" + ";
     else temp+=document.mathformula.CoefficientX.value+" + ";
     if (document.mathformula.ExponentY.value ==1)
          temp+=document.mathformula.CoefficientY.value+"y + ";
     else if (document.mathformula.ExponentY.value != 0)
     temp+=document.mathformula.CoefficientY.value+"y"
     ➥+document.mathformula.ExponentY.value.sup()+" + ";
     else temp+=document.mathformula.CoefficientY.value+" + ";
     if (document.mathformula.ExponentZ.value ==1)
          temp+=document.mathformula.CoefficientZ.value+"z + ";
     else if (document.mathformula.ExponentZ.value != 0)
     temp+=document.mathformula.CoefficientZ.value+"z"
     ➥+document.mathformula.ExponentZ.value.sup()+" + ";
     else temp+=document.mathformula.CoefficientZ.value+" + ";
      temp +=document.mathformula.Constant.value;
     document.mathformula.result.value=temp;
     document.open();
     document.writeln("A view of the HTML code we generated:
     ➥"+document.mathformula.result.value);
     document.close();
}
</script>
</head>

<body>
<h2>Chapter 11 - Demonstration of the sup() Method</h2>
Ok, now we are ready to write some <em>superscript</em> text.<br>
The directions are real easy.  Just enter a numeric value in each of the
boxes below.<br>
After all the boxes are filled, the value of the <b>temp</b> variable
will be shown in the Results box.<br>
The results may surprise you!<br>
<table border=2>
<form name="mathformula" method="POST">
<tr><td>Coefficient of X</td><td><input name="CoefficientX" type="TEXT"
size=2,1 OnChange="create()" value=""></td></tr>
<tr><td>Exponent of X</td><td><input name="ExponentX" type="TEXT"
size=2,1 OnChange="create()" value=""></td></tr>
<tr><td>Coefficient of Y</td><td><input name="CoefficientY" type="TEXT"
size=2,1 OnChange="create()" value=""></td></tr>
<tr><td>Exponent of Y</td><td><input name="ExponentY" type="TEXT"
size=2,1 OnChange="create()" value=""></td></tr>
<tr><td>Coefficient of Z</td><td><input name="CoefficientZ" type="TEXT"
size=2,1 OnChange="create()" value=""></td></tr>
<tr><td>Exponent of Z</td><td><input name="ExponentZ" type="TEXT"
size=2,1 OnChange="create()" value=""></td></tr>
```

continues

Listing 11.2 Continued

```
<tr><td>Constant</td><td><input name="Constant" type="TEXT" size=4,1
OnChange="create()" value=""></td></tr>
<tr><td>Resultant Equation</td><td><input name="result" type="TEXT"
size=60,3 value="- Mathematical formula -"></td></tr>
<tr><td><input name="submit" type="BUTTON" value="True Results"
OnClick="demonstrate() "></td><td><input type="RESET" value="Reset">
</td></tr>
</form>
</table>
</script>
</body>
</html>
```

> **Note:** *Coefficients* are numbers that appear before variables in an equation and specify the multiplier of the variable. For instance, in
>
> 2xy
>
> the coefficient 2 means "multiply xy by 2."
>
> *Exponents* indicate that the variable immediately preceding them are to be raised to their power. For example,
>
> xy^2
>
> means to raise y to the 2nd power (not x).

Figure 11.2 shows the output of an equation that this program created.

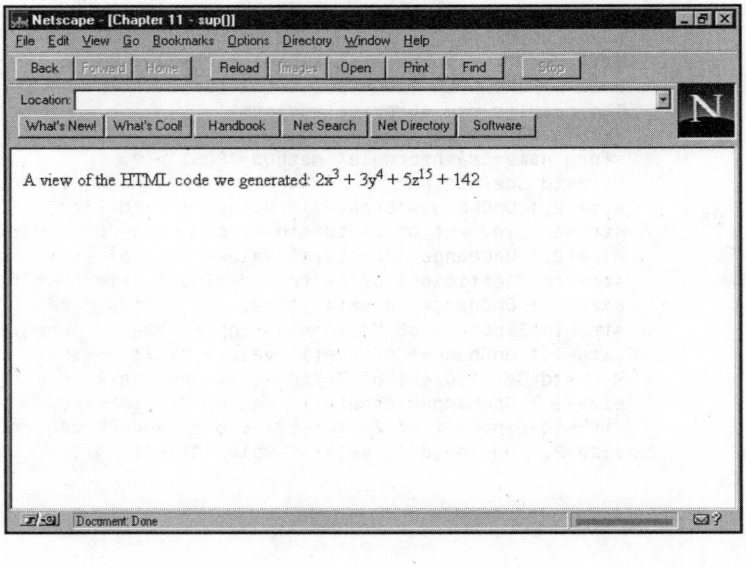

Figure 11.2
The sup.htm file produces this example of superscript text output.

Size Methods

You've already seen how the attribute methods (such as `italics()`, `fontcolor()`, and `bold()`) can be used to make text stand out from the rest of the page. Another way of drawing the surfer's attention to parts of your site is to vary the *size* of the text. With JavaScript, this is done through the `big()`, `fixed()`, `fontsize()`, and `small()` methods.

> **Note:** These methods reflect several new tags (such as `<BIG>` and `<SMALL>`) that have recently been introduced to HTML, either as Netscape *extensions* (new tags that only the Navigator browser recognizes) or as part of HTML 3.0 (the new version of the hypertext standard).

big()

One of the most uniform ways to display larger text has been the `<BIG>` HTML tag. This produces text that's one size larger than the default size. When you create your pages dynamically with JavaScript, the `big()` method replaces the `<BIG>` tag. The syntax is simple (by now, you should be noticing a pattern):

```
string.big();
```

The following is an example of `big()`:

```
var bigString = "A BIG Font";
document.writeln(bigString.big());
```

fixed()

Normally, text you read (like what you're reading now) is *variable-pitch*—a *w* takes up more horizontal space than an *l* or *t*. This type of text is very easy to read, and Web browsers cater to this by using variable-pitch fonts.

There are times, however, when you need to use *fixed-pitch* text (each character has the same horizontal width, as in typewriter text)—like when you're reading program code listings, as in this book. In HTML, this is done with a `<TT>...</TT>` tag pair. In JavaScript, you use the `fixed()` method. The following example shows how the `fixed()` method displays the string in a fixed-pitch font:

```
var fixedSize = "This text is fixed in size";
var noFixSize = "This text is fixed in size - NOT!!";
document.writeln(fixedSize.fixed()+"<br>");
document.writeln(noFixSize+"<hr>");
```

fontsize()

Sometimes you want text to vary (larger or smaller) than just one font size (which `big()` and `small()` handle). Under HTML, you can use the `<FONT SIZE=`*`siz`*`>` tag, replacing *siz* with a number from 1 to 7. With JavaScript, you apply the `fontsize()` method. This method's syntax varies slightly from that of the other methods, because it includes a parameter:

```
string.fontsize(size)
```

The parameter, *size*, represents a numeric value between 1 and 7. A value of 1 specifies a small font size; the greater the value, the larger the font size, with 7 being the largest font size available with `fontsize()`.

> **Note:** You may also specify a *relative* change in font size by passing a signed number to `fontsize()`. For example,
>
> ```
> string.fontsize("-2");
> ```
>
> would make *string* two font sizes smaller than the current default size. You also could use
>
> ```
> string.fontsize("+3");
> ```
>
> to make *string* display three sizes larger than the current default. (By default, your browser "assumes" a <FONT SIZE=3> for your fonts.) Netscape suggests that, when entering relative font sizes, you enclose the size in quotation marks (as shown in these examples).

The following example uses the `fontsize()` method (fig. 11.3 shows the output):

```
var showFontSize = "This is it!";
document.writeln(showFontSize.fontsize(1) + "<BR>");
document.writeln(showFontSize.fontsize(2) + "<BR>");
document.writeln(showFontSize.fontsize(3) + "<BR>");
document.writeln(showFontSize.fontsize(4) + "<BR>");
document.writeln(showFontSize.fontsize(5) + "<BR>");
document.writeln(showFontSize.fontsize(6) + "<BR>");
document.writeln(showFontSize.fontsize(7) + "<BR>");
document.writeln(showFontSize.fontsize(-2) + "<HR>");
```

small()

The other uniform method of displaying text is the `small()` method, which has the same use as the <SMALL> HTML tag. Just as the `big()` method increases the font size by one size, `small()` decreases the font size by one. The syntax is consistent with that of other methods:

```
string.small()
```

The following example uses the `small()` method:

```
var smallString = "A small FONT";
document.writeln(smallString.small());
```

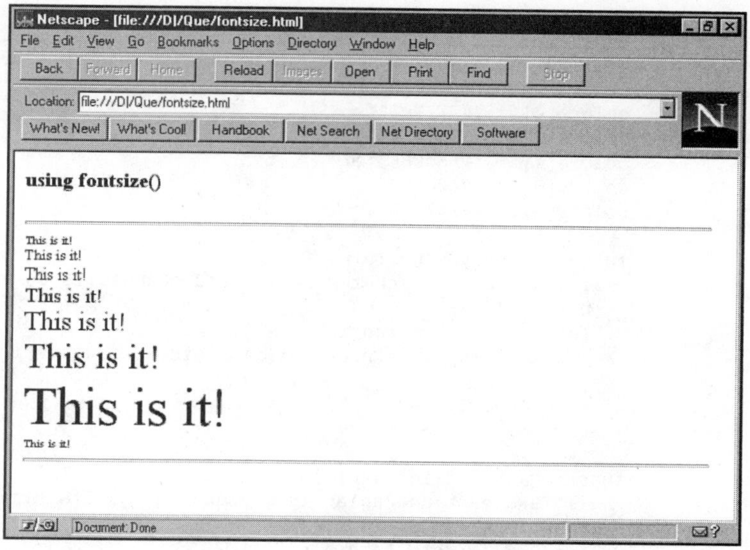

Figure 11.3

Varying the size of text using the `fontsize()` method.

Combining Methods

By using JavaScript, you can combine the string methods that so far you've seen used only individually. For example, you can specify that a string be not only bold and blinking, but also colored, superscript, and more. And you can achieve all this in one line of code, without having to mess with HTML tags.

Combining string methods is quite simple. After finishing one method, you simply add another period and attach the next method, just as though the previous method were the string itself. Listing 11.3 presents several examples.

Listing 11.3

```
<html>
<head>
<script language="JavaScript">
function MakeArray(size) {
   this.length = size;
   for(i = 1; i <= size; i++) {
      this[i] = '';
   }
   return this;
}

colors = new MakeArray(7);
colors[0] = "#FF0000";
```

continues

Listing 11.3 Continued

```
colors[1] = "#00FF00";
colors[2] = "#777700";
colors[3] = "#0000FF";
colors[4] = "#FF00FF";
colors[5] = "#00FFFF";
colors[6] = "#777777";

function crazyColors(str) {
   // Take each character in str and change its color
   newString = "";
   for(i=0 ; i<str.length ; i++) {
      newString += str.charAt(i).fontcolor(colors[i % 7]);
   }
   return newString;
}

function crazySizes(str) {
   // Take each character in str and change its size
   newString = "";
   for(i=0 ; i<str.length ; i++) {
      newString += str.charAt(i).fontsize((i % 7) + 1);
   }
   return newString;
}

function crazyEmphasis(str) {
   // Take each character in str and change its size and color
   newString = "";
   for(i=0 ; i<str.length ; i++) {
      var ch = str.charAt(i);
      var which = i % 7;
      if(which == 0)
         newString += ch.big();
      else if(which == 1)
         newString += ch.small();
      else if(which == 2)
         newString += ch.italics();
      else if(which == 3)
         newString += ch.bold();
      else if(which == 4)
         newString += ch.strike();
      else if(which == 5)
         newString += ch.sub();
      else
         newString += ch.sup();
   }
   return newString;
}
```

```
function crazyEverything(str) {
   // Take each character in str and change its size and color
   newString = "";
   for(i=0 ; i<str.length ; i++) {
      var ch = str.charAt(i);
      var which = i % 7;
      if(which == 0)
         newString += ch.big().fontsize((i % 7) + 1).
         ➥fontcolor(colors[i % 7]);
      else if(which == 1)
         newString += ch.small().fontsize((i % 7) + 1).
         ➥fontcolor(colors[i % 7]);
      else if(which == 2)
         newString += ch.italics().fontsize((i % 7) + 1).
         ➥fontcolor(colors[i % 7]);
      else if(which == 3)
         newString += ch.bold().fontsize((i % 7) + 1).
         ➥fontcolor(colors[i % 7]);
      else if(which == 4)
         newString += ch.strike().fontsize((i % 7) + 1).
         ➥fontcolor(colors[i % 7]);
      else if(which == 5)
         newString += ch.sub().fontsize((i % 7) + 1).
         ➥fontcolor(colors[i % 7]);
      else
         newString += ch.sup().fontsize((i % 7) + 1).
         ➥fontcolor(colors[i % 7]);
   }
   return newString;
}

</script>
</head>
<body bgcolor=ffffff>
<script language="JavaScript">
var displayString = "JavaScript is fun to use!
➥Just look what you can do!";
document.write(crazyColors(displayString) + "<BR>");
document.write(crazySizes(displayString) + "<BR>");
document.write(crazyEmphasis(displayString) + "<BR>");
document.write(crazyEverything(displayString) + "<BR>");
</script>
</body>
</html>
```

Figure 11.4 shows the output of this page. Now that you've combined methods, they definitely might not do what the text implies!

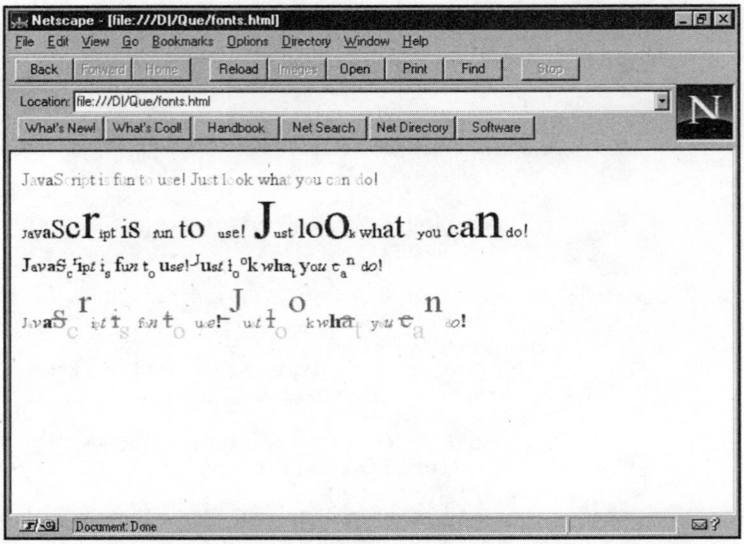

Figure 11.4
With a little creativity and a bit of JavaScript, you can have your pages dance!

Summary

JavaScript allows you to do many of the same things with text (such as change size, emphasize, and change colors) that you can accomplish through HTML tags. However, unlike HTML, you don't have to remember to close tag pairs, and you can have your pages dynamically change—either based on user input or everything the page loads—without having to create a separate page for every possible output. Part of this power comes from JavaScript's capability to manipulate strings and *substrings* (parts of strings), either by hacking them into little pieces or by tacking them back together.

Review Questions

Answers to the review questions can be found in Appendix D.

1. What are the six types of string methods?
2. How can you draw the user's attention to part of your site?
3. What are some of the methods that allow you to control the visual display of text?
4. How can you convert the case of a string?
5. What is an example use for a fixed-pitch font?

6. How can you "extract" part of a string from a larger string?
7. What is an anchor? A link?

Exercises

1. Write a function that takes a string as a parameter and returns that string backward.
2. Write a function that displays a string that grows (gets bigger) at the middle and smaller at both ends (resembling a bell curve).
3. A *palindrome* is a phrase that, when spelled backward, still spells the same phrase (for example, *A man, a plan, a canal, Panama*), ignoring any capitalization or punctuation. Write a page that takes a string from the user and determine whether it's a palindrome.
4. By using the `random()` function introduced in the last chapter, write a page that's even crazier than listing 11.3, where everything happens randomly. As a bonus, have the background color change randomly every time the page is loaded.
5. Write a page that takes input from the user and counts the number of words that were entered. Remember, for these purposes, a *word* is anything separated by a space or punctuation.
6. Again using `random()`, write a page that contains several anchors and links, where the links randomly point to various anchors.
7. Listing 11.2 isn't the cleanest example of using superscripts. Create a new program that handles equations better (don't display coefficients or exponents of 1; if a coefficient is negative, don't display a + in front of it; and so on).

CHAPTER 12

Date Methods

In this chapter, you learn how to use the methods associated with date objects. Associated to math and string methods, date methods add another dimension to your scripting ability and flexibility. The similarities among the form and function of the three types of methods quickly become apparent. Combined with your knowledge of math and string methods, the knowledge of date methods that you gain in this chapter will allow you to perform calculations on dates and display them in an aesthetically pleasing manner.

Date Objects

Date methods are used to manipulate date objects, JavaScript's encapsulation of an interface to the user's system clock (the clock running on the user's computer). With date objects, you can

- Determine what the current time and date are
- Perform calculations between dates or times
- Control the display of your pages based on this information

Before you can manipulate a date object, you must create one with the `new` keyword. You can create date objects in three ways:

- `*dateObjectVariable* = new Date()` creates a date object that holds the current date and time.
- If you want to create a date object for a specific date in the past or future, you can use

```
dateObjectVariable = new Date("month day, year hours:minutes:
➥seconds")
```

if you know the date in string format, as in

```
birthday = new Date("September 7, 1970 13:00:00")
```

> **Note:** In JavaScript, time is stored in *military* or *24-hour* format, where 1 p.m. is 13:00, 2 p.m. is 14:00, and so on.

- If you know the date numerically, you can use

```
dateObjectVariable = new Date(year, month, day, hours, minutes,
seconds)
```

as in

```
birthday = new Date(9, 7, 70, 13, 0, 0)
```

In all cases, `dateObjectVariable` is the variable that becomes your new date object.

> **Note:** Whether you're creating a date from a string or from integers, you can omit the hours, minutes, or seconds. If you do, those values are set to zero. So the preceding examples,
>
> ```
> birthday = new Date("September 7, 1970")
> birthday = new Date(9, 7, 70)
> ```
>
> are both valid, and would set the time to 0:00:00 (midnight).

Date Methods

There are three broad categories of date methods: *set*, *get*, and *conversion*. The first two categories are easy to find because each begins with `set` or `get` followed by the remainder of the method name. They're also easy to understand, as they either "set" (change) the date variable or "get" (receive) the date into a variable.

The conversion methods, however, are slightly different and less intuitive. Conversion methods include `parse()`, `toGMTString()`, `toLocaleString()`, and `UTC()`. `parse()` and `UTC()` convert a given date object into the number of milliseconds since January 1, 1970, 00:00:00. `ToGMTString()` and `toLocaleString()` convert a given number of milliseconds into a date, again since January 1, 1970, 00:00:00.

getDate()

The `getDate()` method returns the day of the month for the date object that you give the method. Therefore, the value that `getDate()` returns is a number between 1 and 31. The method's syntax should look familiar:

```
dateVariable.getDate()
```

The following code section assigns the variable `dayNumber` a value of 14:

```
vDay = new Date("February 14, 1996 12:00:01")
dayNumber = vDay.getDate()
```

getDay()

The `getDay()` method returns the day of the week for the date object that you give the method. You might expect that this method returns a string value, such as *Sunday* or *Monday*. However, the return value is instead a number, beginning at zero, corresponding to the day of the week, as follows:

Return Value	*Day Represented*
0	Sunday
1	Monday
2	Tuesday
3	Wednesday
4	Thursday
5	Friday
6	Saturday

The syntax for the `getDay()` method is as follows:

```
dateVariable.getDate()
```

The following example code section assigns the variable `dayOfWeek` a value of 3 (because February 14, 1996, fell on a Wednesday that year):

```
vDay = new Date("February 14, 1996 12:00:01");
dayOfWeek = vDay.getDay();
```

Although a number representation is useful for calculations on the time period between dates, the representation that most people usually want is the actual day of the week. Converting the `getDay()` value to a text string of the name of the day is quite simple. In fact, the companion CD provides the file convdate.htm, which contains the functions `convertDay()` and `convertDayShort()`, which perform this conversion:

```
document.writeln(convertDay(dayOfWeek));
document.writeln(convertDayShort(dayOfWeek));
```

A single call to `convertDay()` and `convertDayShort()` in the following examples yields *Wednesday* and *Wed,* respectively, as listing 12.1 shows.

Listing 12.1

```
function convertDay(dayValue) {
   // This function takes a dayValue (usually returned from the
   // getDay() method) and converts that numeral into the string
   // text for the day of the week.
   strDay.length = 7; // necessary to 'allocate' array space
   strDay[0] = "Sunday";
   strDay[1] = "Monday";
   strDay[2] = "Tuesday";
   strDay[3] = "Wednesday";
   strDay[4] = "Thursday";
   strDay[5] = "Friday";
   strDay[6] = "Saturday";
   return strDay[dayValue];
}
function convertDayShort(dayValue) {
   // This function takes a dayValue (usually returned from the
   // getDay() method) and converts that numeral into the string
   // text for abbreviation of the day of the week.
   strDay.length = 7; // necessary to 'allocate' array space
   strDay[0] = "Sun";
   strDay[1] = "Mon";
   strDay[2] = "Tue";
   strDay[3] = "Wed";
   strDay[4] = "Thr";
   strDay[5] = "Fri";
   strDay[6] = "Sat";
   return strDay[dayValue];
}
```

The code segment in listing 12.2 demonstrates the use of these functions and their return values. (Notice that the program also incorporates string methods introduced in Chapter 11, "String Methods.")

Listing 12.2

```
document.writeln("Here is day 0 Long: " +
➥convertDay(0).fontcolor("red") + "<br>");
```

```
document.writeln("Here is day 1 Long: " + convertDay(1) +  "<br>");
document.writeln("Here is day 6 Long: " +
➥convertDay(6).fontcolor("blue") + "<br><hr>");
document.writeln("Here is day 2 Short: " +
➥convertDayShort(2).fontcolor("green") +  "<br>");
document.writeln("Here is day 4 Short: " +
➥convertDayShort(4).fontcolor("yellow") +  "<br>");
document.writeln("Here is day 3 Short: " +
➥convertDayShort(3).fontcolor("purple") +  "<br><hr>");
document.writeln("<br>");
```

Figure 12.1 shows the resulting output.

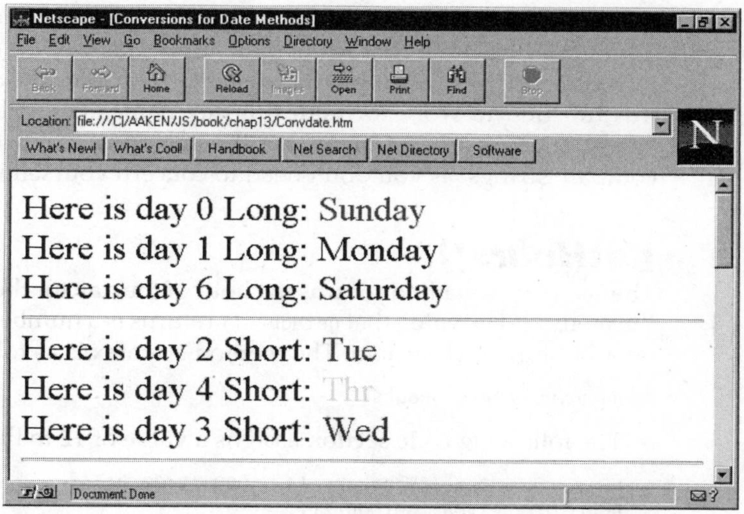

Figure 12.1
This example demonstrates the combined use of date and string methods.

You also could convert from the day string to the numerical representation, as listing 12.3 shows.

Listing 12.3

```
function convertToDay(dayString) {
   // This function converts a dayString (the text of the day of
   // the week) into the corresponding numeric code of the day of
   // the week.
   searchValue = dayString.substring(0,3).toLowerCase();
   if(searchValue == "sun")
      return 0;
   if(searchValue == "mon")
      return 1;
```

continues

Listing 12.3 Continued

```
    if(searchValue == "tue")
      return 2;
    if(searchValue == "wed")
      return 3;
    if(searchValue == "thu")
      return 4;
    if(searchValue == "fri")
      return 5;
    if(searchValue == "sat")
      return 6;
}
```

Notice that the first line of this function creates a substring (`searchValue`) consisting of the first three characters of `dayString` (as well as converts the substring to lowercase). This substring is then used to determine the day of the week, allowing this function to work for both full day names (*Wednesday*) and three-character "short" names (*Thu*). Converting the substring to lowercase makes it easier to compare strings, as you don't need to concern yourself with capitalization.

getHours()

The `getHours()` method returns the hour of the day for the date object that you give the method. The value that `getHours()` returns is a number between 0 and 23, based on a 24-hour clock system. The method's syntax is as follows:

```
dateVariable.getHours()
```

The following code section assigns a value of 12 to the variable `hourOfDay`:

```
vDay = new Date("February 14, 1996 12:00:01");
hourOfDay = vDay.getHours();
```

getMinutes()

The `getMinutes()` method returns the minutes from the time of day for the date object that you give the method. The value that `getMinutes()` returns is a number between 0 and 59. The method's syntax is as follows:

```
dateVariable.getMinutes()
```

The following code section assigns a value of zero to the variable `minutes`:

```
vDay = new Date("February 14, 1996 12:00:01");
minutes = vDay.getMinutes();
```

getMonth()

The `getMonth()` method returns the month of the year for the date object that you give the method. The value that `getMonth()` returns is a number between 0 and 11, with

0 representing January and 11 representing December. The method's syntax is as follows:

```
dateVariable.getMonth()
```

The following code segment assigns a value of 1 to the variable `month`:

```
vDay = new Date("February 14, 1996 12:00:01");
month = vDay.getMonth();
```

The file convdate.htm on the companion CD includes two functions, `convertMonth()` and `convertMonthShort()`, that convert `getMonth()`'s return value to a long or short textual version, respectively (see listing 12.4).

Listing 12.4

```
function convertMonth(monthValue) {
   // This function converts a monthValue (usually returned from
   // the getMonth() method) numeral into the string text for the
   // month of the year.
   strMonth.length = 12; // necessary to 'allocate' array space.
   strMonth[0] = "January";
   strMonth[1] = "February";
   strMonth[2] = "March";
   strMonth[3] = "April";
   strMonth[4] = "May";
   strMonth[5] = "June";
   strMonth[6] = "July";
   strMonth[7] = "August";
   strMonth[8] = "September";
   strMonth[9] = "October";
   strMonth[10] = "November";
   strMonth[11] = "December";
   return strMonth[monthValue];
}
function convertMonthShort(monthValue) {
   // This function converts a monthValue (usually returned from
   // the getMonth() method) into the string text for the
   // abbreviation of the month of the year.

   strMonth.length = 12; // necessary to 'allocate' array space.
   strMonth[0] = "Jan";
   strMonth[1] = "Feb";
   strMonth[2] = "Mar";
   strMonth[3] = "Apr";
   strMonth[4] = "May";
   strMonth[5] = "June";
   strMonth[6] = "July";
   strMonth[7] = "Aug";
   strMonth[8] = "Sep";
   strMonth[9] = "Oct";
```

continues

Listing 12.4 Continued

```
    strMonth[10] = "Nov";
    strMonth[11] = "Dec";
    return strMonth[monthValue];
}
```

Using the two functions in listing 12.5 yields the output shown in figure 12.2.

Listing 12.5

```
document.writeln("Month 0 (long format): " +
➥convertMonth(0) + "<br>");
document.writeln("Month 11 (long format): " +
➥convertMonth(11) + "<br>");
document.writeln("Month 6 (long format): " +
➥convertMonth(6) + "<br><hr>");
document.writeln("Month 3 (short format): " +
➥convertMonthShort(3) + "<br>");
document.writeln("Month 7 (short format): " +
➥convertMonthShort(7) + "<br>");
document.writeln("Month 9 (short format): " +
➥convertMonthShort(9) + "<br><hr>");
```

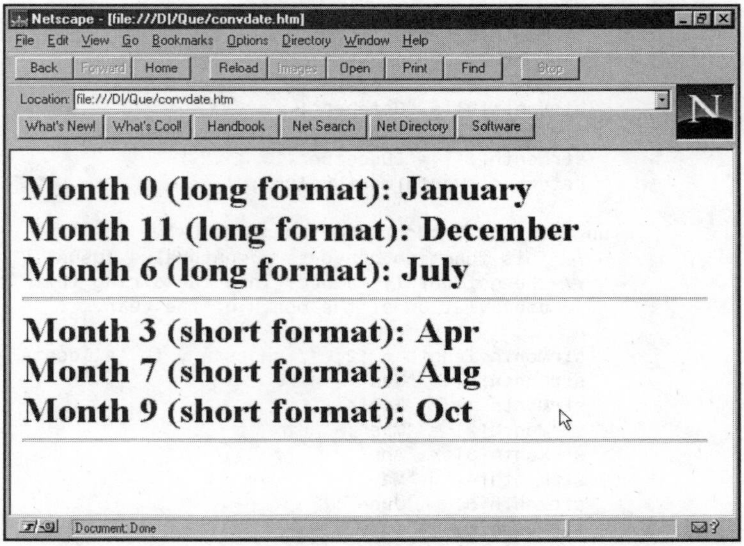

Figure 12.2

This example demonstrates the use of the `convertMonth()` and `convertMonthShort()` functions found in the convdate.htm file.

getSeconds()

The `getSeconds()` method returns the seconds from the time of day for the date object that you give the method. The value that the method returns is a number between 0 and 59. The syntax for `getSeconds()` is as follows:

```
dateVariable.getSeconds()
```

The following code section assigns a value of 1 to the variable `seconds`:

```
vDay = new Date("February 14, 1996 12:00:01")
seconds = vDay.getSeconds()
```

getTime()

The `getTime()` method returns a numeric value corresponding to the number of milliseconds that have elapsed since January 1, 1970, 00:00:00. This number isn't very useful or intuitive, as the example later in this section indicates.

As with other areas of computing, however, such less-intuitive values often possess great computational power. By using two `getTime()` statements and subtracting their results, for example, you can get the exact time between two events. You then need only to convert the milliseconds into a more readable format. This is much less a hassle than having to count days and remember how many days are in each month and whether the time frame includes any leap years.

> **Caution:** As with the `getYear()` method discussed later in this chapter, `getTime()` now supports dates only from 1/1/1970 to 12/31/1999. Passing any other dates is an illegal operation that will crash the browser.

The following example demonstrates the use of `getTime()`'s format:

```
vDay = new Date("February 14, 1996 12:00:01");
document.writeln(vDay.getTime());
```

The rather obscure return value for this example (which, of course, will vary depending on the exact millisecond that you execute it) is as follows:

```
824317201000
```

getTimeZoneOffset()

Greenwich Mean Time (GMT), also called Coordinated Universal Time (or UTC), is the global standard for time. GMT is the current time at the Prime Meridian (or longitude 0°), which runs through the Royal Observatory just outside Greenwich, England (hence the name). Starting from the Prime Meridian, GMT establishes time zones around the world based on 24 one-hour segments.

Establishing the time based on a standard instead of using local time zones is often desirable or even necessary. For example, if you sell merchandise on your Web page, you want to know the precise times when customers have placed their orders. By keeping track of these times, you can ensure the promptness, priority, and efficiency of your service. Suppose, however, that your Web page's captured time is based on the user's local time zone. With orders coming in from all over the world, you couldn't accurately distinguish and sort the placed orders according to the time of entry, because the times wouldn't be based on a standard time zone format. An order placed simultaneously from California and New York would register the Californian order as entered before the one from New York. Your Web page needs to use a base time to record the actual moment at which each customer has placed an order.

Although you could use your local time zone as the standard time for your Web page, you would then have to convert the user's local time to GMT, and then convert from GMT to your local time. To avoid having to perform this double conversion, Internet applications often simply adopt the GMT standard.

The `GetTimeZoneOffset()` method provides a way to set times to a standard zone format. This method doesn't actually do the conversion—instead, it returns the difference (in minutes) between the user's local time and GMT.

Because all other date methods measure time in milliseconds, you need to remember to convert the value returned by `GetTimeZoneOffset()` to milliseconds before you use it for time computations—either by multiplying the value by 60,000, or by using a function such as `SetStandardTime()`, which you can find on the companion CD in the file convdate.htm:

```
function setStandardTime(zoneDay) {
   offset = zoneDay.getTimezoneOffset(); // Get time zone offset
   offset *= 60000;                      // convert to milliseconds
   offset += zoneDay.getTime(); // combine offset and current day
                                // in numeric format
   zoneDay.setTime(offset);     // set zoneDay to date now in
                                // standardized time
   return zoneDay;
}
```

The following code calls the `SetStandardTime()` function:

```
vDay = new Date("February 14, 1996 12:00:01");
vDay2 = new Date(vDay);
standardDay = setStandardTime(vDay);
strDay1 = vDay2.toString();
strDay2 = standardDay.toString();
document.writeln("Standardized time for<br>");
document.writeln(strDay1.fontcolor('blue') + "<br>");
document.writeln(" is <br>");
document.writeln(strDay2.fontcolor('red') + "<hr>");
```

Note that this example requires two variables for the original date. Two "copies" are required because JavaScript transfers the variable's *address*, not its *contents*, to a function (in the programming world, this is called *passing by reference*). This means that any manipulation done *on* a variable (such as calling an object's method to modify the object) will change the variable—even outside the function. Because you want to send the same date value to two different functions (the first of which actually changes the object), you use `new` to make a second copy.

When this code calls `SetStandardTime()`, it produces the results shown in figure 12.3.

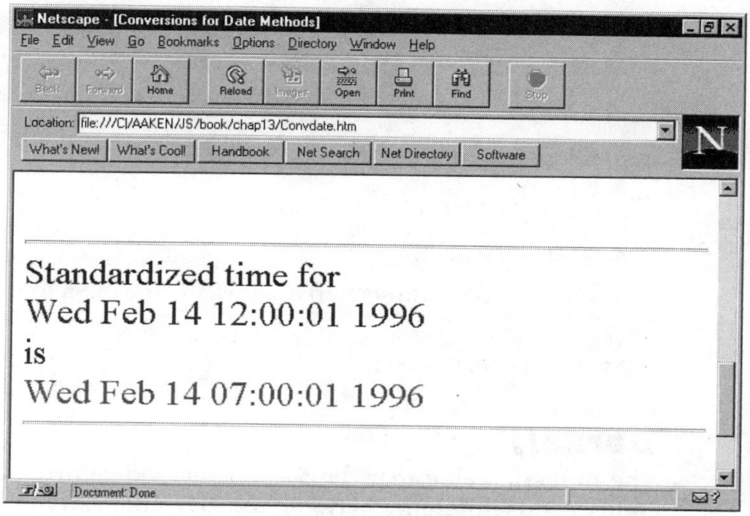

Figure 12.3
The example program displays this output after converting the date for Valentine's Day 1996 from Eastern Standard Time to GMT.

> **Note:** Although JavaScript date objects output strings and take strings as input, they aren't really strings. As a result, you can't use string manipulation methods (such as `fontcolor()`) on them directly. That's why (in the previous example) temporary string copies of the dates were made by using the `toString()` method (discussed later in the chapter).

getYear()

The `getYear()` method returns the year from the date object that you give the method. The value that `getYear()` returns is a number computed by subtracting 1900 from the year in the date object.

> **Caution:** As with `getTime()`, only dates ranging from 1970 to 1999 are valid entries. A date outside that range causes Netscape 2.0 to perform an illegal

operation and terminate itself (see fig. 12.4). A page that does that to its visitors won't be frequented often.

Obviously, this limited range will have to change by the year 2000; otherwise, major problems will arise. Look for newer Web browser releases to incorporate changes to address this problem.

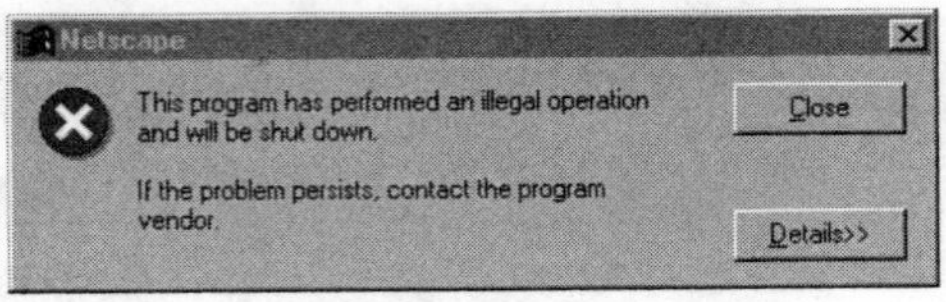

Figure 12.4
To avoid displaying this dialog box to your visitors while manipulating date methods, you must carefully ensure that you use proper coding.

`getYear()`'s syntax is as follows:

```
dateVariable.getYear()
```

The following code section assigns a value of 96 to the variable `Year`:

```
vDay = new Date("February 14, 1996 12:00:01");
Year = vDay.getYear();
```

parse()

The numeric value that the `parse()` method returns represents the number-of-milliseconds difference between the given date and January 1, 1970. The method calculates the date by using the local time zone, not a standard time such as GMT.

Note: The `parse()` method *assumes* that the date object is in the local time and bases its computations accordingly. If the date object is in GMT time, the result returned by `parse()` will be off by the difference between local time and GMT time. For example, in the Central Time Zone of the United States, `parse()` would return a value that's six hours ahead of the actual local time. It's good practice to use GMT time for all your date object operations, converting to local time only when you need to display a date on the page.

Notice the difference in the syntax that this method uses:

```
Date.parse(dateVariable)
```

This difference arises from `parse()` being a static method of `Date`, not a method of a date object that has been created.

The following example uses `parse()`:

```
vDay = new Date("February 14, 1996 12:00:01");
document.writeln(Date.parse(vDay));
```

This example returns the following numeric value:

```
824317201000
```

The numeric value from `parse()` is useful when combined with the `setTime()` method (described later in this chapter), which returns the numeric value to a date.

setDate()

The `setDate()` method is the opposite of the `getDate()` method. It allows you to change the day of the month for a date object, and has the following syntax:

```
dateVariable.setDate(dayNumber)
```

`dayNumber` is any valid numeric integer ranging from 1 to 31 representing the day of the month.

The following code section is the same as the one shown for the `getDate()` method, except that after extracting `dayNumber`, this program changes it and places it back into `vDay`:

```
vDay = new Date("February 14, 1996 12:00:01");
dayNumber = vDay.getDate();
document.writeln("Date before change is  " + vDay + "<br>");
dayNumber = 6;
vDay.setDate(dayNumber);
document.writeln("Date is now changed to " + vDay + "<br>");
```

The program produces this output:

```
Date before change is Wed Feb 14 12:00:01 1996
Date is now changed to Tue Feb 06 12:00:01 1996
```

Note, however, the effect of changing the date to an unacceptable number. If you set `dayNumber = 6` to `dayNumber = 31`, your output is as follows:

```
Date before change is Wed Feb 14 12:00:01 1996
Date is now changed to Sat Mar 02 12:00:01 1996
```

The program automatically updates the day of the week in both examples, but in the second example, the program also updates the month. Although you use and treat dates as strings, the dates are actually numeric codes presented in a more understandable form. At the same time, however, dates aren't strictly numbers, because you can't add or subtract them without first changing them by using a method such as `parse()` or `UTC()`.

setHours()

The complement to `getHours()`, `setHours()` lets you change the hours for a date object. It has the following syntax:

```
dateVariable.setHours(hoursOfDay)
```

`hoursOfDay` is any valid numeric integer ranging from 0 to 23, representing the 24 hours of the day.

The following code section is the same as the one shown for the `getHours()` method, except that after extracting `hoursOfDay`, the program changes it and puts it back into `vDay`:

```
vDay = new Date("February 14, 1996 12:00:01");
dayNumber = vDay.getHours();
document.writeln("Hours before change is  " + vDay + "<br>");
hoursOfDay = 6;
vDay.setHours(hoursOfDay);
document.writeln("Hours is now changed to " + vDay + "<br>");
```

This program's output is as follows:

```
Hours before change is Wed Feb 14 12:00:01 1996
Hours is now changed to Wed Feb 14 06:00:01 1996
```

Note, however, the effect of changing the hours to an unacceptable number. If you set `hoursOfDay = 6` to `hoursOfDay = 31`, you get the following results:

```
Hours before change is Wed Feb 14 12:00:01 1996
Hours is now changed to Thu Feb 15 07:00:01 1996
```

Notice that the second example automatically updates the day of the month from 14 to 15.

setMinutes()

You already have seen how to extract the minutes from a date object. The `setMinutes()` method allows you to change the minutes for a date object. It has the following syntax:

```
dateVariable.setMinutes(minutes)
```

`minutes` is any valid numeric integer ranging from 0 to 59, representing the minutes in the hour.

The following code section is the same as the example for the `getMinutes()` method, except after extracting `minutes`, this program changes it and puts it back into `vDay`:

```
vDay = new Date("February 14, 1996 12:00:01")
minutes = vDay.getMinutes()
document.writeln("Minutes before change is  " + vDay + "<br>")
minutes = 6
vDay.setMinutes(minutes)
document.writeln("Minutes is now changed to " + vDay + "<br>")
```

The program's output is as follows:

```
Minutes before change is Wed Feb 14 12:00:01 1996
Minutes is now changed to Wed Feb 14 12:06:01 1996
```

Note, however, the effect of changing the minutes to an unacceptable number. If you set `minutes = 6` to `minutes = 74`, you get the following results:

```
Minutes before change is Wed Feb 14 12:00:01 1996
Minutes is now changed to Wed Feb 14 13:14:01 1996
```

Notice that the second example automatically updates the hour from 12 to 13.

setMonth()

You've seen how to extract the month from a date object. The `setMonth()` method reverses the process, allowing you to set or change the month in a date object. Its syntax is

```
dateVariable.setMonth(month)
```

where *`month`* is any valid numeric integer ranging from 0 to 11, representing the month of the year for the date (0 equals January, 11 equals December).

The following code section is the same one you saw for the `getMonth()` method, except that after extracting `month`, the program changes it and puts it back into `vDay`:

```
vDay = new Date("February 14, 1996 12:00:01");
month = vDay.getMonth();
document.writeln("Month before change is  " + vDay + "<br>");
month = 6;
vDay.setMonth(month);
document.writeln("Month is now changed to " + vDay + "<br>");
```

This program's output is as follows:

```
Month before change is Wed Feb 14 12:00:01 1996
Month is now changed to Sun Jul 14 13:00:01 1996
```

You expect the change from Feb to Jul, but why did the hours change from 12 to 13? Daylight savings time.

Note, however, the effect of changing the month to an unacceptable number. If you set `month = 6` to `month = 14`, you get the following results:

```
Month before change is Wed Feb 14 12:00:01 1996
Month is now changed to Fri Mar 14 12:00:01 1997
```

Notice that the program automatically updates the month, changes the year to 1997, and keeps the hours at 12 because the two months fall "outside" daylight savings time.

setSeconds()

You've already seen how to extract the seconds from a date object. The `setSeconds()` method allows you to set a date object's seconds to a specific value. Its syntax is as follows:

```
dateVariable.setSeconds(seconds)
```

`seconds` is any valid numeric integer ranging from 0 to 59, representing the seconds of the minute.

The following code section is the same as the example shown for the `getSeconds()` method, except that after extracting `seconds`, the program changes it and puts it back into `vDay`:

```
vDay = new Date("February 14, 1996 12:00:01");
seconds = vDay.getSeconds();
document.writeln("Seconds before change is  " + vDay + "<br>");
seconds = 6;
vDay.setSeconds(seconds);
document.writeln("Seconds is now changed to " + vDay + "<br>");
```

This program's output is as follows:

```
Seconds before change is Wed Feb 14 12:00:01 1996
Seconds is now changed to Wed Feb 14 12:00:06 1996
```

Note, however, the effect of changing the seconds to an unacceptable number. If you set `seconds = 6` to `seconds = 124`, you get the following results:

```
Seconds before change is Wed Feb 14 12:00:01 1996
Seconds is now changed to Wed Feb 14 12:02:04 1996
```

Notice that the program automatically updates the minutes. Because 124 seconds equals 2 minutes and 4 seconds, the change adds 2 minutes to the output's display of minutes.

> **Caution:** Although the last example works quite well, use the technique of adding more than the specific range with care. JavaScript date objects are limited to dealing with dates between January 1, 1970, and December 31, 1999. If your manipulation pushes the date outside that range, the browser will crash.

setTime()

You've seen how to extract from a date object the number of milliseconds that have elapsed since January 1, 1970. Using the `setTime()` method, you can convert that number to a date object. The method's syntax is as follows:

```
dateVariable.setTime(timeValue)
```

timeValue is any valid numeric integer representing the number of milliseconds elapsed since January 1, 1970.

The following code section does the opposite of the example program shown for the `getTime()` method. This example uses the output from the `getTime()` example as the variable `timeValue` for `setTime()`.

```
vDay = new Date();
document.writeln(vDay +"<br>");
vDay.setTime(824317201000);
document.writeln(vDay);
```

This program's output is as follows:

```
Mon Mar 18 16:42:27 1996
Wed Feb 14 12:00:01 1996
```

Notice that `vDay` was originally a date other than Valentine's Day 1996, but that the `setTime()` method changed `vDay` to that date. The value returned by `getTime()` (and used by `setTime()`) is commonly used to compute a new date that's some time before or after a given date, as in the following example:

```
vDay = new Date();
week = 7 * 24 * 60 * 60 * 1000;
document.writeln(vDay +"<br>");
vDay.setTime(vDay.getTime() + week * 2);
document.writeln(vDay);
```

which computes the date 14 days from today. *week* is the amount of milliseconds in one week (7 days, 24 hours/day, 60 minutes/hour, 60 seconds/minute, 1,000 milliseconds/second). The output,

```
Fri Apr 19 17:56:03 1996
Fri May 03 17:56:03 1996
```

shows that `setTime()` correctly handles date changes that span months (it could have as easily spanned years).

setYear()

You've already seen how to extract the year from a date object. The `setYear()` method allows you to set the year of a date object to a specific value.

The syntax for `setYear()` is as follows:

```
dateVariable.setYear(year)
```

year is any valid numeric integer ranging from 70 to 99, representing the current year minus 1900.

> **Caution:** At the risk of sounding repetitive, remember that the year of a date object is restricted to the range of 1970 to 1999, inclusive. Trying to manipulate or

create date objects with a year before 1970 or after 1999 will have unpredictable results (and may even crash the browser). Not making sure the date object stays within the range is probably one of the more common JavaScript programming errors.

The following code section is the same as the example for the `getHours()` method, except that after extracting `hoursOfDay`, this program changes it and puts it back into `vDay`:

```
vDay = new Date("February 14, 1996 12:00:01");
Year = vDay.getYear();
document.writeln("Year before change is  " + vDay + "<br>");
Year = 75;
vDay.setYear(Year);
document.writeln("Year is now changed to " + vDay + "<br>");
```

This example's output is as follows:

```
Year before change is Wed Feb 14 12:00:01 1996
Year is now changed to Fri Feb 14 12:00:01 1975
```

Remember the range limitation on the values that *year* can use. If you enter an unacceptable number, you get an error in the browser.

toGMTString()

The `toGMTString()` method converts a date to a string and uses the GMT conventions. Nothing much more concrete can be said about `toGMTString()`. The exact format of this method's output varies according to the platform on which it executes.

The method's syntax is as follows:

```
dateVariable.toGMTString()
```

The following code section continues in the same vein as previous examples:

```
vDay = new Date("February 14, 1996 12:00:01");
document.writeln(vDay.toGMTString());
```

This script results in the following output (on a Windows 95 platform):

```
Wed, 14 Feb 1996 17:00:01 GMT
```

toLocaleString()

The `toLocaleString()` method is similar to `toGMTString()`, except that it converts the given date using the rules of the current locale. Again, the exact format varies depending on the platform (and locale) under which you execute the method. Its syntax is

```
dateVariable.toLocaleString()
```

> **Note:** *Locale* means "where you are," both geographically and politically (country-wise). Dates are represented differently in different parts of the world. For example, *March 14, 1996*, is the way dates are represented in the United States (and other countries), whereas the same day in Europe would be represented as *14 March 1996*.
>
> Although `toLocaleString()` is an excellent way to have a date displayed in a user's native format, if you want to perform comparison operations, it's better to use `getHours()`, `getMinutes()`, `getSeconds()`, and so on.

The following example uses `toLocaleString()`:

```
vDay = new Date("February 14, 1996 12:00:01")
document.writeln(vDay.toLocaleString())
```

This program results in the following output (on a Windows 95 computer running in the United States):

```
02/14/96 12:00:01
```

toString()

Although `toLocaleString()` and `toGMTString()` can be used to output strings for display, they aren't really "strings"—that is, they aren't true JavaScript *string objects*. If you remember from Chapter 11, "String Methods," JavaScript string objects have a collection of methods available that allow you to control such things as color, font size, emphasis, and so on. If you want the same kind of control over the display of a date object, you must first convert it to a string object. To manipulate the locale or GMT format of the date as a string, simply assign the output of `toLocalString()` or `toGMTString()` to a string variable, as in

```
strLocaleString = vDay.toLocalString();
strGMTString = vDay.toGMTString();
```

where *vDay* is your date object. If you want to manipulate the output you get from displaying the date object directly, as in

```
document.write(vDay);
```

you can use the `toString()` method in the same fashion:

```
strDay = vDay.toString();
```

After it's converted to a string, you can use string object methods:

```
document.write(strLocalString.fontcolor("red") + "<br>");
document.write(strLocaleString.fontsize(6) + "<br>");
document.write(strDay.foncolor("blue").big() + "<br>");
```

UTC()

`UTC()` (like `parse()`) returns a numeric value that represents the number of milliseconds that have elapsed since January 1, 1970, and the given date. However, the `UTC()` method handles the date in terms of *Coordinated Universal Time,* also known as Greenwich Mean Time, or GMT. Using this global standard makes comparison of date objects work properly, regardless of which time zone a user is in.

Note that `UTC()`'s syntax varies from that of all date methods expect `parse()`:

```
Date.UTC(year, month, day)
```

or

```
Date.UTC(year, month, day, hours, minutes, seconds)
```

In this syntax, *`year`*, *`month`*, *`day`* (and optionally, *`hours`*, *`minutes`*, and *`seconds`*) are integers.

You also can use

```
Date.UTC(myDateObject)
```

where *`myDate`* is a date object (created by a call to `new Date()`).

The reason for this different syntax is that `UTC()` is a static method of `Date` rather than a method of a date object that has been created.

The following example uses `UTC()`:

```
vDay = new Date("February 14, 1996 12:00:01");
document.writeln(Date.UTC(vDay));
```

This program returns the following numeric value:

```
824335201000
```

This numeric value is quite useful when combined with the `setTime()` method (described earlier in this chapter), which returns the numeric value to a date.

Summary

The JavaScript date object provides a means of accessing the current date and time (with respect to the user's computer) and manipulating that value. With date objects, you can track when someone last accessed your site, or how many days until a particular date in the future (or past). The methods that make up the date object provide for setting and/or getting various parts of the date, as well as converting between the user's local time and that of GMT.

Although several date methods output strings, they aren't true string objects (as in JavaScript string objects). If you want to be able to manipulate a date as a string, you must first convert it to a string.

Review Questions

The answers to the review questions are in Appendix D.

1. What are the three types of date methods?
2. What are two examples of the use of date methods?
3. What is a *locale*?
4. What is GMT? What's another name for it?
5. How do you convert a date to local time? to GMT?
6. Why would you want to convert a date to GMT?

Exercises

1. Write a page that takes the users' birth dates as input, and then tells them what day of the week their birthdays will be on at the end of the century. For this example, assume the end of the century to be 1999.
2. Write a page that tells the user what zodiac sign a particular date falls in. Most newspapers have horoscopes that provide the dates of the 12 signs of the zodiac, or you can find them on the Internet (an exercise in itself).
3. Write a page that changes its heading based on the day of the week and whether it's a holiday.
4. Write a function that displays the number of shopping days until Christmas.
5. Write a "world clock" that displays the current time in several different cities around the globe, such as London; Washington, D.C.; Moscow; San Francisco; Tokyo; Sydney, Australia; Toronto; and Honolulu.

CHAPTER 13

Window Methods

In JavaScript, a *window* is a physical representation of what's going on inside the browser, where documents retrieved from the Web are displayed. Until now, you've been working in the part of the browser window where HTML pages are shown (called the *client area*), but you also can actually create and control windows by calls to JavaScript methods. This chapter introduces you to those methods and provides examples on how to use them.

Predefined Windows (Dialog Boxes)

JavaScript provides three methods that produce "simple" windows (or *dialog boxes*): `alert()`, `confirm()`, and `prompt()`. Although you have no control over placement, buttons, or size of these dialog boxes, they provide a rudimentary mechanism for informing the user or getting simple input. The following sections examine each method in detail.

alert()

The `alert()` method creates a separate message window through which the initiating window displays needed information to the user. The syntax of this command is

```
alert("message")
```

where `"message"` is any text string to be displayed in the alert window. The companion CD has a file (simpwin.htm) that demonstrates the following `alert()` example in action:

```
<INPUT TYPE="button" VALUE="Alert me about something!!"
onClick="alert('You have just been ALERTED!!')"><P>
```

Figure 13.1 shows the result of clicking this button.

Some things can be noted about the window created by `alert()`:

- ◆ It has only one control button—OK.
- ◆ It has no other buttons that allow you to close, minimize, or size the window. The only way to rid the screen of this window is to choose OK.

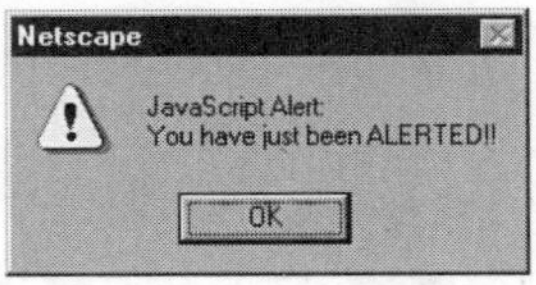

Figure 13.1

The `alert()` method in action. You can use `alert()` to greet users, warn them of a problem, or provide other information.

> **Note:** Until OK is clicked, nothing else can be done in this window (meaning, your browser). So if the program is about to do something (such as close a window or load a graphic), nothing will happen until the alert box is closed. This means that having an alert box pop up before a page is totally drawn will have users staring at a half-created page until they click OK. This is not a fatal problem, but it's one that might not be aesthetically pleasing. If you're familiar with programming Windows or the Macintosh, this type of window is called a *modal dialog box*.

- ◆ If you're not using a Macintosh, the alert window can be moved. Macintosh alert boxes have no title bar by which to drag them.

A real-world example of the `alert()` method in action comes from the world of plug-ins. As mentioned earlier in the book, a *plug-in* is a special program that hooks itself into the browser, providing additional functionality by handling a specific type of data from inside the browser window (rather than have to launch a separate program to view, say, Macromedia Director programs, you can have a plug-in that displays the programs inset with your Web page).

Unfortunately, not everyone has the same collection of plug-ins (you have to find them, download them, and install them yourself), so there's always a chance that a user won't have the correct plug-in and your hard work will be for naught. JavaScript helps correct this by providing a way for you to query the browser to see just what plug-ins are installed, allowing you to act appropriately. This function is shown in listing 13.1.

Listing 13.1

```
function hasPlugin(strPluginName) {
  if(navigator.appVersion.lastIndexOf('3.') != -1) {
    var nplug = navigator.plugins.length;
    var i = 0;
```

```
    while (i < nplug) {
      if (navigator.plugins[i].name.
      ➥indexOf(strPluginName) != -1) {
        return true;
      }
      i++;
    }
  }
  else if(navigator.appVersion.lastIndexOf('2.') != -1) {
    return true;
  }

  return false;
}
```

The `navigator` object is discussed in Chapter 14, "Miscellaneous Methods and Functions," but basically it contains information about the current browser configuration. For your purposes here, it holds an array of strings listing the names of all installed plug-ins. With this function you can check for the existence of a particular plug-in after the pages loads, to warn users that things might not work:

```
...
<body onload="if(!hasPlugin('Shockwave')
➥alert('This page uses Shockwave, which you don't have!');">
...
```

> **Note:** Whereas the `navigator` object "exists" (is recognized) under Navigator 2.0, the `plugins` array is available only under Navigator 3.0. This is why the code in listing 13.1 checks the `appVersion` property to determine what version of the browser is being used. If Navigator 2.0 is used, the code assumes that the users have the correct plug-in installed (in which case, if they don't, they'll see the "broken graphic" icon).
>
> This is another example of how JavaScript is constantly evolving and becoming more powerful, even though it can cause problems for earlier versions of JavaScript-enabled browsers.

confirm()

The `confirm()` method requests confirmation from the user before it proceeds with an event. This gives the user a chance to stop the event from occurring. The syntax of this command is

```
confirm("message")
```

where `"message"` is any text string. A call to the `confirm()` method returns the value of true if the OK button is clicked, and false if Cancel is clicked. `confirm()` appears on the companion CD in the file simpwin.htm, as follows:

```
<INPUT TYPE="button" VALUE="Confirm This First"
onClick="confirm('Well, do you want the value to be TRUE??')">
```

Figure 13.2 shows the results of this button click.

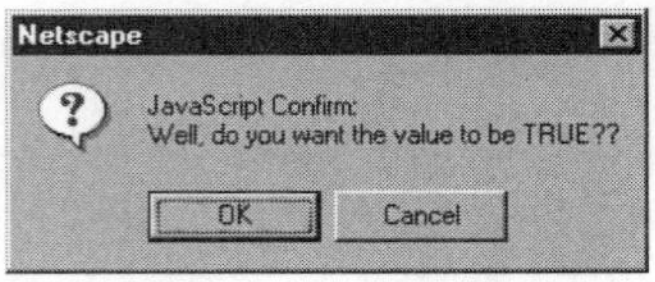

Figure 13.2
Using `confirm()` to prompt the user to answer a yes/no question is useful when submitting form information or asking for passwords ("Are you sure you want to send this?").

Some things can be noted about the window created by `confirm()` as well:

- It has only two control buttons—OK and Cancel.
- It has the option button to be closed, but it can't be minimized or resized.

> **Note:** When the user clicks the Close button in the upper right corner (or presses the Esc key) rather than OK or Cancel, the `confirm()` method returns a value of false, just as if Cancel was chosen.

- The `confirm()` window can be moved (unless, as with `alert()`, you're using a Macintosh).

Suppose that you create a form and want to provide users one last chance to cancel submission *after* they click the Submit button. With JavaScript, you can code the Submit button to do this by using the `OnSubmit` event:

```
<form method=POST>
...
<input type=SUBMIT value="Submit This Form"
onSubmit="return confirm('Submit this information?');">
</form>
```

You may remember that `OnSubmit` will cancel the form submission if you return a value of false within the event handler. Because the `confirm()` method returns true or false, it's perfectly designed to control whether or not a form is submitted.

prompt()

The `prompt()` method receives feedback from users that they can enter from the keyboard, or accepts the default value by a mouse click if it's acceptable to them. The syntax of this command is

```
prompt("message")
```

Or if you want to specify a default value,

```
prompt("message", inputDefault)
```

`"message"` is any text or numeric value. Users can enter any value they want. Therefore, a variable expecting a numeric value on which to perform calculations can receive text input instead. If Cancel or the Close button is chosen, `prompt()` returns the value of null.

> **Note:** Because the input can be text *or* numeric (there's no way to program `prompt()` to only accept one type or the other), it's your responsibility to make sure that what the user typed is the correct kind of information (if you plan on using it in calculations, for example). You can check for numeric data by using the `parseInt()` and `parseFloat()` methods (covered in Chapter 14, "Miscellaneous Methods and Functions"). For string data, the `length` property (in Chapter 11, "String Methods") can be used to make certain that at least *some* characters have been input.

You can test `prompt()` return values by executing the prompt.htm file on the companion CD. Specific code on the companion CD in the file prompt.htm contains the following references to the `prompt()` command:

```
number=prompt("What number would you like for me to display??.", 7);
document.writeln("Here is your number input: <font color='red'>",
➥number, "</font><p>");
character=prompt("What text would you like displayed??", "Nothing
➥at all");
document.writeln("Here is your character input: <font color='red'>",
➥character, "</font><br>");
```

Figure 13.3 shows the results of this script executing when it's at the second `prompt()` command using default input.

Figure 13.3
Example of a prompt window and the output to the screen of a return value from a previous `prompt()` usage.

Some things can be noted about the window created by `prompt()` as well:

- It has only two control buttons—OK and Cancel.
- It has only the option button to be closed; it can't be minimized or resized.

> **Note:** When the user clicks the Close button rather than OK or Cancel, the `prompt()` method returns a value of null, just as if Cancel was chosen.

- The confirm window can be moved (unless, like `alert()` and `confirm()`, you're using a Macintosh).

As you can see, `prompt()` rounds out the collection of JavaScript "simple windows," providing a mechanism to get typed input from users. This method, along with `alert()` and `confirm()`, creates a good basic user interaction "tool kit." However, sometimes you need to design windows and have a bit more control over what goes into them. For that, you need to deal with custom windows.

Custom Windows

The following sections will expound on the customization available in creating and using windows.

`alert()` and `confirm()` windows serve their purposes well, but often you'll need greater flexibility than such limited, controlled windows offer. Looking at the following methods will empower you with the needed skills to successfully command windows in your JavaScripts.

You'll now work through each method concerning a window's operation. The first thing that's needed to know is how to create a window.

open()

The `open()` method will create a new window. It creates this new window just as choosing New Web Browser from the File menu does. The difference is that, with `open()`, you as the programmer control how this new window will appear and what it will contain. As a result, you save the user from having to bother with extra steps. The syntax is as follows:

```
windowVar = window.open("URL","windowName")
```

Or if you want to define a window's attributes,

```
windowVar = window.open("URL","windowName","windowAttributes")
```

windowVar is the name by which you'll reference this window.

URL is a text string specifying a valid URL that will be called when the new window is created. If no URL is specified (using a pair of empty quotation marks), the window will be empty.

windowName can contain only alphanumeric characters (letters and numbers) and/or the underscore (_) character; no spaces are permitted. This is the name used in the `target` attribute for a `<FORM>` or `<A>` tag, and is equivalent to the `NAME` attribute for those tags.

windowFeatures are optional features you can assign to the window, such as a toolbar, location field, directories, status bar, menu bar, scroll bars, resizability, width, and height (see table 13.1). They will appear as a comma-separated list of options describing the new window, the entire list enclosed in a single pair of quotation marks.

> **Note:** *Features* are different from HTML *attributes* in that they also control different parts of the browser (like the toolbar) that are outside the page display area.

Table 13.1 Window Features

Feature	*Description*
`toolbar`	Controls the display of the button bar
`location`	Controls the display of the current location field
`status`	Controls the display of the status bar
`menubar`	Controls the display of the menu bar
`scrollbars`	Controls the display of scroll bars
`resizable`	Controls whether the user can change the window's size
`width`	Specifies window width (in pixels)
`height`	Specifies window height (in pixels)

These features are of the following form:

```
feature=value
```

`feature` is the desired feature. *`value`* (for all features *except* `width` and `height`) is either `yes` (or `1`) to activate the feature, or `no` (or `0`) to deactivate it. For example, if you wanted a menu bar and location field but no status bar, you could use

```
menubar=yes,status=no,location=yes
```

The syntax for `width` and `height` is of the form

```
feature=pixels
```

where *`pixels`* is any positive integer (or positive integer equivalent, such as the value from a JavaScript variable) that specifies the dimension of your new window in pixels.

Figure 13.4 shows an example of opening windows using different combinations of features.

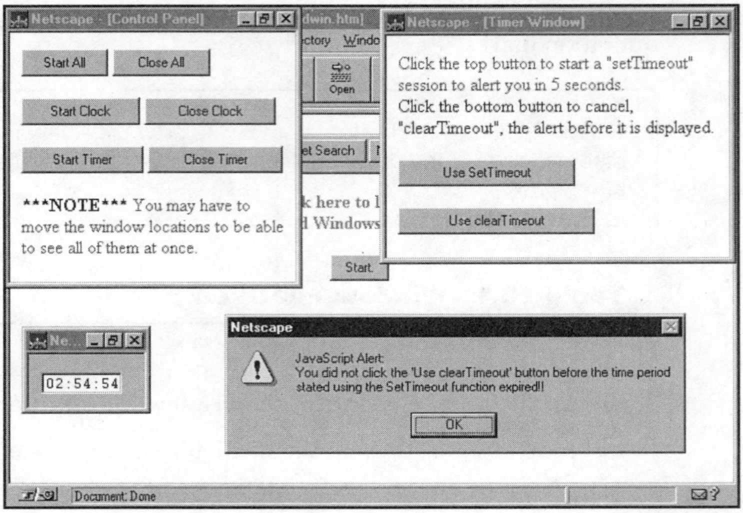

Figure 13.4
Multiple windows created using the `window.open()` command and demonstrating other windowing options discussed in this chapter.

> **Note:** If no window features are specified, all features are set to equal `yes`. If any one window feature is specified, the remaining features will be defaulted to equal `no`. If `width` and `height` aren't specified (or only one of the two is given), the window is sized to fill the screen.

A complete understanding of the `open()` method and its function is fundamental to all window operations. All windows require the use of this command to be brought into existence, at which time a window's visual presentation is defined by using the defined (or default) features.

All examples from the advanced windows section (found on the companion CD as adwin.htm, adcont.htm, adclock.htm, and adtime.htm) except adwin.htm are used as the script for a newly created window (adwin.htm being the initial script run in the original browser window). Here's a sample listing of the `open()` command method:

```
<input type="button" name="ControlButton" value="Start."
onClick="window.open('adcont.htm','ControlWindow',
'width=250,height=225')">
timerw=open("adtime.htm","TimerWindow","width=300,height=200");
clockw=open("adclock.htm","ClockWindow","width=50,height=50");
```

> **Note:** The `open()` method may be the object of an `OnClick` event handler of a button or as a stand-alone command. This allows you to control whether a window

> is automatically created as a script executes or in response to some action by the user, such as a button click.

In the provided examples found on the companion CD, adwin.htm is contained in the root or top window. It's the parent window of ControlWindow, which in turn is the parent window of ClockWindow and TimerWindow.

close()

Of course, the opposite of creating a window is terminating a window. Terminating a window is accomplished by using the `close()` method. The syntax is as follows:

```
windowReference.close()
```

> **Note:** As with any other method (or user-created function), even though `close()` doesn't take any parameters, the parentheses are still required.

`windowReference` can be any valid way of referring to a window. For example, to close the current window, you could use any of the following:

```
window.close()
self.close()
close()
```

> **Note:** When a specific window isn't defined by using a particular variable or the keywords `window` and `self` (both refer to the current window), JavaScript assumes that you mean the current window.

You can close a separate window by referencing it by the *`windowVar`* name it was given with the `open()` command. If a window had been created by the command

```
windowB=open("","anotherWindow","width=80,height=40");
```

it could be closed from within any other window by using the command

```
windowB.close()
```

Closing the root or topmost window is accomplished by the following method:

```
top.close()
```

Of course, you can use any of the self-close commands if it's the current window of operation.

In much the same way, window features (as discussed earlier for the `open()` method) can be seen as *properties* of the `window` object from inside JavaScript. This makes it possible to later access and change a window's attributes if necessary. This is accomplished in the following form (using the name given earlier):

```
window.toolbar="yes";
windowB.resizable="no";
clockw.width=100;
timerw.menubar="no";
```

By examining figure 13.4 and running adwin.htm (the initial file behind all the windows), you can see the remote use of `close()` for a window. The clock and timer windows can be closed individually or simultaneously from the control window by using the appropriate buttons. These commands appear together as

```
clockw.close();
timerw.close();
```

Also note how they're referenced by the variable name assigned them in their respective `open()` commands:

```
timerw=open("adtime.htm","TimerWindow","width=300,height=200");
clockw=open("adclock.htm","ClockWindow","width=50,height=50");
```

Summary

There are three simple windows (or dialogs) that you can bring up from JavaScript: an alert box, a confirm dialog box, and a prompt dialog box. With them, you can warn users of something, ask a yes/no question, or request input.

JavaScript also allows you to open other browser-type windows from inside your scripts. You also can control different features of the window you're opening, such as the size of the window and whether it has a toolbar, menu bar, or status bar. This allows you to customize your windows and create such things as control panels, timer boxes, and display areas.

Review Questions

Answers to the review questions are in Appendix D.

1. What are the three "simple" windows you can create with JavaScript?
2. What are the possible values returned by the `confirm()` method?
3. True or false: A new window can be created from any other window.
4. What kind of response could be held in the variable containing the results from a `prompt()` method?

5. What are the possible options facing a user when an alert window appears?

6. What may be considered the most critical window method? (*Hint:* It sets a window's attributes.)

7. What features can you control when you create a window?

Exercises

1. Design a simple form that asks the user to input several strings, and then checks the fields to make sure the user has entered something in every field. Have an alert issued if the user doesn't completely fill out the form.

2. Design another form that allows the user to control the features of a window (generated when the user clicks the Submit button).

3. Add buttons to the adwin.htm file to allow the closing of the control, clock, and timer windows. Add buttons to all windows that will permit open and close of any other window.

4. Now the control window has no toolbar. Add direct script to either the clock or the timer window that will add a toolbar to the control window. Maybe make one put the toolbar there, and the other to remove it. Open both and see what happens (which function prevails); can you predict the results?

CHAPTER 14

Miscellaneous Methods and Functions

Chapter 6, "More Programming Basics," introduced the concept of a *function* (a collection of JavaScript statements that produce a single result). From earlier chapters, you've also seen *methods*, or specialized functions that act on specific JavaScript objects. This chapter covers the various methods and functions not covered in earlier chapters.

The *history* Object

After you use Netscape Navigator for a while, use of the Back, Forward, Open, and Home buttons becomes understood. The usefulness of these buttons lies in Navigator remembering where it has been during the current session (the *history list*, which is displayed as options under the Go menu). The `history` object is the JavaScript interface into the history list.

The only property of a `history` object is `length`, which returns the number of entries (URLs that were visited) in that window's `history` object. If you create a new window through JavaScript (via the `window.open()` method) or by using the File menu's New Web Browser command, it won't possess the information regarding the parent's history but instead will have its own history beginning with any URL that may have been loaded by default on opening.

Using the Navigator and its buttons to move throughout a history is fine, as long as you're the user. To cause a user's browser to navigate throughout its history automatically, you can apply certain history methods. These methods should sound familiar, because they mirror the names and functionality of the common browser buttons used for history navigation—`go()`, `back()`, and `forward()`.

go()

Within the browser, the history list (previously visited URLs) shows up as menu selections appended to the brower's Go menu (see fig. 14.1), the first 10 of which can be accessed via hotkeys 0 through 9.

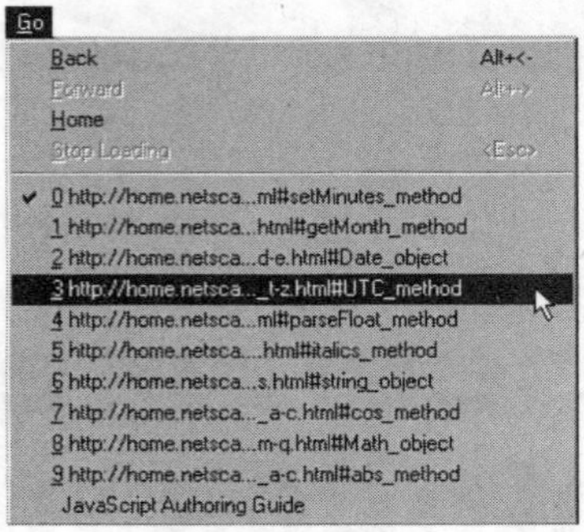

Figure 14.1

Only the first 10 (the 10 most recent) URLs are hotkey-accessible. You must use the mouse to select an URL that's farther "back" in the list.

The `go()` method allows you to jump to a specific URL in the history list, and has the following syntax:

```
history.go(target)
```

where *`target`* identifies the URL from the history list to go to, and can be either of the following:

- An *integer* value that corresponds to the position of the target URL relative to the current URL in the history list. A value of 0 causes the current page to reload (like choosing Reload from the View menu). A positive or negative integer loads the URL that many entries forward or backward in the history list.
- A *string* value that corresponds to all or part of an URL from the history list. The entire URL isn't necessary; if *`string`* is found as a substring of an URL in the list, that URL will be loaded.

> **Note:** When using `go()` with a string parameter, the *first* URL that contains the string will be loaded (case doesn't matter). For example, the menu shown in figure 14.1 has the word *object* in several URLs (indexes 2, 6, and 8). If the following call were made,
>
> ```
> history.go("object");
> ```
>
> the URL at index 2 would be loaded.

back()

To return to the page you just left, you can use

- The browser's Back button
- `history.go(-1);`
- The `back()` method

As its name implies, `back()` reloads the previous URL from the history list. The syntax is as follows:

```
history.back();
```

The `back()` method will go back only one URL at a time and can't be specified to jump backward in the history list beyond that (subsequent calls can be used to perform this operation). For example, to go back two URLs, the following commands could be initiated:

```
history.back()
history.back()
```

However, this coding technique doesn't work—you can use `back()` to go back only one URL. You should use the `go()` method (discussed earlier) for more concise scripting.

> **Note:** If you're at the last URL in your history list, a call to `history.back()` will do nothing.

forward()

Just as `back()` will take you back one URL, `forward()` will reload the next URL from the history list. The syntax is as follows:

```
history.forward()
```

This is equivalent to

```
history.go(1)
```

The `forward()` method goes only one URL ahead at a time and can't be specified to jump in the history list beyond one URL. You should use the `go()` method in situations requiring forward moves of greater than one increment through the history list.

> **Note:** When surfing, you may notice that the Forward button is deactivated (dimmed) most of the time, unless you use Back to back up in your history list. The `forward()` method has the same restriction: If you're at the "top" (most recent URL) of your history list, a call to `history.forward()` will do nothing.

The *password*, *text*, and *textarea* Objects

The `password`, `text`, and `textarea` objects all permit user input to be collected in one form or another. These are valuable tools for gathering data and requests, with each possessing specific attributes making them useful in different situations. The following sections discuss each object in detail.

> **Note:** `password`, `text`, and `textarea` are all form elements and therefore must be contained within an HTML `<FORM>` tag. To access one of these objects from within JavaScript, you would use the following syntax:
>
> ```
> form.objectName
> ```
>
> where `form` is the `form` object and *`objectName`* is the name of the respective object (as defined with a `NAME=` attribute).

text

A `text` object is normally an input field on an HTML form. However, with JavaScript it can act as a display window for values returned to the user. You define a `text` object with the HTML `<INPUT>` tag as follows:

```
<INPUT TYPE="text" NAME="textName" [VALUE="textValue"]
       [SIZE=integer] [onBlur="handlerText"]
       [onChange="handlerText"] [onFocus="handlerText"]
       [onSelect="handlerText"]>
```

> **Note:** The HTML syntax of the `text` object lists several attributes enclosed in brackets (`[]`). This is a common method of identifying *optional* attributes. If you don't want to include an attribute, don't. If you do, remember *not* to type the brackets—just what's between them.

`NAME="textName"` assigns a specific name to the object through which it can be referenced.

`VALUE="textValue"` designates an optional initial value.

`SIZE=integer` specifies the number of characters that the field can accommodate without the user having to scroll.

> **Note:** A `text` object permits entry on only a single line. For multiple-line entry, see the discussion on the `textarea` object.

Also, the `text` object supports the `OnBlur`, `OnChange`, `OnFocus`, and `OnSelect` event handlers. (For more information on event handlers, see Chapter 4, "Understanding Events.")

Once a text object has been defined with HTML, you can manipulate it from JavaScript through the following properties:

- `defaultValue` returns the `VALUE` attribute of a `text` object.
- `name` returns the `NAME` attribute of a `text` object.
- `value` returns the current text contained in the `text` object.

password

The `password` object is a specialized text object, the difference being that a `text` object echoes the characters entered onto the field, whereas a `password` object echoes asterisks (`*`) when the user enters text into the field.

> **Tip:** You don't need to use a `password` object just for entering passwords. You can also use it for any information that you may not want to appear on-screen, such as a credit-card number or other secure information.

The `password` object is defined the same way a `text` object is (with the same HTML attributes and JavaScript properties), except that the `TYPE` attribute is set to `password` rather than `text`. The following example demonstrates the use of the password object:

```
<html>
<body>
<form method="post">
Enter your password:
<input type="password" name="secret" size=8><br>
<input type="submit" name="access" value="Let Me In!">
</form>
</body>
</html>
```

> **Note:** If you set or change a `password` object's `value` property from within JavaScript, you'll be able to view the `value` property and see what you've set it to. However, if users enter information into a `password` object, you won't be able to use `value` to see what they've entered (for security). However, when the form is submitted to the server, the value users have entered will be passed to the server correctly.

textarea

You can use a `textarea` object to acquire user input where it's conceivable that multiple entry lines would be necessary. An example of this might be contained in an online ordering system where you may want to grant the buyer some space to leave a brief comment or special instructions.

The general syntax of the `textarea` object is as follows:

```
<TEXTAREA NAME="textareaName" ROWS=integer
  COLS=integer [onBlur="handlerText"]
  [onChange="handlerText"] [onFocus="handlerText"]
  [onSelect="handlerText"]>
  textToDisplay
</TEXTAREA>
```

`NAME="textareaName"` assigns a specific name to the object through which it can be referenced.

`ROWS=integer` and `COLS=integer` establishes the dimensions of the `textarea` field in terms of number of characters.

`textToDisplay` designates a default initial value that may be composed only of ASCII text, and can be changed by using the `defaultValue` property.

> **Note:** A `textarea` object permits multiple lines of entry. If you want only a single line of input, use the `text` object, discussed in the preceding section.

The *select* Object

When you want to obtain input from the user but limit that input to certain predefined choices, you can use the `select` object. Providing such an option standardizes the input values that will be returned from a form, thus reducing the amount of error checking and data manipulation necessary to compile the user input to a standardized format. The `select` object provides a selection or scrolling list from which users can choose their desired input.

To create a `select` object, use the following format:

```
<SELECT NAME="selectName" [SIZE=integer]
  [MULTIPLE] [onBlur="handlerText"]
  [onChange="handlerText"] [onFocus="handlerText"]>
  options
</SELECT>
```

`NAME="selectName"` assigns a name for the current `select` object. As with the other JavaScript objects, the name you assign allows you to access the `select` object by referencing its `name` property.

`SIZE=integer` is an optional attribute that provides the integer value for the number of options visible when the form is on-screen.

`MULTIPLE` is an optional attribute. If specified, the options of the `select` object will be displayed as a scrolling list; otherwise, the object is displayed as a drop-down list box. `MULTIPLE` also specifies that more than one option may be selected at a time.

`options` are the actual options to be displayed within the `select` object. They are defined by using the `<OPTION>` tag (one tag per option), as follows:

```
<OPTION VALUE="optionValue" [SELECTED]>textToDisplay
```

`VALUE="`*`optionValue`*`"` specifies the return value for the option. When the form is submitted, the `select` object will be set to whatever option(s) have been selected. You can access this value via the `value` property.

`SELECTED` is an optional attribute denoting that the given option is the one selected by default. Within JavaScript, you can override this attribute and force another option to be the default with the `defaultSelected` property.

`textToDisplay` is the text displayed in the list. To change this value, use the `text` property.

Listing 14.1 shows a page that demonstrates the different kinds of select objects you can create. Its output is shown in figure 14.2.

Listing 14.1

```
<html>
<body>
<h2>Using the SELECT object</h2>
<hr>
<form>
<table>
 <tr>
   <td>
      This is a multiple selection list.<br>
      You can select more than one option.
   </td>
   <td>
   <select name="colors" multiple>
      <option value="blue">blue
      <option value="green">green
      <option value="red">red
      <option value="yellow">yellow
      <option value="black">black
   </select>
   </td>
 </tr>
 <tr>
   <td>This is a 'drop-down' selection list:</td>
   <td>
   <select name="direction">
      <option value="north">north
      <option value="south">south
      <option value="east">east
```

continues

Listing 14.1 Continued

```
        <option value="west">west
    </select>
    </td>
  </tr>
 </table>
 </form>
 </body>
 </html>
```

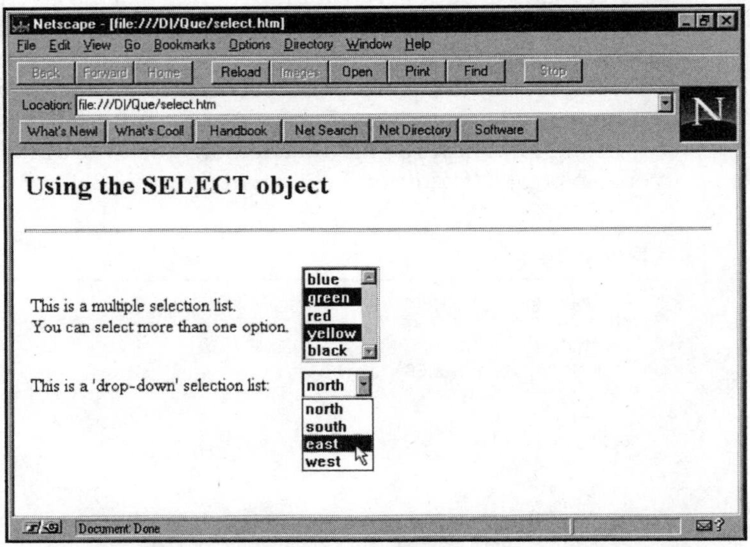

Figure 14.2
Selection objects can be single-selection (represented as a drop-down list) or multiple-selection (represented as a scrolling list).

The *length* Property

To obtain information about the number of options in a `select` object, use the `length` property to access this information:

```
selectName.length
```

Earlier in listing 14.1, for example, the first selection object (named `colors`) has five options, so

```
document.write(colors.length);
```

would display 5.

The *options* Property

The actual options within a `select` object are contained in the `options` property, which is actually an array with one index per `<OPTION>` tag. Again using the `colors` object from listing 14.1 (and assuming that `green` and `yellow` are selected as shown in fig. 14.2), you could iterate through the options of that object with the following:

```
for(i=0; i<colors.length; i++) {
   document.writeln("Option " + i + " is ");
   document.writeln(colors.options[i].name + "<br>");
}
```

This would display the following:

```
Option 0 is blue
Option 1 is green
Option 2 is red
Option 3 is yellow
Option 4 is black
```

You have to use the `value` property, because each index in the `options` array is itself an object.

The *selectedIndex* Property

To access the index of the selected option (shown visually as a highlighted option in a multiple list, or the current option in a drop-down list), the `selectedIndex` property is used. The `selectedIndex` property returns the index of either the selected option or, if more than one option is selected, the first selected option.

From listing 14.1, the second `select` object (named `direction`) shows `north` as the currently selected option (`east` is highlighted, but until the list closes it doesn't replace the current selection). Inside JavaScript, this means the statement

```
document.writeln(direction.selected);
```

would display 0, because indexes start at zero.

To identify all selected options in a multiple list (like `colors` from listing 14.1), there is a `selected` property that's attached to *each* element of the `options` array. This means that

```
for(i=0; i<colors.length; i++) {
   document.writeln("Option " + i + " is ");
   if(colors.options[i].selected) {
      document.writeln("selected <br>");
   } else {
      document.writeln("NOT selected <br>");
   }
}
```

would display

```
Option 0 is NOT selected
Option 1 is selected
Option 2 is NOT selected
Option 3 is selected
Option 4 is NOT selected
```

The *options* Array

You've already seen some of the properties of the `options` array. Additional properties include

- `defaultSelected`, which returns the `SELECTED` attribute of an option
- `index`, which returns the index for that option
- `length`, which returns the number of options in a `select` object
- `name`, which returns the `NAME` attribute of an option
- `selected`, which allows you to select an option
- `selectedIndex`, which returns the index of the selected option
- `text`, which returns the *`textToDisplay`* that follows an `<OPTION>` tag
- `value`, which returns the `VALUE` attribute of an option

Methods That Apply to Forms Objects

The `password`, `select`, `text`, and `textarea` objects are all part of an HTML form (or JavaScript `form` object). As such, they share a collection of methods that help JavaScript identify when their values change: `blur()`, `focus()`, and `select()`.

blur()

The `blur()` method removes focus from the specified object. Removing the focus will cause the execution of the handler text contained in the `OnBlur` and possibly the `OnChange` (if the value has been changed) attributes.

The `blur()` syntax is as follows:

```
passwordName.blur()

selectName.blur()

textName.blur()

textareaName.blur()
```

Each `blur()` prefix represents a valid name assigned at the creation of each object using the `"NAME="` attribute for the object.

focus()

The `focus()` method restores focus to the specified object. Returning the focus will cause the execution of the handler text contained in the `OnFocus` and possibly the `OnChange` (if the value where the focus was has been changed) attributes.

The syntax of `focus()` is as follows:

```
passwordName.focus()

selectName.focus()

textName.focus()

textareaName.focus()
```

Each `focus()` prefix represents a valid name assigned at the creation of each object using the `"NAME="` attribute for the object.

select()

The `select()` method causes the selection of the input area of the specific `password`, `text`, or `textarea` object. This will cause the execution of the handler text contained in the `OnSelect` attribute.

The syntax of `select()` is as follows:

```
passwordName.select()

textName.select()

textareaName.select()
```

Each `select()` prefix represents a valid name assigned at the creation of each object using the `"NAME="` attribute for the object.

> **Note:** The `select()` method applies only to `password`, `text`, and `textarea` objects. It does *not* apply to the `select` object.

System Functions

Certain methods and functions can't be classified as belonging to any one object, nor even to a small group of objects. These functions are inherent in JavaScript and thereby have no prefix attached to them. The `escape()`, `eval()`, `parseFloat()`, `parseInt()`, and `unescape()` system functions shall be examined in this section.

> **Note:** Remember, *functions* are collections of JavaScript statements (or built-in collections provided by JavaScript). A *method* is a special case of a function in that it (the method) is attached to a JavaScript object and works on the content of that object (functions, in general, are global and work on anything).

escape()

Behind the characters normally seen on-screen or printed out are unique codes representing each specific character. In addition to the codes for the normal character set of numbers, letters, and symbols are specialized codes that perform miscellaneous functions. These functions can include a carriage return amid text to begin a new paragraph, specialized symbols, a way to clear the screen, as well as operations to printers such as form and line feeds.

The code behind each character or action is called an *escape code*. The two most common forms of representing escape codes are ASCII (American Standard Code for Information Interchange) and EBCDIC (Extended Binary-Coded Decimal Interchange Code). JavaScript uses an ASCII representation based on the ISO Latin-1 character set. Normally, escape codes aren't considered and very little attention is paid to them simply because they usually aren't needed. They perform their job of formatting text and displaying it properly, so that there's no need to think about them.

JavaScript represents ASCII codes through their numeric number assignment prefixed with a percent symbol (`%`).

> **Note:** A numeric code representation isn't always returned by the `escape()` function in JavaScript. The passing of an alphanumeric character returns that same character.

The value for the ampersand symbol (`&`) is `"%26"` and the value for the letter F is `"F"`. Thus, the results from the following script yield `"%26"` and `"F"` respectively.

```
escape("&")
escape("F")
```

A concatenation of characters produces a sequence of escape codes. The following produces the string `"%26F%23"`:

```
escape("&F#")
```

eval()

At times, the data type of a variable and whether it's a string, a number, or a date can be confusing and hard to discern. Performing a "math" operation on a string will result in the two values in the variables being concatenated together rather than added, as you may have hoped.

The `eval()` function performs an evaluation of a given string, treating it as though it were an actual JavaScript statement. The syntax is as follows:

```
result = eval(string)
```

string can be any string expression (even a JavaScript statement or statements) and can include variables as well as properties of objects. The following two `eval()` statements each set `z` to 14:

```
var x=5;
var y=3;
z = eval("x + y + y + y");
z = eval("x * y -1");
```

Evaluating a variable by itself returns the value contained in it, as in

```
var x=15;
z = eval("x");
```

This would set `z` to 15. Also, `eval()` can handle JavaScript methods and functions, as in

```
z = eval("Math.round(3.14156)");
```

where `z` would be set to 3.

parseFloat()

Along with being able to evaluate strings as though they were numerical, sometimes being able to extract the numeric value from a string is useful. For example, if you're planning to evaluate a string entered by the user, it's entirely possible that characters that aren't digits have been entered. Unless you test the string to see whether it evaluates (or that part of it evaluates) to a number of some sort, your calculations may not work—or, worse yet, crash the browser.

The `parseFloat()` function will return the floating-point representation of a string value it's given. For example,

```
var x="3.14";
var y="abc3.14def";
var z="3.14cd";
document.writeln(parseFloat("3.14")+"<BR>");
document.writeln(parseFloat("314e-2")+"<BR>");
```

```
document.writeln(parseFloat(".0314e+2")+"<BR>");
document.writeln(parseFloat(x)+"<BR>");
document.writeln(parseFloat(y)+"<BR>");
document.writeln(parseFloat(z)+"<BR>");
```

These statements return the following values:

```
3.1400000000000001
3.1400000000000001
3.1400000000000001
3.1400000000000001
0
3.1400000000000001
```

It doesn't matter whether the string is passed directly or through a variable. As soon as `parseFloat()` hits a non-numeric character, it stops returning what it has found (last example); if it has found no numerals by that point, it returns 0 on a Windows platform (next-to-last example) and `NaN` on any other platform.

> **Note:** The returned value of `NaN` from a function indicates that the value sent to that function is "not a number". This value is seen on all platforms except Windows, which returns a zero instead.

parseInt()

The `parseInt()` function operates on the same premise as `parseFloat()`, except that `parseInt()` tries to return an integer value of a set base in place of a floating-point number. The syntax is as follows:

```
parseInt(string[,radix])
```

`string` is, again, any string value wanting parsed. The optional *`radix`* argument denotes the base in which the return value shall be.

The following statements all return the value 12:

```
document.writeln(parseInt("C",16)+"<BR>");
document.writeln(parseInt("14", 8)+"<BR>");
document.writeln(parseInt("12", 10)+"<BR>");
document.writeln(parseInt("12.99")+"<BR>");
document.writeln(parseInt("CPA", 16)+"<BR>");
document.writeln(parseInt("1100", 2)+"<BR>");
document.writeln(parseInt("12*7", 10)+"<BR>");
```

Most of the reasons for returning 12 are straightforward. The fourth example (document.writeln(parseInt("12.99")+"<BR>")) demonstrates the option of not adding the *`radix`* number, and it defaults to a base 10 because that's the common standard.

> **Note:** The `parseInt()` function doesn't round numbers—it truncates them at the decimal because `parseInt()` sees a string, not a decimated numeral.

The fifth example (`document.writeln(parseInt("CPA", 16)+<BR>"))` shows that `parseInt()` will interpret numerals until it hits a non-numeric value for the given base number system. Here it encounters a P, which isn't contained in the hexadecimal number system. The inclusion of any letters in base 10 and including even the number 2 in binary will cause the `parseInt()` function to halt its interpretation.

The last example (`document.writeln(parseInt("12*7", 10)+"<BR>"))` illustrates further that `parseInt()` views the input as strings, not as numerical data. Most of you will look at this example, expect a value of 84 to be returned, and be surprised when it comes back as 12.

> **Note:** Remember that `parseInt()` doesn't perform arithmetic or decimal operations. Such values (the +, –, and decimal point) are seen as non-numeral input, and parsing is halted.

Based on your operating system, the following examples all return 0 or `NaN` (except the last, which returns 4):

```
document.writeln(parseInt("Hello World!", 8)+"<BR>");
document.writeln(parseInt("0x4", 10)+"<BR>");
document.writeln(parseInt("D", 10)+"<BR>");
document.writeln(parseInt("1002", 2)+"<BR>");
```

The second example (`document.writeln(parseInt("0x4", 10)+"<BR>"))` shows that given the wrong base of interpretation—10 instead of 16—a usual number scheme for one base will be regarded in a different base just as any other string input.

The last example returns 4 because `parseInt()` sees the value "100" as the integer to parse (1 and 0 are the only digits in base 2, so the integer stops before the 2), and 100 in base 2 is equivalent to 4.

unescape()

The reverse of the `escape()` function is the `unescape()` function, which will return the ASCII string for a specified value. The syntax is as follows:

```
unescape("string")
```

`string` is a number between 0 and 255 preceded by a percent symbol (`%`). *`string`* can also be a hexadecimal number between 0x0 and 0xFF, which doesn't need the percentage symbol. For example, the following calls to `unescape()`

```
unescape("%26")
unescape("F")
unescape("%26%46%23")
```

would return the values `&`, `F`, and `&F#`, respectively. Notice in the last `unescape()` that the value `%46` was substituted for `F`, yet still returned the same value as the second line did with `F`. This just illustrates the way characters are represented "behind the scenes" in the computer.

Summary

In HTML, a form allows you to retrieve input from the user. In JavaScript, you manipulate different parts of a form with unique objects—`select`, `text`, `textarea`, and `password`, to name a few. Each of these objects has its own properties that control what information is within the object. Also, these objects respond to various system events, notifying JavaScript that the content of the object has changed or that the user is moving from one object to the next.

JavaScript also has several system-level functions that allow you to manipulate input and output, convert between ASCII and displayed text, and evaluate a string as though it were a JavaScript expression.

Review Questions

The answers to the review questions can be found in Appendix D.

1. How do you access the browser's history list?
2. What are three different objects that can take user input?
3. What are the components of a `select` object?
4. How do you define a `select` object where you can select more than one option?
5. What are three functions that can be used to convert a string to a numeric representation?
6. How do you convert from ASCII to characters?
7. True or false: System functions vary depending on which operating system they are executed under.
8. True or false: The `length` function applies only to the `select` object.
9. Describe the operation of the `escape()` function.

10. How does the value returned by the `unescape()` function relate to the `escape()` function?

11. True or false: `NaN` will be a return value that occurs only under a Windows operating system.

12. What are the three properties of a `password` object?

13. `blur`, `focus`, and `select` are all methods of which objects?

Exercises

1. Write a simple calculator that allows the user to enter an expression for evaluation.

2. Write a function that converts from one number system to another (from base 10 to base 2, for example), and allows the user to specify the target base (from a list). If users enter something that can't be converted, tell them so.

CHAPTER 15

Properties

Properties are JavaScript attributes that tie everything together and make JavaScript the language that it is. Properties are used to define object colors; show the location of objects, references, and resources; specify which object; and provide constants used in calculations. This chapter is devoted to the properties not already covered in other chapters.

Common Properties for All Objects

All JavaScript objects have two properties that you'll use on a regular basis within your scripts—`name` and `length`.

name

The `name` property identifies the particular object to JavaScript, and is the value set with the `NAME` attribute of that object's HTML tag. This property serves a second (and more important) duty in that it matches the variable name you use to access the object. For example, if you defined an HTML form with a text object,

```
<form method="POST">
   Enter your name: <input type="text" name="userName">
</form>
```

`userName` would not only be the value stored in the `name` property, it would be the *variable* used to manipulate this object through JavaScript. To print out the contents (what the user typed) of the text object, you would use

```
document.write(form.userName.value);
```

which tells JavaScript to display the contents (`value`) of the `userName` object within the `form` object.

length

The `length` object, generally speaking, indicates "how big" or "how much data" a particular object contains. What this actually means varies depending on the object type. For example, in string objects, `length` is set to the number of characters in the string. The following code fragment would display `Your name is 7 characters long, Kenneth.`

```
Var strName="Kenneth";
document.writeln("Your name is " + strName.length +
➥" characters long, " + strName + ".");
```

On the other hand, in array-type objects (such as `form`, `anchor`, `history`, `frames`, and other objects where the object contains multiple subobjects), `length` is the number of objects within the form.

For predefined objects (those that come with JavaScript, such as `form` and `string`), `length` is a read-only property and can't be directly modified (but, as in the case of strings, you can change the value by changing the string itself). For arrays you create yourself, `length` is used to initialize the array, as in

```
myArray.length = 10;
```

which defines `myArray` to be an array variable of 10 elements.

Arrays are covered in more detail in Chapter 9, "Building Arrays." See Chapter 14, "Miscellaneous Methods and Functions," for more examples of `length`.

Document Object Properties

The `document` object encompasses all the elements within an HTML page. This complex object has other JavaScript objects attached to it (such as `anchor`, `form`, `history`, and `link`), as well as its own properties.

> **Note:** The `anchor` and `link` objects are discussed in Chapter 8, "JavaScript Objects." The `history` and `form` objects are covered in Chapter 14, "Miscellaneous Methods and Functions." Additional information on the `form` object is also found later in this chapter.

Informational Properties

Several `document` properties hold information about the document itself:

- `location` holds the complete URL of the document.
- `referrer` contains the complete URL of the calling document (the document that contained the link to the current document, or where the user was before he arrived at the current document).

> **Note:** A complete (or *absolute*) URL has the format
>
> `http://www.winternet.com/~sjwalter/javascript/index.html`
>
> which contains the protocol, domain, directory path, and document name of the document.

- `title` contains the document title and is equivalent to the `<TITLE>` tag.
- `lastModified` holds the date the document was last changed.
- `cookie` contains a document cookie or cookies—special data that's unique to each user. (Cookies are covered in detail in Chapter 16, "Cookies.")

One example use of the `lastModified` property is to display this date somewhere on the page (giving the user a visual indication of when things have last changed), as in the following code fragment:

```
document.writeln("This document was last modified: ");
document.writeln(document.lastModified + "<br>");
```

This would produce the following output:

```
This document was last modified: Wed May 07 11:39:34 1996
```

Display Properties

The `title` property isn't the only property that equates to an HTML tag or attribute. Five other `document` properties match attributes of the `<BODY>` tag:

- `bgColor` The document's background color; equates to the `BGCOLOR` attribute
- `fgColor` The document's default text (foreground) color; equates to the `TEXT` attribute
- `linkColor` The color of a hypertext link; equates to the `LINK` attribute
- `alinkColor` The color of an active link; equates to the `ALINK` attribute
- `vlinkColor` The color of a visited link; equates to the `VLINK` attribute

> **Color My Link**
>
> Hypertext links within a document are colored (as well as underlined) to identify them from the rest of the text on a page. A link can be thought of as a button in that it can have two "states"—active and inactive.
>
> The *active* state happens when the user clicks a link. The link is "active" for as long as the user holds the mouse button down.

> The *inactive* state covers the rest of the time (when the mouse button isn't being held down). To further delineate things, links in the normal state can be two types—a link the user has *visited* (clicked) and one the user hasn't (called a *normal* link).

Colors can be defined either as *hexadecimal* values,

```
document.linkColor = "#0000FF"; // make links blue
```

or as strings:

```
document.linkColor = "blue";  // also makes links blue
```

> **Note:** For a complete listing of common colors, their JavaScript strings, and their hexidecimal equivalents, see Appendix C, "Colors."

> **Tip:** You can change a document's color values (even the background and foreground colors) on the fly from within JavaScript, as long as you follow these rules:
>
> ◆ Link colors (`alinkColor`, `vlinkColor`, and `linkColor`) must be set *before* the document finishes formatting (that is, before it starts displaying itself). To change link colors after a document is displayed, you have to force the document to reload itself.
>
> ◆ Background color can be changed at any time.

Content Properties

In addition to the displayed text, `document` objects also contain links, anchors, and (possibly) forms. Within JavaScript, this additional content is grouped into three array properties that are actually arrays of other JavaScript objects:

◆ `anchors` An array of the document's `anchor` objects

◆ `links` An array of the document's `link` objects

◆ `forms` An array of the document's `form` objects

As with all arrays in JavaScript, the `length` property of each of these objects identifies the number of elements within the array.

> **Note:** The `anchor` and `link` objects are covered in more detail in Chapter 8, "JavaScript Objects."

Form Object Properties

Chapter 14, "Miscellaneous Methods and Functions," introduced the different objects (`text`, `password`, `select`, and so on) that make up an HTML form. Like any other JavaScript object, the `form` object has `name` and `length` properties, as well as five properties of its own:

- `encoding` holds the value set by the `ENCTYPE` attribute.
- `method` holds the value set by the `METHOD` attribute.
- `action` holds the value set by the `ACTION` attribute.

> **Note:** The `ACTION` attribute is often used to direct the output of a form to either a CGI program or to a mail address, as in
>
> ```
> <form method="post" action="mailto:sjwalter@winternet.com">
> ```
>
> which would cause the form's output to be e-mailed to the address specified.

- `target` holds the value set by the `TARGET` attribute.

The fifth property, `elements`, is an array that contains all the objects within the `form`. Because `elements` itself is an array, its `length` property is set to the number of elements (form objects). You can use the `elements` array to access individual form objects, but referencing a text field with

```
form.elements[0]
```

is less clear than

```
form.userName
```

and requires you to remember the order in which the objects are defined within the form. A better use would be to provide the user with a review of the data entered into a form before submission, as shown in listing 15.1.

Listing 15.1

```
<html>
<head>
<script language="JavaScript">
<!-- hide from non-JavaScript browsers
function verify(theForm) {
   strOut = "\n\n";

   for(i = 0; i < theForm.elements.length; i++) {
      strOut += theForm.elements[i].name + ": "
```

```
            +  theForm.elements[i].value + "\n";
    }

    strOut += "\nIs this information correct?";

    return confirm(strOut);
}// end hide -->
</script>
</head>
<body>
<h2>Please complete the following:</h2>
<form method="post" onSubmit="return verify(this)">
<table>
 <tr>
  <td>Name:</td>
  <td><input type="text" name="userName" size=25></td>
 </tr>
 <tr>
  <td>email address:</td>
  <td><input type="text" name="eMail" size=25></td>
 </tr>
 <tr>
  <td align=center colspan=2>
  <input type="submit" name="submit" value="Submit">
  </td>
 </tr>
</table>
</form>
</body>
</html>
```

When the user clicks the Submit button, the `confirm()` dialog box appears (see fig. 15.1), asking for final confirmation before completing the form submission.

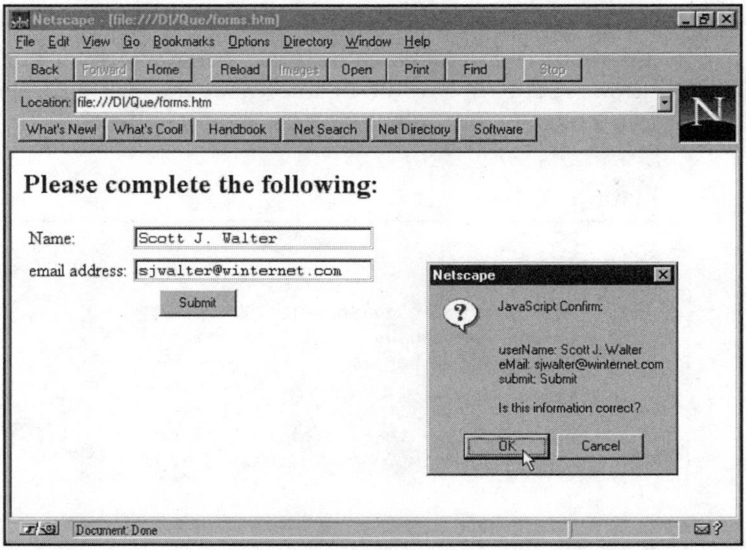

Figure 15.1

One use of the `elements` array. Notice that the Submit button is also an element of the form.

Note: You also can iterate through all the objects within a form using the `for...in` statement, which would replace the `for` loop in the `verify()` function in listing 15.1 with

```
for (object in theForm) {
   strOut += object.name + ": "
          +  object.value + "\n";
}
```

For more information on `for...in`, see Chapter 6, "More Programming Basics."

Forms and Function

You can have more than one form—and more than one `form` object—within a single HTML document. Like any other HTML tag, the `NAME` attribute helps identify one form from another:

```
<form name="form1">
...
</form>
...
<form name="form2">
...
</form>
```

From JavaScript, individual forms can be accessed two different ways:

- By using the value specified by the `NAME` attribute as a variable to access the form and its objects:

  ```
  form1.formObject
  ```

- By using the `forms[]` array:

  ```
  forms[0].formObject  // access the first form
  forms[1].formObject  // access the second form
  ```

Like all other arrays in JavaScript, `forms` has a `length` property that indicates the number of forms in the document. You access a particular form by referencing its index (as shown above).

The `form` keyword seen so often in JavaScript is a shorthand way of accessing `forms[0]`. If you have multiple forms, you can still use `form`, but it will refer only to the first form in the file.

Math Object Properties

The properties of the `Math` object are discussed in more detail in Chapter 10, "Math Methods," but for review purposes table 15.1 lists them here.

Table 15.1 Math Properties

Property	*Meaning*	*Approximate Value*
`E`	Euler's constant *e*	2.71828
`LN2`	Natural log of 2	0.693
`LN10`	Natural log of 10	2.302
`LOG2E`	Base 2 log of *e*	1.442
`LOG10E`	Base 10 log of *e*	0.434
`PI`	Ratio of a circle's circumference to its diameter	3.14159
`SQRT1_2`	Square root of 1/2	0.707
`SQRT2`	Square root of 2	1.414

All these properties are *constants* (values to be used in computations) and are therefore read-only. You access them through the `Math` object, as in

```
circumference = Math.PI * radius * radius;
```

which uses the `PI` property to compute a circle's circumference.

checked

The `checked` property reflects the Boolean status of a `checkbox` or `radio` object. When one of these objects is highlighted, the `checked` property returns a value of true. This status can be updated at any time and will immediately be reflected on-screen, verifying such status has been changed.

The syntax for the `checked` property is as follows:

```
objectName.checked
```

`objectName` may be a valid `NAME` attribute or array element for a `checkbox` or `radio` object.

defaultChecked

The `defaultChecked` property allows you to control which option in a group of check boxes or radio buttons is selected (checked) by default. From HTML, you would do this with the `CHECKED` attribute of the `<INPUT>` tag:

```
<input type=checkbox checked> This is checked by default
<input type=checkbox> This is not
```

If, however, you want to change the default value dynamically, you can override the `CHECKED` attribute by using the `defaultChecked` property, as in

```
objectName.defaultChecked = true;
```

This would set the object referenced by *`objectName`* to the checked state. As with the *`checked`* property, *`objectName`* is the name assigned to a check box or radio button object with the `NAME` attribute of the `<INPUT>` tag.

defaultStatus

The *status bar* is the message area at the very bottom of the browser window that normally displays either the phrase `Document: Done` or the URL of the link the cursor is currently over. You're already familiar with the `status` property, which allows you to put special messages in the status bar when the user is over a link:

```
<a href="next.html"
   onMouseOver="window.status='Click me!'; return true;">
```

This would display `Click me!` instead of `next.html` on the status bar.

The `Document: Done` message is the default message, which you can change as well with the `defaultStatus` property. For example, the following code fragment would display `Go to Netscape` or `Go to Que` if the user moved the mouse over one of the two URLs, and `Click Something!` when the mouse is elsewhere on the page:

```
<script language="JavaScript">
function setStatus(statusString) {
   window.defaultStatus = "Click Something!";
   window.status = statusString;
   return true;
}
</script>
...
<a href="http://www.netscape.com/"
   onMouseOver = "return setStatus('Go to Netscape');">Netscape</a>
<a href="http://www.mcp.com/que/"
   onMouseOver = "return setStatus('Go to Que');">Que</a>
```

Note: When using `OnMouseOver`, remember that you must return a value of true to the handler—either by having the function do it, or by adding the line

```
return true;
```

after the function call. If you don't do this, any operations you perform in the body of the handler (in this case, setting `status` and `defaultStatus`) won't actually happen.

href

Just as in HTML, the JavaScript `href` property specifies the full URL as a string. You can set the `href` property at any time. The syntax for this property is as follows:

```
location.href
```

The `location` object can be attached to several different JavaScript objects. For example,

```
windowName.location.href
```

displays the full URL reference of the specified window's current position.

Summary

Properties are elements of JavaScript objects that define certain characteristics of the objects they are attached to, such as the name of the object and the value it holds. Some objects are *complex*, and consist of multiple properties, which may be objects in their own right, with their own properties and subobjects.

Properties may be read-only (as in the case of the `Math` object properties), or they may be modifiable (as in the `value` property of most objects). Properties may also have *limited modifiability* (they can only be changed at certain times, like the link color properties of the `document` object).

Review Questions

The answers to the review questions are in Appendix D.

1. What is a property?
2. What properties contain information about a document?
3. How do you reference the elements of a form?
4. How can you control the color of a document?
5. True or false: All the properties of objects can be changed using JavaScript at any time—that's why JavaScript is such a powerful language.
6. True or false: `alinkColor` and `linkColor` are the same property.
7. When you set the background color using a HTML tag, you can change it by using which property?

Exercises

1. By using these new properties, revise one of your current Web pages, removing as many HTML tags as you can and replacing them with JavaScript properties.
2. Listing 15.1 not only displays the text-entry fields the user filled out, but also the Submit button (because it's an element of the form). Rewrite listing 15.1 to "filter out" the button and not display it in the `confirm()` dialog box.
3. Design a page that changes color each time it's loaded.
4. Design a page that enumerates the entire "tree" of a document, displaying all the properties of the `document` object, any subproperties, sub-subproperties, and so on.

Cookies

Cookies were originally used only by server-side scripts, but through JavaScript they're now accessible from the client side. The term *cookie* applies to the objects used on the Web to store information on the client's system. All this information is kept in a single file—cookies.txt—with one cookie per line. Cookies are transported between the server and the client in the HTTP headers (the packets that the server and clients use to identify themselves). Because not all browsers support cookies yet, it's a good idea to check out the following Web page from time to time, to see who does and who doesn't support them:

http://www.research.digital.com/nsl/formtest/stats-by-test/NetscapeCookie.html

As you can see in figure 16.1, the browser has stored three cookies so far. One of the cookies is from Microsoft's home page, and the other two are from Netscape.

What are cookies used for? Well, let's use the MSN home page as a starting point. The cookie stores ID information that's passed to the server at **http://www.msn.com** when I contact the site. A CGI script on the server searches a server-side file to determine my setup. It remembers what stock quotes I want to see, what search sites I want listed, and what news services I want to see.

Cookies store registration information for the browser. Many of the search utilities use cookies to store your search preferences. Two notable examples of such sites are InfoSeek and search.com. Look at your cookies.txt file, and then visit either of these two sites and set a particular search preference.

Note: In Navigator, you must close the browser for the cookie information to actually be written to the file. Until the browser is shut down, any new or changed cookies are kept in memory.

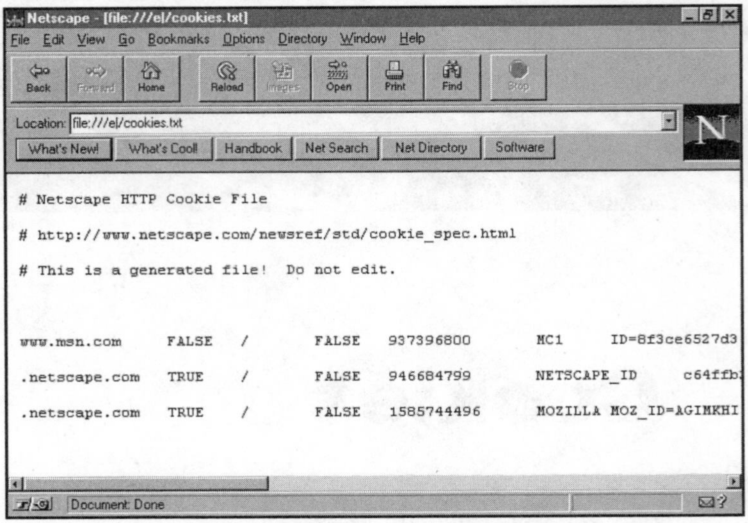

Figure 16.1
Example of the information that can be stored in cookies.txt.

Now thanks to JavaScript, you too can set cookies from your pages. Cookies can be used in a multitude of ways, but the most important use is to store data across multiple pages. If index1.hmtl has a script that captures a user's first name, wouldn't you like to use that information later on, like perhaps on index2.html? Well, you know that functions and variables are lost if you change pages or reload the original. Now you just set a cookie and change the pages! The new page can read the cookie information from the client's side and pass it to a variable in the new script.

Particulars

Each cookie has six elements, at most: `name`, `value`, `expires`, `domain`, and `secure`. These elements store the scope of the cookie's reach and the actual data stored.

The *name* Element

Each cookie *must* have a name. Without a name, how can you address it? The name is a string of characters, excluding the semicolon, comma, and space. If you must use one of these characters, some form of encoding must be used. Cookies are named just like you name variables; `myCookie`, `lastTimeVisited`, and `card5` are all valid cookie names. For more information on variable names, check out Chapter 5, "Programming Basics."

The *value* Element

Just as every cookie must have a name, it also *must* have a value. The value is the information that's actually stored in the cookie, and is a string made of any combination of characters (`21`, `Wednesday`, and `Navigator2.0` are all valid values).

The *expires* Element

Can a cookie live forever? That depends on what you set the expiration date to. All computers have a problem with dates after the year 1999—a hardware limitation that you must view as your own also. Cookies without a set expiration date expire at the end of the user's session. The cookie is alive until the user closes his or her browser.

Just because a cookie has expired doesn't mean it will be removed from the cookie text file. It may live there until its space is required to store another cookie. It just won't be sent to a requesting server.

An expiration date string looks like this:

```
Wdy, DD-Mon-YY HH:MM:SS GMT
```

Specifying an expiration date for a cookie is optional.

The *domain* Element

It wouldn't do for a cookie created by my site to affect a script on your site, so each cookie must have a domain entry. For top-level domains such as .com, .edu, or .mil, the domain name must have at least two periods (.) in it. For lower-level domains such as .ga, .uk, or .ca, the domain must have three periods. The domain is automatically set to the basic domain of your site's location. If you had pages at http://www.dscga.com/~user, then by default any cookie you set will be valid for the dscga.com domain. If you want your cookies to apply only to visits on the www3.dscga.com server, you have to specify that when the cookie is set.

Only sites within a particular domain can set cookies for that domain.

The *path* Element

A cookie can be particular to only a certain level of a site. If you have a Web site that caters to registered and unregistered clients, your cookie information may apply only to users who can enter your "registered" pages.

The path is optional and, if missing, is assumed to be the path of the page that set the cookie.

The *secure* Flag

The `secure` flag is a Boolean value (either true or false). By default, it's considered to be false. If it's set to true, the cookie will be presented only to a server your browser considers to be secure.

Limitations

There's a limit to the number of cookies a site can set for a single client. Only 20 cookies can be set for each server or domain. If you have two servers—www.dscga.com and www3.dscga.com—and fail to specify the domain, the cookie defaults to dscga.com. If you specify the exact server address, however, each site can set 20 cookies—not 20 combined.

> **Note:** Keep in mind that if you have your site on a popular server such as aol.com, it's entirely possible that other subscribers to that service may have already set 20 cookies from that server's domain (through visiting all the other pages on that server). The only alternative is to register your own domain, thus giving yourself 20 cookies.

Not only are you limited by the number of cookies that can be set by each server, but each client is only required to store a maximum of 300 cookies. If a client has 300 cookies and a site sets a new cookie, one of the previously existing cookies will be removed.

Each individual cookie has a limit of its own. The cookie can't exceed 4K (4,096 bytes) in size, including the name and the other information combined.

JavaScript and Cookies

Now that you understand the basics, let's get down to business. Various JavaScript functions have been created to set, read, and delete cookies. Because of the simple nature of the functions, many of them look quite similar. The cookies in this chapter are patterned after the public domain versions authored by Bill Dortch. In keeping with the cookie theme, I have given the functions unique names.

Baking a Cookie

The very first task that you must perform is to actually set—or, as I like to say, *bake*—the cookie. Figure 16.2 shows how the `BakeCookie()` function (in listing 16.1) allows for the use of all the possible arguments.

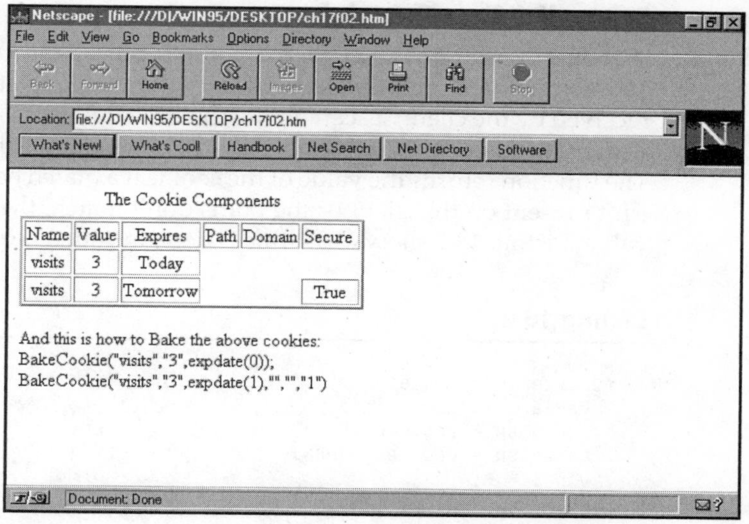

Figure 16.2
The recipe on how to properly bake a cookie.

Listing 16.1

```
function BakeCookie(name, value) {
  var argv = BakeCookie.arguments;
  var argc = BakeCookie.arguments.length;
  var expires = (argc > 2) ? argv[2] : null;
  var path = (argc > 3) ? argv[3] : null;
  var domain = (argc > 4) ? argv[4] : null;
  var secure = (argc > 5) ? argv[5] : false;
  document.cookie = name + "=" + escape (value) +
    ((expires == null) ? "" : ("; expires=" + expires.toGMTString())) +
    ((path == null) ? "" : ("; path=" + path)) +
    ((domain == null) ? "" : ("; domain=" + domain)) +
    ((secure == true) ? "; secure" : "");
}
```

`BakeCookie()` requires only the cookie name and value, but you can set the other four arguments, if needed, without changing the function's design. The optional arguments must be used in the proper order. If an argument is skipped, an empty placeholder must be set. For example, if you want to create a secure cookie but don't want to set `expires`, `path`, or `domain`, you call `BakeCookie()` as follows:

```
BakeCookie("MyNewCookie", "My Value", "", "", "", true);
```

Reading a Cookie

A cookie doesn't do much good if you can't recall the information. So to gain any "nourishment" from the baked cookie, you must "eat" it. When a cookie request is received by the client, it searches its cookies.txt file for a match. It first matches the name. If the name is found and a second cookie exists, it then tries to match the path. The function returns the value of the cookie if a match has been made. If the cookie isn't present on the client or the paths don't match, the function returns a NULL value. Listing 16.2 shows how this is done in code.

Listing 16.2

```
function EatCookie(name) {
  var arg = name + "=";
  var alen = arg.length;
  var clen = document.cookie.length;
  var i = 0;
  while (i < clen) {
    var j = i + alen;
    if (document.cookie.substring(i, j) == arg)
      return EatCookieVal (j);
    i = document.cookie.indexOf(" ", i) + 1;
    if (i == 0) break;
  }
  return null;
}
```

Unless you want to parse the cookie value manually, it's recommended that you use the `EatCookieVal()` function (in listing 16.3), which complements the `EatCookie()` function. `EatCookieVal()` breaks the cookies.txt file into "bite-sized" pieces, returning the correct cookie out of the "batch."

Listing 16.3

```
function EatCookieVal(offset){
  var endstr=document.cookie.indexOf(";",offset);
  if (endstr == -1)
    endstr = document.cookie.length;
  return unescape(document.cookie.substring(offset,endstr));
}
```

Deleting a Cookie

Deleting a cookie is quite simple—set its expiration date to `NULL` (which effectively deletes the expiration date). When the user's session is completed, the cookie is expired (cookies with no expiration date are deleted when the browser is closed). Listing 16.4 shows how to delete a cookie.

Listing 16.4

```
function TossCookie(name) {
  var exp = new Date();
  exp.setTime (exp.getTime() - 1);  // This cookie is history
  var cval = GetCookie (name);
  document.cookie = name + "=" + cval + "; expires=" +
  ➥exp.toGMTString();
}
```

Uses of Cookies

The ability to store information about a specific user that relates to an individual Web page makes cookies very powerful things. Some of the possible uses for cookies include the following:

- Tracking how many times a user has visited your page
- Notifying users that the page has changed since the last time they viewed it
- Storing a collection of items temporarily, like a shopping basket, until the user wants to "check out"
- Remembering whether a user prefers the framed or non-framed version of your site

Of these examples, the following sections examine the first two.

How Many Times Have I Been Here?

In this first example, shown in listing 16.5, I'll track the total number of visits a user has made to your page. This is accomplished by using a cookie to store the value between sessions.

Listing 16.5

```
<html>
<head>
<script language="Javascript">
<!-- hide from non-JavaScript browsers
function getCookieVal (offset) {
  var endstr = document.cookie.indexOf (";", offset);
  if (endstr == -1)
    endstr = document.cookie.length;
  return unescape(document.cookie.substring(offset, endstr));
```

continues

Listing 16.5 Continued

```
}

function GetCookie (name) {
  var arg = name + "=";
  var alen = arg.length;
  var clen = document.cookie.length;
  var i = 0;
  while (i < clen) {
    var j = i + alen;
    if (document.cookie.substring(i, j) == arg)
      return getCookieVal (j);
    i = document.cookie.indexOf(" ", i) + 1;
    if (i == 0)
      break;
  }
  return null;
}

function SetCookie (name, value) {
  var argv = SetCookie.arguments;
  var argc = SetCookie.arguments.length;
  var expires = (argc > 2) ? argv[2] : null;
  var path = (argc > 3) ? argv[3] : null;
  var domain = (argc > 4) ? argv[4] : null;
  var secure = (argc > 5) ? argv[5] : false;
  document.cookie = name + "=" + escape (value) +
    ((expires == null) ? "" : ("; expires=" + expires.toGMTString())) +
    ((path == null) ? "" : ("; path=" + path)) +
    ((domain == null) ? "" : ("; domain=" + domain)) +
    ((secure == true) ? "; secure" : "");
}

function DeleteCookie(name) {
  var exp = new Date();
  FixCookieDate (exp); // Correct for Mac bug
  exp.setTime (exp.getTime() - 1);  // This cookie is history
  var cval = GetCookie (name);
  if (cval != null)
    document.cookie = name + "=" + cval + "; expires=" +
    ➥exp.toGMTString();
}

var expdate = new Date();
var num_visits;
expdate.setTime(expdate.getTime() + (5*24*60*60*1000));
if (!(num_visits = GetCookie("num_visits")))
  num_visits = 0;
num_visits++;
```

```
SetCookie("num_visits",num_visits,expdate);
document.write("Thank you for visiting us.<br>");
document.write("You have loaded this page <font size=5>"+num_visits+"
➥</font> times.<br>");
// end hide -->
</script>
</html>
```

Notice the lines

```
if (!(num_visits = GetCookie("num_visits")))
  num_visits = 0;
```

If you just tried to pull a cookie value but the cookie didn't exist, the interpreter would return a `num_visits is undefined` error. You can circumvent this problem by using the NOT (`!`) operator. Figure 16.3 illustrates how cookies can work on a Web page.

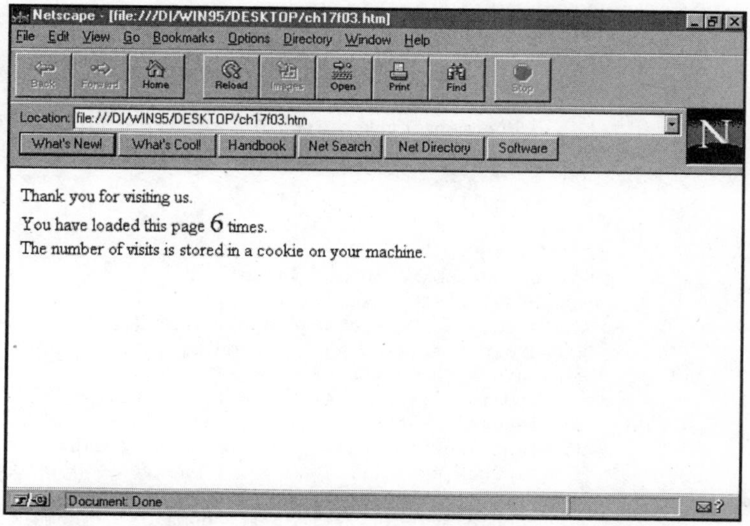

Figure 16.3
This shows a viewer the total number of visits to that page.

Has This Page Changed Since my Last Visit?

Although the preceding cookie can be useful, it may appear as nothing more than a cheap gimmick to your visitors. Not many Web surfers really care how many times they have hit a page. On the other hand, a dedicated Web surfer does like to know when a certain page has changed. Although it's perhaps not as efficient as a Web spider or robot might be, the example in listing 16.6 uses a cookie to determine whether a page has changed since the last visit.

Listing 16.6

```
<html>
<head>
</head>
<script language="JavaScript">
<!-- hide from non-JavaScript browsers
function getCookieVal (offset) {
  var endstr = document.cookie.indexOf (";", offset);
  if (endstr == -1)
    endstr = document.cookie.length;
  return unescape(document.cookie.substring(offset, endstr));
}

function GetCookie (name) {
  var arg = name + "=";
  var alen = arg.length;
  var clen = document.cookie.length;
  var i = 0;
  while (i < clen) {
    var j = i + alen;
    if (document.cookie.substring(i, j) == arg)
      return getCookieVal (j);
    i = document.cookie.indexOf(" ", i) + 1;
    if (i == 0) break;
  }
  return null;
}

function SetCookie (name, value) {
  var argv = SetCookie.arguments;
  var argc = SetCookie.arguments.length;
  var expires = (argc > 2) ? argv[2] : null;
  var path = (argc > 3) ? argv[3] : null;
  var domain = (argc > 4) ? argv[4] : null;
  var secure = (argc > 5) ? argv[5] : false;
  document.cookie = name + "=" + escape (value) +
    ((expires == null) ? "" : ("; expires=" + expires.toGMTString())) +
    ((path == null) ? "" : ("; path=" + path)) +
    ((domain == null) ? "" : ("; domain=" + domain)) +
    ((secure == true) ? "; secure" : "");
}

function DeleteCookie(name) {
  var exp = new Date();
  FixCookieDate (exp); // Correct for Mac bug
  exp.setTime (exp.getTime() - 1);  // This cookie is history
  var cval = GetCookie (name);
  if (cval != null)
    document.cookie = name + "=" + cval + "; expires=" +
    ➥exp.toGMTString();
}
```

```
var cookie_date=new Date(document.lastModified);
var expdate = new Date();
expdate.setTime(expdate.getTime()+(5*24*60*60*1000));

document.write("This page last updated on: "+document.lastModified);
document.write("<br>");
if (!(cookie_date == GetCookie("cookie_date"))){
  SetCookie("cookie_date",cookie_date,expdate);
  document.write("<font color='Red'>This page has changed since
  ➥your last visit!</font><br>");
}
// end hide -->
</script>
</html>
```

Just as listing 16.5 checked for the existence of the cookie, the same thing is done here. But rather than use an integer value, I used a date value in the cookie. The test is as simple as comparing the `document.lastModified` value, located in the cookie, to the current `document.lastModified`. If it matches, the page hasn't been modified; if it's different, the cookie's value is reset, and the visitor is alerted. Figure 16.4 shows how this code works.

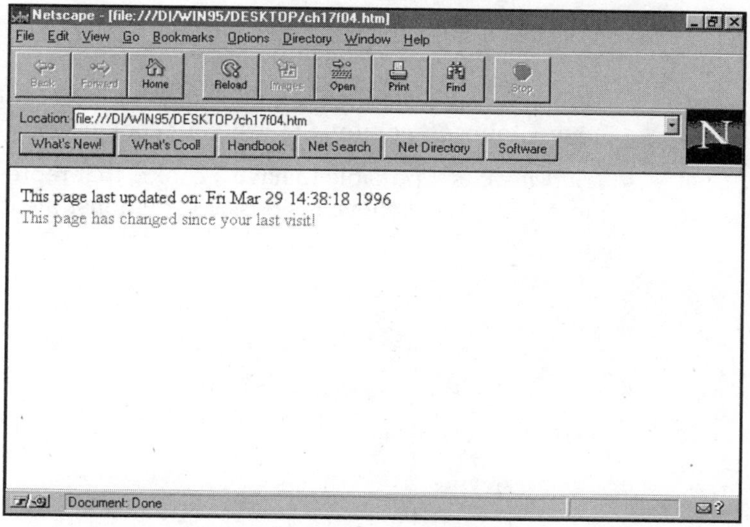

Figure 16.4
Here, the viewer sees how many days it's been since the page was last changed.

Review Questions

The answers to the review questions are in Appendix D.

1. How are cookies transported?
2. What are the only two required attributes of a cookie?

3. Which system reads the cookie—the server or the client?
4. Where is the cookie stored?
5. What are the minimum number of cookies a client should be ready to receive?
6. Can cookie names have spaces in them?
7. Can a page loaded from the HTTP server at www.gatech.com set a cookie with a `DOMAIN` attribute valid for only www.psu.com?

Exercises

1. Create a cookie that stores the name of the state you live in. Have the cookie expire one week from today.
2. Now delete your new cookie, using a function call (of course).
3. Write a cookie with the following attributes:

    Name = JSbE
    Domain = lobosoft.com
    Path = /que/jsbe.htm

    When finished setting the cookie to your local cookies.txt file, visit **http://www.lobosoft.com/que** to test your cookie!
4. *Advanced:* Is it possible to have a cookie that represents an array of information? If you believe it's possible, demonstrate it.

Part IV

Sample Applications

Building a Marquee

As I've emphasized throughout this book, JavaScript provides you with many terrific resources for building that "I've-got-to-see-it-again!" Web site. Scrolling text has always been a great eye-catcher. You see it in flight information displays at airports and, of course, on TV screens. The text may be important information, such as emergency routes or weather reports, or it may be advertising. Whatever the subject, scrolling text attracts attention.

Microsoft's *<Marquee>* Tag

Before delving too deeply into using JavaScript to build marquees, I feel obligated to tell you that there's a much easier way to scroll text by using Microsoft's <MARQUEE> tag. This chapter briefly looks at this tag (and explains why you can't use it) next.

Original Intent

Microsoft incorporated a new HTML tag into its Internet Explorer. You can use the <MARQUEE> tag to scroll or slide text from left to right or right to left (see listing 17.1). The text can start at a specific location and end at a specific location. All in all, the <MARQUEE> is the easiest way to scroll text on the Internet Explorer.

Listing 17.1

```
<html>
<head>
</head>

<body bgcolor="White">
<marquee behavior=scroll direction=right height=10% width=50%>
-----------------------</marquee>
<marquee behavior=scroll direction=left height=10% width=50%>
------------------------</marquee>
<marquee behavior=slide direction=right>This text slides from left to
right.</marquee>
<marquee behavior=slide direction=left>This text slides from right to
left.</marquee>
</body>
</html>
```

Figure 17.1 shows how this code would look on-screen.

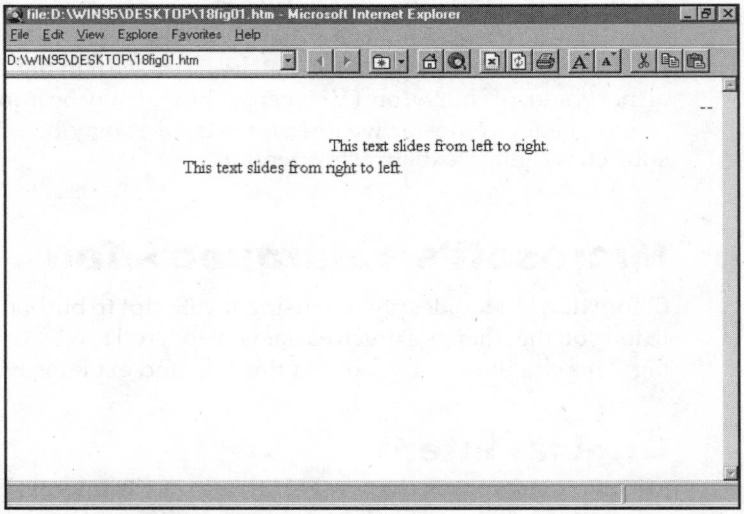

Figure 17.1
The Microsoft <MARQUEE> tag in action. With <MARQUEE>, you can scroll text into place, or create a banner that constantly scrolls.

The only problem with <MARQUEE> is that its supported only by Internet Explorer, not by Netscape Navigator. For your purposes, you need to come up with another way to create a scrolling marquee, as demonstrated next.

Dynamic Marquees

But what does dynamic have to do with JavaScript? Very simply, *dynamics*. One of JavaScript's best features is its capability to create dynamic HTML. Although you may be designing Web pages only for clients who expect you to have only MSIE

(Microsoft Internet Explorer) visitors, you can still use JavaScript to create some fairly fancy screens.

The example in listing 17.2 can't actually be demonstrated. Because Microsoft has yet to completely implement the `document.write()` function, you can only view the code at this time.

Listing 17.2

```
<html>
<head>
</head>
<body bgcolor="White">
<script language="JavaScript">
vday = new Date()
minutes = vday.getMinutes()
if ((minutes > 0) && (minutes < 15 )) {
   document.write("<marquee
   ➥behavior=scroll direction=right>Our next demonstration is
   ➥at one-quarter past the hour.</marquee>");
 elseif ((minutes >15) && (minutes < 30)) document.write("<marquee
 ➥behavior=scroll direction=right>Our next demonstration is at half
 ➥past the hour.</marquee>");
 elseif ((minutes >30) && (minutes < 45)) document.write("<marquee
 ➥behavior=scroll direction=right>Our next demonstration is
 ➥at one-quarter till the hour.</marquee>");
 else document.write("<marquee behavior=scroll direction=right>Our
 ➥next demonstration is on the hour.</marquee><br>");
}
</script>
</body>
</html>
```

By using the `Date` object, you determine what the "minute" was when the page was loaded. If you assume that every 15 minutes you have a small demonstration, the script will compare the current time to when the next demonstration is. Based on that, you can change the scrolling text as needed.

Scrolling Text Bars

Not all Internet surfers use Microsoft Explorer. Some use Mosaic, AOL, Netscape Navigator, or any one of dozens of other browsers. As a Web-page designer, you'll need to write pages that most surfers can use. The simplest marquee for Navigator is the scrolling text block. You simply manipulate the value of a form text object. The basic marquee will update the value of a text object located within a form. The code can be easily modified to accommodate your various string lengths and speeds:

```
<html>
<head>
<script language="JavaScript">
<!-- hide from non-JavaScript browsers
```

The first thing you do is declare a new object type, `statusMessageObject`. As an object, its properties, which you have declared, can be used. Creating this new object type is shown in the following code fragment:

```
function statusMessageObject(p,d){
this.msg = MESSAGE
this.out = " "
this.pos = POSITION
this.delay = DELAY
this.i = 0
this.reset = clearMessage}
function clearMessage(){
this.pos = POSITION}
var POSITION = 100
var DELAY = 50
var MESSAGE = "Welcome to the JavaScript by Example"
     +" Marquee Demonstration."
var scroll = new statusMessageObject()
function scroller(){
  for (scroll.i = 0; scroll.i < scroll.pos; scroll.i++) {
    scroll.out += " "
  }
```

The next code fragment in this function determines whether it needs to remove characters from the front or add them to the rear of the string, which depends on whether the beginning or ending characters are about to scroll off the screen.

```
if (scroll.pos >= 0)
  scroll.out += scroll.msg
else
  scroll.out = scroll.msg.substring(-scroll.pos,scroll.msg.length)
```

After `scroll.out` is correctly set, you write its value into `scrollbox`:

```
document.scrollform.scrollbox.value = scroll.out
```

Finally, reset your variables for the next run:

```
scroll.out = " "
scroll.pos--
```

If you find yourself at the end of your message, you must reset the variables so you can start again. The following function resets the variables as noted:

```
if (scroll.pos < -(scroll.msg.length)) {
   scroll.reset()
  }

  setTimeout ('scroller()',scroll.delay)
```

```
// -->
</script>
</head>

<body onLoad="scroller()">
<form name="scrollform">
This is where your text will scroll:<br>
<input type=text name="scrollbox">
</body>
</html>
```

Figure 17.2 shows how your first JavaScript text marquee would look using this code.

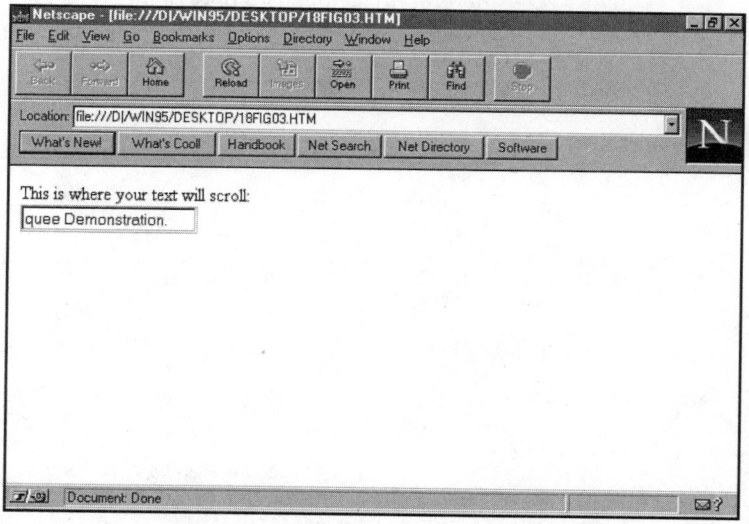

Figure 17.2
Your first JavaScript text marquee.

Using the Status Bar

Another popular location for scrolling text is the Netscape status bar. As you'll remember from the discussions on window objects in Chapter 13, "Window Methods," you can access the properties and values of the status bar. I'll discuss two of the more popular techniques of accessing values in the status bar in this chapter.

The JavaScript Alternative

The first status bar example will be written entirely in JavaScript, although this method has some drawbacks. Because the string manipulation to create the scroll effect uses memory, and because Netscape hasn't fixed a problem with the manner in which memory is reused, this script can crash Navigator 2.0 if run for a long period of time (or display a confusing `Lengthy JavaScript still running...` message to the user). Granted, not too many visitors are going to just sit on one page for hours on end. But if you have a large document that users want to read, it isn't advisable that you use this script there. Let's hope that the problem will be fixed in the next release of Navigator.

The first JavaScript example, which follows, is very simple. Nothing in it will be created dynamically, but let's move on to that a little later on.

```
<html>
<head>
<script language="JavaScript">
```

The first thing you do is declare a new object type called `statusMessageObject`. An object uses the properties that you have declared. The code in listing 17.3 is an example of this.

Listing 17.3

```
function statusMessageObject(p,d){
this.msg = MESSAGE
this.out = " "
this.pos = POSITION
this.delay = DELAY
this.i = 0
this.reset = clearMessage}
function clearMessage(){
this.pos = POSITION}
var POSITION = 100
var DELAY = 50
var MESSAGE = "Welcome to the JavaScript by Example"
    +" Marquee Demonstration."
var scroll = new statusMessageObject()
function scroller(){
  for (scroll.i = 0; scroll.i < scroll.pos; scroll.i++) {
    scroll.out += " "
  }
```

The following portion of the function determines whether it needs to remove characters from the front or add them to the end of the string. This all depends on whether the beginning characters are about to exit the screen or if the tail characters are about to do the same.

```
if (scroll.pos >= 0)
  scroll.out += scroll.msg
else scroll.out = scroll.msg.substring(-scroll.pos,scroll.msg.length)
```

The following line is what makes this listing different from the preceding example. If you haven't noticed by now, the engine is basically the same. The only difference is where you write the results to.

```
window.status = scroll.out
```

The following segment of code resets the variables for the next run:

```
scroll.out = " "
scroll.pos--
```

If you find yourself at the end of the message, you must reset the variables so you can start again:

```
<script>
if (scroll.pos < -(scroll.msg.length)) {
   scroll.reset()
  }

  setTimeout ('scroller()',scroll.delay)
}

// -->
</script>
</head>

<body onLoad="scroller()">
</body>
</html>
```

Figure 17.3 shows how this text would look on-screen.

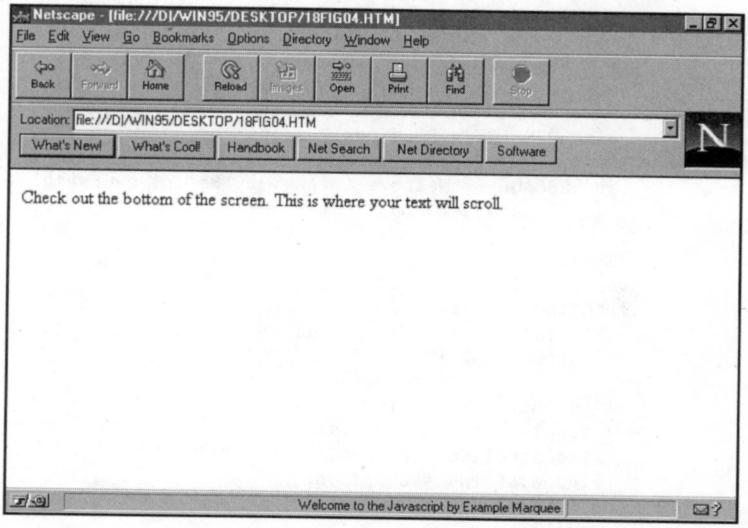

Figure 17.3
Your first JavaScript status bar marquee.

You can dynamically change the message based on the time that the page was first loaded. The code in listing 17.4 shows how this is done.

Listing 17.4

```
<html>
<head>
<script language="JavaScript">
function statusMessageObject(p,d){
this.msg = MESSAGE
this.out = " "
this.pos = POSITION
this.delay = DELAY
this.i = 0
this.reset = clearMessage}
function clearMessage(){
this.pos = POSITION}
var POSITION = 100
var DELAY = 50
```

At this point, you add your code to dynamically change the message. The code snippet in listing 17.5 is almost identical to the one you used earlier.

Listing 17.5

```
var MESSAGE=" "
vday = new Date()
minutes = vday.getMinutes()
if ((minutes > 0) && (minutes < 15 )) MESSAGE = "Our next
➥demonstration is at one quarter past the hour."
 elseif ((minutes >15) && (minutes < 30)) MESSAGE = "Our next
 ➥demonstration is at half past the hour."
 elseif ((minutes >30) && (minutes < 45)) MESSAGE = "Our next
 ➥demonstration is at one quarter till the hour."
 else MESSAGE = "Our next demonstration is on the hour."

var MESSAGE = "Welcome to the JavaScript by Example"
     +" Marquee Demonstration."

<script>
var scroll = new statusMessageObject()
function scroller(){
  for (scroll.i = 0; scroll.i < scroll.pos; scroll.i++) {
    scroll.out += " "
  }
if (scroll.pos >= 0)
   scroll.out += scroll.msg
  else scroll.out = scroll.msg.substring(-scroll.pos,scroll.msg.length)
  window.status = scroll.out
scroll.out = " "
  scroll.pos--
```

```
if (scroll.pos < -(scroll.msg.length)) {
   scroll.reset()
  }
  setTimeout ('scroller()',scroll.delay)
}
//-->
</script>
</head>
<body onLoad="scroller()">
</body>
</html>
```

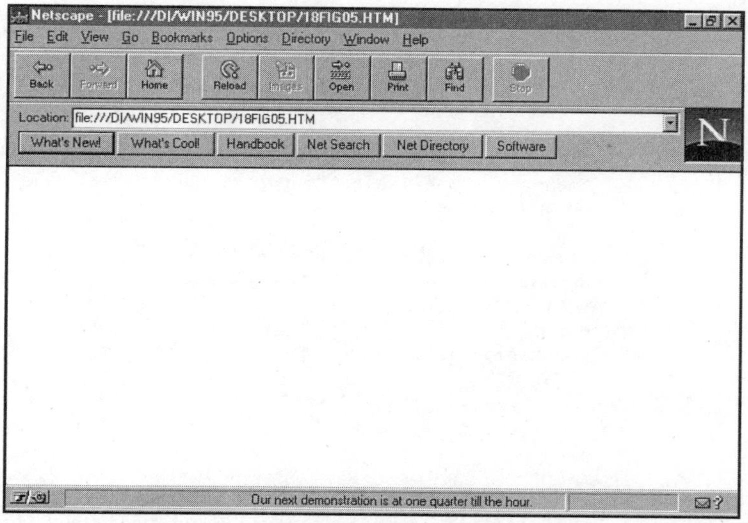

Figure 17.4

The dynamic status bar marquee.

Java and JavaScript

The second example will use a Java binary to handle the scrolling text. A couple of limitations and disadvantages are that Java is supported only on the 32-bit version of Navigator, and hasn't yet been fully implemented in Internet Explorer. But because Netscape's original press release claimed that JavaScript would be like a "glue" that would tie Java to HTML, I decided maybe I should see whether this will really work.

You could build a really simple page that just used the Java applet, but how would that demonstrate JavaScript? It wouldn't, so let's bounce back to the original example in the preceding section. You'll use JavaScript to build the HTML that will "hold" the Java applet in place. The code in listing 17.6 shows just how this will be done. It uses a Java class file, `MsgScroll.class`, that needs to be included in the same directory as the HTML document.

Listing 17.6

```
<html>
<head>
</head>
<body bgcolor="White">
<script language="JavaScript">
<!-- hide
vday     = new Date();
minutes  = vday.getMinutes();

document.write('<applet code="MsgScroll.class" width=0 height=0>' +
               '<param name=delay value=5>' +
               '<param name=line1 ');

if ((minutes > 0) && (minutes < 15 ))
   document.write('value="Our next demonstration is at one quarter
   ➥past the hour.">');
else
if ((minutes >15) && (minutes < 30))
   document.write('value="Our next demonstration is at half past
   ➥the hour.">');
else
if ((minutes >30) && (minutes < 45))
   document.write('value="Our next demonstration is at one quarter
   ➥till the hour.">');
else
   document.write('value="Our next demonstration is on the hour.">');

document.write('<param name=line2 value=" ">');
document.write('</applet>')
// -->
</script>
<b><i>
   This listing demonstrates implementing a Java applet through
   JavaScript. This technique is unique to Netscape Navigator.
</i></b>

<hr>

</body>
</html>
```

Summary

Scrolling banners (marquees) are ways to draw the user's attention to particular messages (such as notifications of new features or products for sale). Although Internet Explorer has a built-in HTML extension that makes creating marquees a breeze, you've seen that a little JavaScript coding can achieve similar results. With JavaScript, you can either scroll the text directly, or control a Java applet to do the work for you.

Review Questions

The answers to the review questions are in Appendix D.

1. What's a marquee?
2. Name a problem with the status bar marquees.
3. How are marquees implemented with Internet Explorer?
4. What line of code determines whether you create a form-based marquee or a status bar marquee?

Exercises

1. Using what you've learned up to now, create your own marquee that scrolls the text from left to right instead of right to left.
2. Create a marquee that is form-based and dynamic in nature (for example, one that allows the user to specify the scrolling text).

CHAPTER 18

Creating an Online Store

Online commerce is one of the most popular new areas of the Net—to such an extent that Netscape has even created a Web server dedicated to servicing business needs. However, a small business may not be able to justify the cost of a dedicated Internet server to handle small sales issues. The CGI interface, with its capability to handle database interaction, can handle online pricing and has been around for years, but you still need access to the Internet service provider's (ISP's) server to make any changes (which, if available, is usually not inexpensive).

JavaScript may be the answer to this growing dilemma. As you've discovered in previous chapters, JavaScript, although new, is very robust. You've seen how to use its mathematical methods and string methods to create unique and vibrant pages. In this chapter, I'll tie a few of those methods together to form the foundation for an online store.

I've chosen to use a computer *reseller* (market-speak for a "store" such as Best Buy, CompUSA, Computer City, and many others) as the model for the example business. Because the number of options possible with buying a computer (Mac or IBM, how much RAM, what size monitor, what software, and so forth) is rather extensive, let's limit the number of possibilities from which the "buyer" (the user) can choose through the use of HTML forms and JavaScript.

> **Tip:** When you're designing a Web page that will use forms, it's much easier to design the forms in standard HTML and *then* add your JavaScript code. Forms aren't straightforward, and trying to correct problems in the form design *and* bugs in JavaScript at the same time make the whole process more difficult than necessary.

Building the Basic Store

The online store will sell computer systems, using a "build-your-own" menu format. For the purposes of this chapter, a PC will consist of five basic parts:

- Base system (the CPU, motherboard, disk drive, keyboard, and mouse)
- Hard drive
- Memory
- Monitor
- Operating system

The Form

Using the five parts just outlined, buyers will be able to "build" their own system by selecting from the available options for each of these parts. The various options are displayed through an HTML form, as shown in figure 18.1. After an option for each part is selected, buyers can click the Calculate the Cost button to determine the total system price.

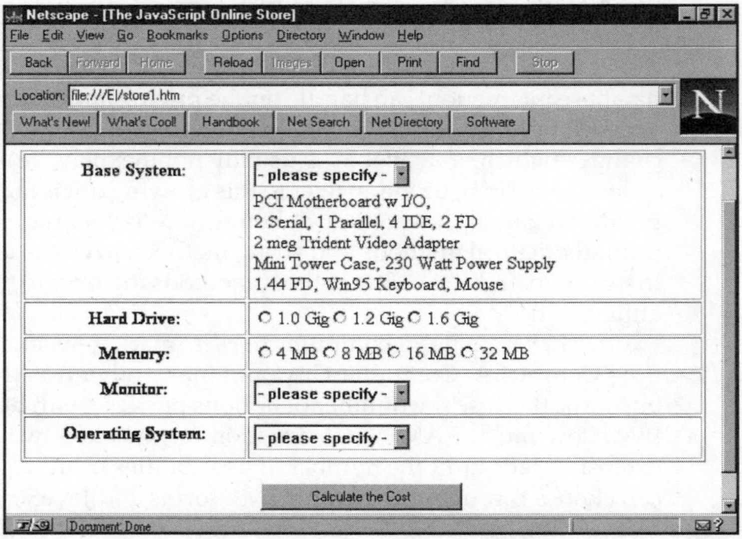

Figure 18.1
The form of the online store uses a combination of drop-down list boxes and radio buttons to handle the different selections.

Listing 18.1 shows the code for the form, and there are a couple of important points to note. Rather than specify `<SELECT>` and `<INPUT>` tags directly, you use JavaScript to build them.

Listing 18.1

```
<FORM NAME="order1" METHOD=POST>
<CENTER>
<TABLE WIDTH=99% CELLPADDING=4 BORDER>
 <TR>
    <TH VALIGN=TOP>Base System:</TH>
    <TD>
      <SCRIPT LANGUAGE="JavaScript">
      <!-- begin hide
        document.write(createSelect("base", baseList)
                        + "<BR>");
      // end hide -->
      </SCRIPT>
      PCI Motherboard w I/O,<BR>
      2 Serial, 1 Parallel, 4 IDE, 2 FD<BR>
      2 meg Trident Video Adapter<BR>
      Mini Tower Case, 230 Watt Power Supply<BR>
      1.44 FD, Win95 Keyboard, Mouse
    </TD>
  </TR>
  <TR>
    <TH VALIGN=TOP>Hard Drive:</TH>
    <TD>
      <SCRIPT LANGUAGE="JavaScript">
      <!-- begin hide
        document.write(createRadio("hdrive", driveList)
                        + "<BR>");
      // end hide -->
      </SCRIPT>
    </TD>
  </TR>
  <TR>
    <TH VALIGN=TOP>Memory:</TH>
    <TD>
      <SCRIPT LANGUAGE="JavaScript">
      <!-- begin hide
        document.write(createRadio("memory", memList)
                        + "<BR>");
      // end hide -->
      </SCRIPT>
    </TD>
  </TR>
  <TR>
    <TH VALIGN=TOP>Monitor:</TH>
    <TD>
      <SCRIPT LANGUAGE="JavaScript">
      <!-- begin hide
        document.write(createSelect("monitor", monList)
                        + "<BR>");
      // end hide -->
      </SCRIPT>
    </TD>
```

continues

Listing 18.1 Continued

```
    </TR>
    <TR>
      <TH VALIGN=TOP>Operating System:</TH>
      <TD>
        <SCRIPT LANGUAGE="JavaScript">
        <!-- begin hide
          document.write(createSelect("os", osList)
                          + "<BR>");
        // end hide -->
        </SCRIPT>
      </TD>
    </TR>
  </TABLE>
  </CENTER>
  <BR>
  <INPUT TYPE=button NAME="compute"
         VALUE="Calculate the Cost" ONCLICK="calculate()">
  </FORM>
```

Tip: Although it's not required, you should actually name each of your forms. Remembering a name is much easier than remembering `form[0]` or `form[1]`.

Because the inventory of a computer store can change from time to time, the form would have to be updated (which can be time-consuming and fraught with error). To overcome this, JavaScript is used to actually build the `<SELECT>` and `<INPUT>` tag blocks, based on a "database" of components. This centralizes all the component information in one place in the document, so any additions or changes to the database have to be done only once.

The next sections look at these "custom HTML" functions more closely, but first you need to examine how the database is constructed.

A JavaScript Database

Chapter 9, "Building Arrays," showed how to create arrays in JavaScript. By using this technique, and the capability to add properties to JavaScript objects that can be arrays themselves, you can build an "array of parts" that holds the name and cost of each part as a separate element. All that's needed is to take the `MakeArray()` function and extend it to make an array of objects (see listing 18.2).

Listing 18.2

```
function MakeArray(size) {
   this.length = size;

   for(i = 1; i <= size; i++)
```

```
        this[i] = null;

    return this;
}

function Part(strName, iCost) {
    this.name    = strName;
    this.cost    = iCost;
}
```

The `Part()` function creates a `Part` object, with a `name` and a `cost`. Each of the five components of the computer system will have its own array of parts, created similarly to the base system array (see listing 18.3).

Listing 18.3

```
baseList       = new MakeArray(3);
baseList[1]    = new Part("AMD DX4/100", 420);
baseList[2]    = new Part("Pentium 75" , 522);
baseList[3]    = new Part("Pentium 100", 609);
```

First, the `baseList` array is set up, and then a `Part` object (with the appropriate name and cost) is created for each element in the array. Because the `MakeArray()` function also creates a `length` property for `baseList`, which holds the number of parts in the list, it's not necessary to remember how many different parts are in a particular list when writing the computation functions. To add a new part, simply change the number specified by `MakeArray()` and add an additional `baselist[?] = new Part(...);` line.

These databases are what permit JavaScript to dynamically build the form displayed to the buyer. Editing the parts array doesn't require editing the HTML farther down the document. How to get JavaScript to create these input fields dynamically is next on the list.

List Boxes and Radio Buttons with JavaScript

It's possible to construct a list box by using nothing but HTML, but that adds to the amount of maintenance the document needs as parts and prices change. By using the parts and prices from listing 18.3, a pure HTML `<SELECT>` block of base systems would look something like the fragment in listing 18.4.

Listing 18.4

```
<SELECT NAME="base">
  <OPTION SELECTED>- please specify -
  <OPTION>AMD DX4/100
  <OPTION>Pentium 75
  <OPTION>Pentium 100
</SELECT>
```

However, no price information can be stored with this, meaning that additional JavaScript code would be needed to keep track of a part and its price. Because this would require an array anyway, it's more efficient to use the `Part()` function from the previous section—and because all that information is available to JavaScript, the next step is to let JavaScript actually generate the HTML code for you. Listing 18.5 shows the `createSelect()` function that does this for `<SELECT>` tags.

Listing 18.5

```
function createSelect(strName, objList) {
  var tStr = "<SELECT NAME=\"" + strName + "\">"
           + "<OPTION SELECTED>- please specify -";

  for(var i=1; i<=objList.length; i++)
    tStr += "<OPTION>" + objList[i].name;

  tStr += "</SELECT>";

  return tStr;
}
```

This function works generically because to JavaScript, an object is an object—no matter what type of object it is. As long as *you* know the properties of the object, you can reference them in *any* object. Each of the different parts arrays has the same structure (a `length` property, and `name` and `cost` properties for each index element), so no matter which parts list is given to `createSelect()`, it will generate a list box based on the information in that array.

In the body of the HTML code itself, all that's needed to have the `<SELECT>` tag generated is one line of JavaScript:

```
document.write(createSelect("base", baseList) + "<BR>");
```

This line generates the `<SELECT>` block shown earlier in listing 18.5.

Creating a block of radio buttons (as used by the "Memory" and "Hard Disk" parts of the form) is done much the same way. The `createRadio()` function uses the same format as `createSelect()`, but generates the appropriate `<INPUT>` tags.

Now that the form creation is complete, the next step is to handle the click of the Compute the Cost button.

Calculating the Cost

The `calculate()` function (see listing 18.6) is the "main driver" for tallying up the cost of the buyer's system, and is run when the Compute the Cost button is clicked.

Listing 18.6

```
totalCost       = 0;
strDesc         = "";

function calculate() {
   totalCost    = 0;
   strDesc      = "";

   if(!calcBase())
      return false;

   if(!calcHDrive())
      return false;

   if(!calcMemory())
      return false;

   if(!calcMonitor())
      return false;

   if(!calcOS())
      return false;

   alert("\nYou have selected the following " +
         "configuration:\n\n" + strDesc +
         "\n with a total cost of $" +
         totalCost + ".");

   return true;
}
```

The phrase *main driver* means that `calculate()` actually calls a separate calculation function for each part of the system and—if each part is calculated properly—continues with the process. For example, listing 18.7 shows the hard disk calculation function, `calcHDrive()`, which adds the cost of the selected hard drive to the running tally. Also, because `calculate()` calls other functions that are adding to the running tally, the `totalCost` and `strDesc` variables are declared as global, so they are accessible to all necessary functions.

Listing 18.7

```
function calcHDrive() {
  var which = 0, j = -1;

  for(var i=0; i<document.order1.hdrive.length; i++) {
    if(document.order1.hdrive[i].checked) {
```

continues

Listing 18.7 Continued

```
      j = i;
      break;
    }
  }

  if(j == -1) {
    alert("\nYou must select a hard disk " +
          "configuration.\n");
    return false;
  }

  for(var i=1; i<=driveList.length; i++) {
    if(document.order1.hdrive[j].value ==
       driveList[i].name) {
      which = i;
    }
  }

  totalCost += eval(driveList[which].cost);
  strDesc   += " - " + driveList[which].name + " HD\n";

  return true;
}
```

Each individual calculation function follows the same basic structure:

- Determine which item has been selected.
- If no item is selected, warn the buyer that a selection must be made.
- Add the cost of the selected item to the running total and its description to the overall system description.

Also, because the individual parts arrays each have `length` properties, adding elements to an array doesn't require changing the calculation function (which uses the `length` property to determine how many parts it has to look through).

Looking at the Final Code

Listing 18.8 shows the final code in its entirety.

Listing 18.8

```
<HTML>
<HEAD>
<TITLE>The JavaScript Online Store</TITLE>
```

```
<SCRIPT LANGUAGE="JavaScript">
<!-- hide from non-JavaScript browsers
function MakeArray(size) {
   this.length = size;

   for(i = 1; i <= size; i++)
      this[i] = null;

   return this;
}

function Part(strName, iCost) {
   this.name   = strName;
   this.cost   = iCost;
}

baseList        = new MakeArray(3);
baseList[1]     = new Part("AMD DX4/100", 420);
baseList[2]     = new Part("Pentium 75" , 522);
baseList[3]     = new Part("Pentium 100", 609);

driveList       = new MakeArray(3);
driveList[1]    = new Part("1.0 Gig", 212);
driveList[2]    = new Part("1.2 Gig", 231);
driveList[3]    = new Part("1.6 Gig", 281);

memList         = new MakeArray(4);
memList[1]      = new Part("4 MB", 76);
memList[2]      = new Part("8 MB", 155);
memList[3]      = new Part("16 MB", 310);
memList[4]      = new Part("32 MB", 620);

monList         = new MakeArray(4);
monList[1]      = new Part("14\" GVC", 242);
monList[2]      = new Part("14\" Samsung", 140);
monList[3]      = new Part("15\" GVC", 385);
monList[4]      = new Part("17\" Samsung", 610);

osList          = new MakeArray(4);
osList[1]       = new Part("Windows 3.11", 80);
osList[2]       = new Part("Windows 95", 90);
osList[3]       = new Part("OS/2 Warp", 76);
osList[4]       = new Part("Linux", 50);

totalCost       = 0;
strDesc         = "";

function createSelect(strName, objList) {
   var tStr = "<SELECT NAME=\"" + strName + "\">"
         + "<OPTION SELECTED>- please specify -";

   for(var i=1; i<=objList.length; i++)
      tStr += "<OPTION>" + objList[i].name;
```

continues

Listing 18.8 Continued

```
   tStr += "</SELECT>";

   return tStr;
}

function createRadio(strName, objList) {
   var tStr = "";

   for(var i=1; i<=objList.length; i++) {
      tStr += "<INPUT NAME=\"" + strName + "\" "
            + "TYPE=radio VALUE=\"" + objList[i].name
            + "\">" + objList[i].name;
   }

   return tStr;
}

function calculate() {
   totalCost   = 0;
   strDesc     = "";

   if(!calcBase())
      return false;

   if(!calcHDrive())
      return false;

   if(!calcMemory())
      return false;

   if(!calcMonitor())
      return false;

   if(!calcOS())
      return false;

   alert("\nYou have selected the following " +
         "configuration:\n\n" + strDesc +
         "\n with a total cost of $" +
         totalCost + ".");

   return true;
}


function calcBase() {
   var which = document.order1.base.selectedIndex;

   if(which == 0) {
      alert("\nYou must select a base system.\n");
      return false;
```

```
    }

    totalCost += eval(baseList[which].cost);
    strDesc   += " - " + baseList[which].name + "\n"
              + " - PCI Motherboard w /I/O\n"
              + " - 2 meg Video card\n"
              + " - Mini Tower Case\n";

    return true;
}

function calcHDrive() {
    var which = 0, j = -1;

    for(var i=0; i<document.order1.hdrive.length; i++) {
        if(document.order1.hdrive[i].checked) {
            j = i;
            break;
        }
    }

    if(j == -1) {
        alert("\nYou must select a hard disk " +
              "configuration.\n");
        return false;
    }

    for(var i=1; i<=driveList.length; i++) {
        if(document.order1.hdrive[j].value ==
            driveList[i].name) {
            which = i;
        }
    }

    totalCost += eval(driveList[which].cost);
    strDesc   += " - " + driveList[which].name
              + " HD\n";

    return true;
}

function calcMemory() {
    var which = 0, j = -1;

    for(var i=0; i<document.order1.memory.length; i++) {
        if(document.order1.memory[i].checked) {
            j = i;
            break;
        }
    }

    if(j == -1) {
        alert("\nYou must select a memory " +
```

continues

Listing 18.8 Continued

```
            "configuration.\n");
        return false;
    }

    for(var i=1; i<=memList.length; i++) {
        if(document.order1.memory[j].value ==
            memList[i].name) {
            which = i;

        }
    }

    totalCost += eval(memList[which].cost);
    strDesc   += " - " + memList[which].name
              + " RAM\n";

    return true;
}

function calcMonitor() {
    var which = document.order1.monitor.selectedIndex;

    if(which == 0) {
        alert("\nYou must select a monitor.\n");
        return false;
    }

    totalCost += eval(monList[which].cost);
    strDesc   += " - " + monList[which].name
              + " Monitor\n";

    return true;
}

function calcOS() {
    var which = document.order1.os.selectedIndex;

    if(which == 0) {
        alert("\nYou must select an operating system.\n");
        return false;
    }

    totalCost += eval(osList[which].cost);
    strDesc   += " - " + osList[which].name + "\n";

    return true;
}
// end hide -->
</SCRIPT>
</HEAD>
<BODY BGCOLOR=#FFFFFF>
```

```
<FORM NAME="order1" METHOD=POST>

<H3>Welcome to "Buy It Online!"</H3>

<CENTER><TABLE WIDTH=99% CELLPADDING=4 BORDER>

   <TR>
      <TH VALIGN=TOP>Base System:</TH>
      <TD>
         <SCRIPT LANGUAGE="JavaScript">
         <!-- begin hide
            document.write(createSelect("base", baseList)
                           + "<BR>");
         // end hide -->
         </SCRIPT>
         PCI Motherboard w I/O,<BR>
         2 Serial, 1 Parallel, 4 IDE, 2 FD<BR>
         2 meg Trident Video Adapter<BR>
         Mini Tower Case, 230 Watt Power Supply<BR>
         1.44 FD, Win95 Keyboard, Mouse
      </TD>
   </TR>

   <TR>
      <TH VALIGN=TOP>Hard Drive:</TH>
      <TD>
         <SCRIPT LANGUAGE="JavaScript">
         <!-- begin hide
            document.write(createRadio("hdrive", driveList)
                           + "<BR>");
         // end hide -->
         </SCRIPT>
      </TD>
   </TR>

   <TR>
      <TH VALIGN=TOP>Memory:</TH>
      <TD>
         <SCRIPT LANGUAGE="JavaScript">
         <!-- begin hide
            document.write(createRadio("memory", memList)
                           + "<BR>");
         // end hide -->
         </SCRIPT>
      </TD>
   </tr>

   <TR>
      <TH VALIGN=TOP>Monitor:</TH>
      <TD>
         <SCRIPT LANGUAGE="JavaScript">
         <!-- begin hide
```

continues

Listing 18.8 Continued

```
            document.write(createSelect("monitor", monList)
                                + "<BR>");
         // end hide -->
         </SCRIPT>
      </TD>
   </TR>

   <TR>
      <TH VALIGN=TOP>Operating System:</TH>
      <TD>
         <SCRIPT LANGUAGE="JavaScript">
         <!-- begin hide
            document.write(createSelect("os", osList)
                                + "<BR>");
         // end hide -->
         </SCRIPT>
      </TD>
   </TR>
</TABLE>

<BR>

<INPUT TYPE=button NAME="compute"
       VALUE="Calculate the Cost"
       ONCLICK="calculate()">

</FORM>
</BODY>
</HTML>
```

After the buyer selects options for all the parts of the system, the total cost is displayed, as shown in figure 18.2.

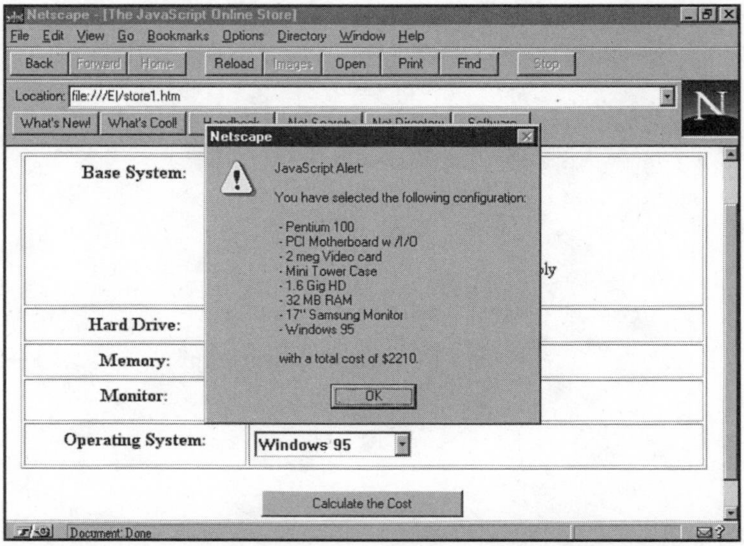

Figure 18.2
The online store in action. Using the new-line character freely allows you to design output with the `alert()` dialog box that's pleasing to the eye.

Submitting the Order

All the tools in the world won't do store owners much good if they can't get the customer's personal information. Displaying the buyer's selection with an `alert()` box is fine for the user, but it doesn't transmit the information back to you. This next add-in function gathers customer information. You'll use this information to build an e-mail message to transport the order.

The simplest way to implement this is to use JavaScript to generate a new custom form (see fig. 18.3) that displays the selected system and permits the buyer to enter a name and address. Listing 18.9 shows the `order()` function that does this.

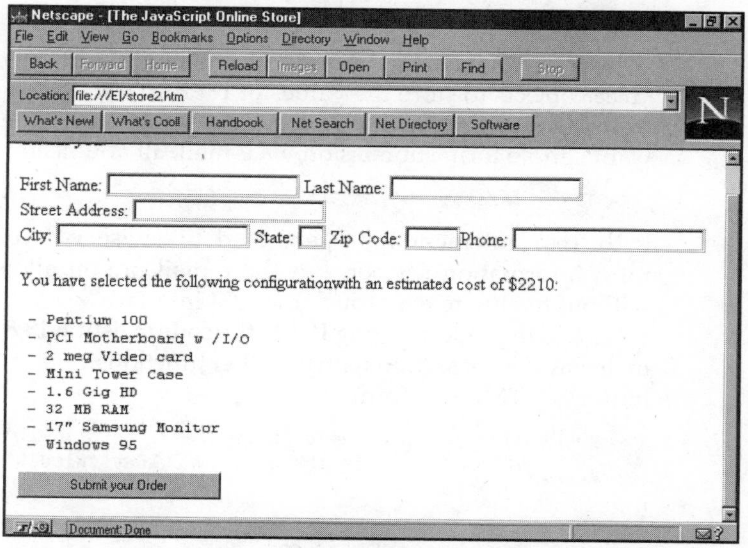

Figure 18.3

Using JavaScript to dynamically create a second form with information collected from the first.

Listing 18.9

```
function order() {
   document.write("<body bgcolor=#ffffff>");
   document.write("<h4>Thank you!</h4>");
   document.write("<FORM name='order2' METHOD=POST>");
   document.write("First Name: <INPUT NAME='first' TYPE=TEXT> ");
   document.write("Last Name: <INPUT NAME='last' TYPE=TEXT><br>");
   document.write("Street Address: <INPUT NAME='street'
   ➥TYPE=TEXT size=40><br>");
   document.write("City: <INPUT NAME='city' TYPE=TEXT> ");
   document.write("State: <INPUT NAME='state' TYPE=TEXT size=2> ");
   document.write("Zip Code: <INPUT NAME='zip' TYPE=TEXT size=5>");
   document.write("Phone: <INPUT NAME='phone' TYPE=TEXT><br><br>");
   document.write("You have selected the following configuration "
```

continues

Listing 18.9 Continued

```
                    + "with an estimated cost of $" +
                    + totalCost + ":"
                    + "<PRE>" + strDesc + "</PRE>");
    document.write("<INPUT value='Submit your Order'
    ➥TYPE=SUBMIT><br>");
    document.write("<INPUT NAME='description' TYPE=HIDDEN>");
    document.write("<INPUT NAME='cost'
    ➥TYPE=HIDDEN></form></body>");

    document.order2.description.value = strDesc;
    document.order2.cost.value = totalCost;
}
```

Because this is the form that will actually be submitted, it's necessary to use two `hidden` objects to store the values of `totalCost` and `strDesc` (while they are hidden from the user, they will be added to the information sent back to the server). If you want simple form submission via e-mail, all you need to do is add

```
ACTION='mailto:...'
```

to the `FORM` statement that's generated. Likewise, you could use CGI to process the form information further, but the e-mail option allows you to run a business without having to ever touch the CGI interface.

To add the code in listing 18.9 to the code in listing 18.8, simply place this function in the JavaScript section with the other functions, and change the Compute the Cost button's HTML line from

```
<INPUT TYPE=button NAME="compute"
       VALUE="Calculate the Cost" ONCLICK="calculate()">
```

to

```
<INPUT TYPE=button NAME="compute"
       VALUE="Calculate the Cost"
       ONCLICK="if(calculate()) order();">
```

This takes advantage of the Boolean value returned by `calculate()` to make certain that the order form is generated only when a complete system has been built.

As a final touch, you may want to replace the `alert()` dialog in the `calculate()` function with a `confirm()` dialog similar to listing 18.10.

Listing 18.10

```
return confirm("\nYou have selected the following
➥configuration:\n\n" +
            strDesc + "\n with a total cost of $" +
            totalCost + ".\n" +
            "\n Do you wish to place an order?");
```

This has the added benefit of giving buyers one last chance to change their minds before placing the order. The complete program, store2.htm, is available on the CD-ROM.

Summary

Although JavaScript can't be used to access a database located on the server, it's possible to craft a "mini-database" that's contained within the HTML document itself. A JavaScript database is nothing more than an array of items where each item is a new, user-defined object type.

This technique can then be used to design a simple "online store" that displays the contents of the database through a form. The buyer can then select items to purchase and submit the resulting "shopping list" through e-mail. It's also possible to have JavaScript not only validate all the information the customer has entered, but generate additional forms for data and tailor the content of the e-mail to exactly what the seller needs.

Exercises

1. Using the information learned from Chapter 13, "Window Methods," move the Customer Information form to a new window. Be sure to access the information gathered from the first form.
2. Add the ability to calculate state sales tax to the Customer Information form.

Verifying Form Input

How many times have you set up a form on your server, and when you scanned the input files, found that 20 percent of the entries weren't filled out correctly? Sometimes people leave important fields blank, and sometimes they give input that makes no sense.

A common solution to this problem is to write a custom CGI script that examines the data, checks its validity, and then takes appropriate action. This action tells users that they need to change their entries or—if they filled out the form correctly—tells the script that it process the data, and then returns confirmation to the users.

As you can imagine, if the load on the server is heavy or bandwidth is especially clogged, the whole process can take a while—especially if users have to resubmit the form more than once. Often, users don't even finish the form; they get frustrated and leave your site.

Obviously there's a solution to the problem, and I'm sure that you can guess that it involves JavaScript. As you'll see, JavaScript is actually the best solution for this problem—much more so than Java or CGI.

Before implementing a solution with JavaScript, let's look at the traditional (non-JavaScript) implementation of form verification, and then make some modifications so that JavaScript can expedite the whole process.

> **Note:** It's important to pay special attention to how the order form will be implemented without JavaScript. Because JavaScript has no effect on browsers that don't support JavaScript, anyone without Netscape 2.0+ won't have the benefits of what will be implemented. You might want to consider still using a CGI to check form input for individuals without a JavaScript-capable browser.

Traditional Methods of Form Verification

Let's build a simple HTML form to act as an online order form for the Obscure Computer Part Manufacturing Company (OCPMC). The form must have fields for item description, quantity, and total cost for each item, as well as total cost for the whole order. Listing 19.1 shows the HTML for the form. You'll build on this form later in the chapter by incorporating JavaScript.

Of course, either you'll have to rely on users to add up the cost themselves, or you can write a CGI script to add up their total and return it to them. Then they can okay that price and resubmit their order, using another call to the script, of course. As you can see, this process is getting pretty intense—I would hate to access a site like this over a 14.4kbps connection!

The HTML for a form like this is pretty simple. Listing 19.1 shows the HTML used to build the order form. To make things look a little snazzier, I put the input fields into a table, and also played with font colors. Figure 19.1 shows what the page looks like in Netscape.

Listing 19.1

```
<!DOCTYPE HTML PUBLIC "-//IETF//DTD HTML 2.0//EN">
<HTML>
<HEAD> <TITLE>Obscure Computer Catalog</TITLE> </HEAD>

<BODY bgcolor=ffffff>
<font color=red>
<h1>On-Line Ordering with</h1>
<h2>The Obscure Computer Part Manufacturing Company</h2><br><br>
<b>Products Offered</b>
<ol>
     <li> Spacely Sprockett  $5.00/each
     <li> Cogswell Cog  $4.00/each
     <li> TRS-80  $1.00/each
     <li> Commodore 128  $0.50/each
     <li> Prime Mainframe  $0.10/each
</ol><br>
</font>
<p>    Please input the item number from above in the Product<br>
     column and fill out the form accordingly</p>
<form name="OrderForm" action=http://www.luke.org/cgi-bin/Obscure.pl
method=post>
<table>
<tr><th>Product</th><th>Quantity</th><th>Total</th></tr>
<tr><td><input type=text size=20 name=product1></td>
     <td><input type=text size=5 name=quantity1 value=0></td>
     <td>$<input type=text size=5 name=total1 value=0></td></tr>
<tr><td><input type=text size=20 name=product2></td>
     <td><input type=text size=5 name=quantity2 value=0></td>
     <td>$<input type=text size=5 name=total2 value=0></td></tr>
<tr><td><input type=text size=20 name=product3></td>
```

```
        <td><input type=text size=5 name=quantity3 value=0></td>
        <td>$<input type=text size=5 name=total3 value=0></td></tr>
<tr><td><input type=text size=20 name=product4></td>
        <td><input type=text size=5 name=quantity4 value=0></td>
        <td>$<input type=text size=5 name=total4 value=0></td></tr>
<tr><td><input type=text size=20 name=product5></td>
        <td><input type=text size=5 name=quantity5 value=0></td>
        <td>$<input type=text size=5 name=total5 value=0></td></tr>
<tr><td></td><td align=right>Total</td>
        <td>$<input type=text size=5 name=total value=0></td></tr>
</table>
<br><input type=submit name=Submit value=Order!><input type=Reset
name=Clear value="Clear Input">
</form>

</BODY>
</HTML>
```

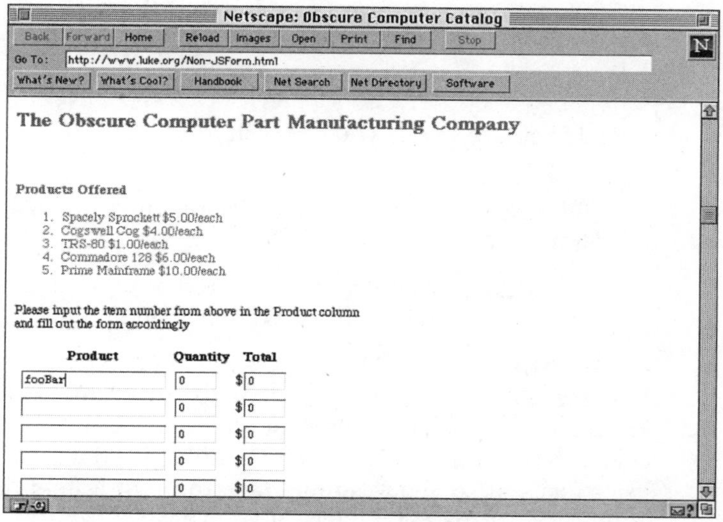

Figure 19.1

The traditional order form. Note how an input of fooBar isn't noticed by the computer. The user would have to wait until the form is submitted to the CGI script to find out that he needs to modify his entry.

Well, the form is a start; it obviously allows people to order any of the five fabulous products offered by OCPMC. What you don't see here is the Perl CGI, Obscure.pl, that processes the data. Let's examine the steps that Obscure.pl would have to take for this form:

1. It parses the input that's sent from the Web browser to the CGI, and then looks at each field in the form.
2. If problems are found, an HTML response that details each problem has to be built.

3. If no problems are found with the input, the CGI simply has to tally up the order and prepare a response to tell the user how much the order is.
4. It returns the response to the user and waits for him to resubmit it.
5. It accepts the new form, if the user was correcting his entries, and goes to step 1; otherwise, it inputs the data into a database, or whatever was required in this situation.

Modifying the Form to Take Advantage of JavaScript

In the previous solution, the constant client / server communication and server-side data analysis make the whole process take much longer than it has to. A better solution can obviously be found using JavaScript.

JavaScript provides a perfect solution to this problem. Let's examine the preceding five steps and decide which can be replaced with JavaScript:

- Because you aren't dealing with the post-input, step 1 isn't necessary.
- To replace step 2, you can wait for the user to change a field, and then call a JavaScript function to examine the input.
- Step 4 can be replaced if you keep a running total of the price and display it on-screen.
- An additional enhancement would be to examine the product number and replace it with the product description.

All the functions you develop do their work after the contents of certain fields are changed. For this reason, you need to embed the `OnChange` event handler in the HTML next to each input element. (`OnBlur` can be used here also, but it's not the best choice. If you use the `OnBlur` event handler, the data is checked every time the field loses focus; if someone simply tabs through a field, its data is still examined.) Although these extra function calls don't cause a noticeable time lag or error, calling unnecessary functions is an example of poor programming techniques.

For the JavaScript solution, you'll develop two principle functions: `setProduct()`, which is called when someone changes a product number in the Product column, and `checkInput()`, which is called whenever someone changes a value in the Quantity column. Of course, helper functions are used to facilitate in the execution of the principle functions. Because the form has room for placement of up to five different orders, you call the principle functions with an integer representing the row that contains the order. This helps when you need to fetch and modify the data in the order's row.

In addition to the two principle functions and their helper functions, you need two global variables. These could be local to the functions, but you really can afford to waste a touch of memory on two globals. The globals are going to be arrays of product numbers and their corresponding prices. To facilitate grabbing the information from the arrays, you make a product's array index identical to its product number.

Actually, you're probably questioning the decision to have an array of product descriptions. Why do you need an array of product descriptions when the order form asks for product numbers? You'll use this array to enhance the form with JavaScript. JavaScript will use the product number to reference the product description and then will replace the number with its description in the form. Let's look at the code you use to set up the global arrays. Listing 19.2 shows two functions, `initProducts()` and `initPrices()`, which fill their corresponding arrays with the product numbers or prices. Listing 19.3 uses the new operator to declare two new array objects—prices (of type `initPrices`) and products (of type `initProducts`).

Listing 19.2

```
function initProducts() {
     this.length = 5;
     this[1] = "1: Spacely Sprockett";
     this[2] = "2: Cogswell Cog";
     this[3] = "3: TRS-80";
     this[4] = "4: Commodore 128";
     this[5] = "5: Prime Mainframe";
}

function initPrices() {
     this.length = 5;
     this[1] = 5;
     this[2] = 4;
     this[3] = 1;
     this[4] = 6;
     this[5] = 10;
}
```

Listing 19.3

```
var prices = new initPrices();
var products = new initProducts();
```

Now that the product and price arrays are all set up, you're ready to look at the `setProduct()` function. Listing 19.5 shows this function. Notice how it uses a series of if statements to find out which row the product order came from. After it determines the proper row, the function snatches the value from the product entry for that row. Users can enter either a valid product number (1–5) or garbage. The garbage comes in one of two forms, and due to the structuring of one of the functions, you have to test for both cases of garbage. One case is when the user enters an out-of-range integer only, and the other case is when the input involves at least one non-integer (3A, for instance).

After you determine which row the call came from, you set the variable `tempID` to the contents of the product field. The function `isDigit()` tests whether `tempID` is an integer. If it isn't—for example, someone enters `G5y` for a product number—an error message appears. If you determine that `tempID` is an integer, you call the function `checkID()`, which returns true if the product number is associated with a product sold by the OCPMC. If it is, you replace the contents of the current order field with the product description. Otherwise, you display an error message telling users that they've entered an incorrect product number. Listing 19.4 shows the `isDigit()` and `checkID()` functions, and listing 19.5 shows the `setProduct()` function.

Listing 19.4

```
function isDigit( n ) {
    var test = "" + n;

    if (test == "0" ¦¦ test == "1" ¦¦ test == "2" ¦¦ test == "3" ¦¦
    ➥test == "4" ¦¦ test == "5" ¦¦ test == "6" ¦¦ test == "7" ¦¦
    ➥test == "8" ¦¦ test == "9")
        { return true; }

    else
         { return false; }
}

function checkID( theID ) {
     theID += "";
     return ( theID >=1 && theID <= 5 );
}
```

Listing 19.5

```
function setProduct( which ) {
     if ( which == 1 ) {
          tempID = document.OrderForm.product1.value;
          if (!isDigit( tempID ))
               { alert(" Invalid Product Number "); }
          else if ( checkID( tempID ) )
               { document.OrderForm.product1.value =
               ➥products[tempID]¦; }
          else
               { alert(" Invalid Product Number "); }
     }
     else if ( which == 2 ) {
          tempID = document.OrderForm.product2.value;
```

```
        if (!isDigit( tempID ))
            { alert(" Invalid Product Number "); }
        else if ( checkID( tempID ) )
            { document.OrderForm.product2.value =
            ➥products[tempID]¦; }
        else
            { alert(" Invalid Product Number "); }
    }
    else if ( which == 3 ) {
        tempID = document.OrderForm.product3.value;
        if (!isDigit( tempID ))
            { alert(" Invalid Product Number "); }
        else if ( checkID( tempID ) )
            { document.OrderForm.product3.value =
            ➥products[tempID]¦; }
        else
            { alert(" Invalid Product Number "); }
    }
    else if ( which == 4 ) {
        tempID = document.OrderForm.product4.value;
        if (!isDigit( tempID ))
            { alert(" Invalid Product Number "); }
        else if ( checkID( tempID ) )
            { document.OrderForm.product4.value =
            ➥products[tempID]¦; }
        else
            { alert(" Invalid Product Number "); }
    }
    else if ( which == 5 ) {
        tempID = document.OrderForm.product5.value;
        if (!isDigit( tempID ))
            { alert(" Invalid Product Number "); }
        else if ( checkID( tempID ) )
            { document.OrderForm.product5.value =
            ➥products[tempID]¦; }
        else
            { alert(" Invalid Product Number "); }
    }
}
```

After you get users to enter a valid product ID, you want them to enter a quantity. Here, you'll implement the `checkID()` function. Again, you'll pass an integer to `checkID()`, which indicates the row from which the order originated. In addition to checking the validity of the input, you also have to update the product total based on the item total.

Listing 19.6 shows the `checkInput()` function, which takes a slightly different approach than the `setProduct()` function. I chose this approach merely to demonstrate stylistic differences, and it has no real functional difference. When you implement this yourself, feel free to choose the method that makes the most sense to you. In this function, the contents of the field in question are placed into a variable called `tempID`. The function `isDigit()` (in listing 19.4) tests whether users placed a non-integer into the quantity field; `isWhole()` (also in listing 19.6) makes sure that the number entered does not have a mantissa. If `tempID` isn't an integer, an appropriate error message is displayed; otherwise, the program searches for the row from which the event was generated.

Listing 19.6

```
function isWhole( testInt ) {
     testInt *= 1;

     if ( Math.floor( testInt ) == testInt )
          { return true; }
     else { return false; }
     }

function checkInput( which ) {
     if ( which == 1 )
          { tempID = document.OrderForm.quantity1.value; }
     else if ( which == 2 )
          { tempID = document.OrderForm.quantity2.value; }
     else if ( which == 3 )
          { tempID = document.OrderForm.quantity3.value; }
     else if ( which == 4 )
          { tempID = document.OrderForm.product4.value; }
     else if ( which == 5 )
          { tempID = document.OrderForm.product4.value; }

     if ( !isDigit( tempID.substring(0,1) ) )
          { alert(" Please Enter A Valid Quantity "); }
     else {
          var tempTotal = 1 * document.OrderForm.total.value;
          if ( which == 1 ) {
               productID = document.OrderForm.product1.value.
               ➥substring(0, 1);
               productCount = document.OrderForm.quantity1.value;
               document.OrderForm.total1.value = 1*(prices[productID])
               ➥*productCount;
               tempVal = ( 1*document.OrderForm.total1.value +
               ➥tempTotal);
               setTotal( tempVal );
          }
          else if ( which == 2 ) {
               productID = document.OrderForm.product2.value.
               ➥substring(0, 1);
               productCount = document.OrderForm.quantity2.value;
               document.OrderForm.total2.value = 1*(prices[productID])
               ➥*productCount;
               tempVal = ( 1*document.OrderForm.total2.value +
               ➥tempTotal);
               setTotal( tempVal );
          }
          else if ( which == 3 ) {
```

```
            productID = document.OrderForm.product3.value.
            ➥substring(0, 1);
            productCount = document.OrderForm.quantity3.value;
            document.OrderForm.total3.value = 1*(prices[productID])
            ➥*productCount;
            tempVal = ( 1*document.OrderForm.total3.value +
            ➥tempTotal);
            setTotal( tempVal );
        }
        else if ( which == 4 ) {
            productID = document.OrderForm.product4.value.
            ➥substring(0, 1);
            productCount = document.OrderForm.quantity4.value;
            document.OrderForm.total4.value = 1*(prices[productID])
            ➥*productCount;
            tempVal = ( 1*document.OrderForm.total4.value +
            ➥tempTotal);
            setTotal( tempVal );
        }
        else if ( which == 5 ) {
            productID = document.OrderForm.product5.value.
            ➥substring(0, 1);
            productCount = document.OrderForm.quantity5.value;
            document.OrderForm.total5.value = 1*(prices[productID])
            ➥*productCount;
            tempVal = ( 1*document.OrderForm.total5.value +
            ➥tempTotal);
            setTotal( tempVal );
        }
    }
}
```

To determine the price for the current item, the program obviously needs to know the quantity desired (`tempID`) and the price of the item being ordered. Remember that the product description was added to the ID number in the previous column. To strip the product ID off the description, the `substring()` function is used to grab the first character off the previous entry; the first character is also the product ID. Because product IDs are equal to the array index of the price for the product, the program simply looks in the prices array for the price of that object. Once the program knows the quantity desired and the cost for each, it simply has to multiply these numbers and place the value in the total box.

Now that there's a total for the item in question, all the program has to do is add the item price to the total price. This part is a little tricky due to the way that JavaScript treats strings and integers. If the current total is simply grabbed from the total field and added to the item total field, the values are treated as strings; when you use the + operator, the two are concatenated. Thus, if the current value is 4 and you add 5 to it, you get a value of 45. To coerce the strings into integers, you multiply them by the identity element for multiplication—1. Now the values are treated as integers, and 4+5 gives 9.

The only function not shown here is `setTotal()`; it is passed the new total value and places this integer into the total field. It's relatively trivial and is contained in the final source listing at the end of this chapter.

Only one more aspect of this form has yet to be covered: The event handlers still have to be embedded in the HTML wherever data analysis is needed. As discussed earlier, the `OnChange` event handler is the best choice for this situation.

Listing 19.7 shows the updated HTML. Notice how the function is passed an integer. This corresponds to the row from which the order originated. Of course, the form input still needs to be passed to a CGI script, because the information needs to be stored server-side. This time, the script is always going to be passed proper information and only has to store the data.

Listing 19.7

```
<form name="OrderForm" action=http://www.luke.org/cgi-bin/Obscure.pl
method=post>
<table>
<tr><th>Product</th><th>Quantity</th><th>Total</th></tr>
<tr><td><input type=text size=20 name=product1
onChange="setProduct(1)"></td>
     <td><input type=text size=5 name=quantity1 value=0
onChange="checkInput(1)"></td>
     <td>$<input type=text size=5 name=total1 value=0></td></tr>
<tr><td><input type=text size=20 name=product2
onChange="setProduct(2)"></td>
     <td><input type=text size=5 name=quantity2 value=0
onChange="checkInput(2)"></td>
     <td>$<input type=text size=5 name=total2 value=0></td></tr>
<tr><td><input type=text size=20 name=product3
onChange="setProduct(3)"></td>
     <td><input type=text size=5 name=quantity3 value=0
onChange="checkInput(3)"></td>
     <td>$<input type=text size=5 name=total3 value=0></td></tr>
<tr><td><input type=text size=20 name=product4
onChange="setProduct(4)"></td>
     <td><input type=text size=5 name=quantity4 value=0
onChange="checkInput(4)"></td>
     <td>$<input type=text size=5 name=total4 value=0></td></tr>
<tr><td><input type=text size=20 name=product5
onChange="setProduct(5)"></td>
     <td><input type=text size=5 name=quantity5 value=0
onChange="checkInput(5)"></td>
     <td>$<input type=text size=5 name=total5 value=0></td></tr>
<tr><td></td><td align=right>Total</td>
     <td>$<input type=text size=5 name=total value=0></td></tr>
</table>
<br><input type=submit name=Submit value=Order!><input type=Reset
name=Clear value="Clear Input">
</form>
```

That wasn't so bad was it? In about 200 lines of JavaScript, you have written code to verify form input. Figure 19.2 shows the completed order form alerting you that fooBar is an incorrect product number. The completed HTML with JavaScript is contained in listing 19.8.

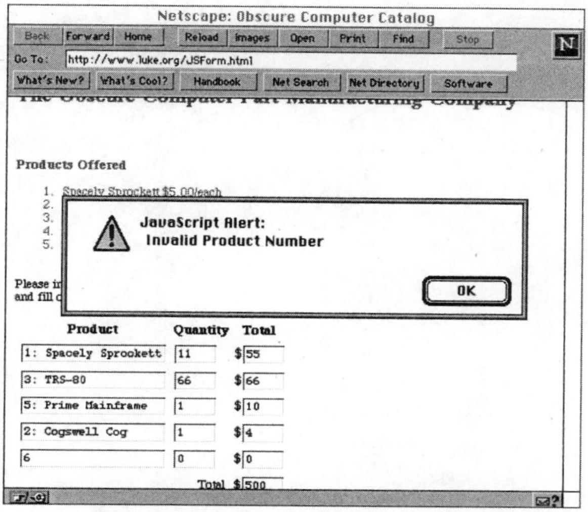

Figure 19.2

The completed order form. The product number fooBar is caught as an incorrect number.

Listing 19.8

```
<!DOCTYPE HTML PUBLIC "-//IETF//DTD HTML 2.0//EN">
<HTML>
<HEAD>

<TITLE>Obscure Computer Catalog </TITLE>

<SCRIPT language="JavaScript">
<!--
     function initProducts() {
          this.length = 5;
          this[1] = "1: Spacely Sprockett";
          this[2] = "2: Cogswell Cog";
          this[3] = "3: TRS-80";
          this[4] = "4: Commadore 128";
          this[5] = "5: Prime Mainframe";
     }

     function initPrices() {
          this.length = 5;
          this[1] = 5;
          this[2] = 4;
```

continues

Listing 19.8 Continued

```
        this[3] = 1;
        this[4] = 6;
        this[5] = 10;
    }

    var prices = new initPrices();
    var products = new initProducts();

    function isDigit( n ) {
        var test = "" + n;

            if (test == "0" || test == "1" || test == "2" || test ==
            ➥"3" || test == "4" || test == "5" || test == "6" ||
            ➥test == "7" || test == "8" || test == "9")
            { return true; }

        else
             { return false; }
    }

    function checkID( theID ) {
         theID += "";
         return ( theID >=1 && theID <= 5 );
    }

    function setProduct( which ) {
         if ( which == 1 ) {
              tempID = document.OrderForm.product1.value;
              if (!isDigit( tempID ))
                   { alert(" Invalid Product Number "); }
              else if ( checkID( tempID ) )
                   { document.OrderForm.product1.value =
                   ➥products[tempID]; }
              else
                   { alert(" Invalid Product Number "); }
         }
         else if ( which == 2 ) {
              tempID = document.OrderForm.product2.value;
              if (!isDigit( tempID ))
                   { alert(" Invalid Product Number "); }
              else if ( checkID( tempID ) )
                   { document.OrderForm.product2.value =
                   ➥products[tempID]; }
              else
                   { alert(" Invalid Product Number "); }
         }
         else if ( which == 3 ) {
              tempID = document.OrderForm.product3.value;
              if (!isDigit( tempID ))
                   { alert(" Invalid Product Number "); }
              else if ( checkID( tempID ) )
```

```
                { document.OrderForm.product3.value =
                ➥products[tempID]; }
            else
                { alert(" Invalid Product Number "); }
        }
        else if ( which == 4 ) {
            tempID = document.OrderForm.product4.value;
            if (!isDigit( tempID ))
                { alert(" Invalid Product Number "); }
            else if ( checkID( tempID ) )
                { document.OrderForm.product4.value =
                ➥products[tempID]; }
            else
                { alert(" Invalid Product Number "); }
        }
        else if ( which == 5 ) {
            tempID = document.OrderForm.product5.value;
            if (!isDigit( tempID ))
                { alert(" Invalid Product Number "); }
            else if ( checkID( tempID ) )
                { document.OrderForm.product5.value =
                ➥products[tempID]; }
            else
                { alert(" Invalid Product Number "); }
        }
    }

    function setTotal( t )
        { document.OrderForm.total.value = t; }

    function checkInput( which ) {
        if ( which == 1 )
            { tempID = document.OrderForm.quantity1.value; }
        else if ( which == 2 )
            { tempID = document.OrderForm.quantity2.value; }
        else if ( which == 3 )
            { tempID = document.OrderForm.quantity3.value; }
        else if ( which == 4 )
            { tempID = document.OrderForm.product4.value; }
        else if ( which == 5 )
            { tempID = document.OrderForm.product4.value; }

        if ( !isDigit( tempID.substring(0,1) ) )
            { alert(" Please Enter A Valid Quantity "); }
        else {
            var tempTotal = 1 * document.OrderForm.total.value;
            if ( which == 1 ) {
                productID = document.OrderForm.product1.value.
                ➥substring(0, 1);
                productCount = document.OrderForm.quantity1.value;
                document.OrderForm.total1.value =
                ➥1*(prices[productID])*productCount;
```

continues

Listing 19.8 Continued

```
          tempVal = ( 1*document.OrderForm.total1.value +
          ➥tempTotal);
          setTotal( tempVal );
     }
     else if ( which == 2 ) {
          productID = document.OrderForm.product2.value.
          ➥substring(0, 1);
          productCount = document.OrderForm.quantity2.value;
          document.OrderForm.total2.value =
          ➥1*(prices[productID])*productCount;
          tempVal = ( 1*document.OrderForm.total2.value +
          ➥tempTotal);
          setTotal( tempVal );
     }
     else if ( which == 3 ) {
          productID = document.OrderForm.product3.value.
          ➥substring(0, 1);
          productCount = document.OrderForm.quantity3.value;
          document.OrderForm.total3.value =
          ➥1*(prices[productID])*productCount;
          tempVal = ( 1*document.OrderForm.total3.value +
          ➥tempTotal);
          setTotal( tempVal );
     }
     else if ( which == 4 ) {
          productID = document.OrderForm.product4.value.
          ➥substring(0, 1);
          productCount = document.OrderForm.quantity4.value;
          document.OrderForm.total4.value =
          ➥1*(prices[productID])*productCount;
          tempVal = ( 1*document.OrderForm.total4.value +
          ➥tempTotal);
          setTotal( tempVal );
     }
     else if ( which == 5 ) {
          productID = document.OrderForm.product5.value.
          ➥substring(0, 1);
          productCount = document.OrderForm.quantity5.value;
          document.OrderForm.total5.value =
          ➥1*(prices[productID])*productCount;
          tempVal = ( 1*document.OrderForm.total5.value +
          ➥tempTotal);
          setTotal( tempVal );
     }
   }
 }
-->
</SCRIPT>
</HEAD>
```

```
<BODY bgcolor=ffffff>
<font color=red>
<h1>On-Line Ordering with</h1>
<h2>The Obscure Computer Part Manufacturing Company</h2><br><br>
<b>Products Offered</b>
<ol>
     <li> Spacely Sprockett  $5.00/each
     <li> Cogswell Cog  $4.00/each
     <li> TRS-80  $1.00/each
     <li> Commadore 128  $6.00/each
     <li> Prime Mainframe  $10.00/each
</ol><br>
</font>
<p>     Please input the item number from above in the Product column<br>
     and fill out the form accordingly</p>

<form name="OrderForm" action=http://www.luke.org/cgi-bin/Obscure.pl
method=post>
<table>
<tr><th>Product</th><th>Quantity</th><th>Total</th></tr>
<tr><td><input type=text size=20 name=product1
onChange="setProduct(1)"></td>
     <td><input type=text size=5 name=quantity1 value=0
onChange="checkInput(1)"></td>
     <td>$<input type=text size=5 name=total1 value=0></td></tr>
<tr><td><input type=text size=20 name=product2
onChange="setProduct(2)"></td>
     <td><input type=text size=5 name=quantity2 value=0
onChange="checkInput(2)"></td>
     <td>$<input type=text size=5 name=total2 value=0></td></tr>
<tr><td><input type=text size=20 name=product3
onChange="setProduct(3)"></td>
     <td><input type=text size=5 name=quantity3 value=0
onChange="checkInput(3)"></td>
     <td>$<input type=text size=5 name=total3 value=0></td></tr>
<tr><td><input type=text size=20 name=product4
onChange="setProduct(4)"></td>
     <td><input type=text size=5 name=quantity4 value=0
onChange="checkInput(4)"></td>
     <td>$<input type=text size=5 name=total4 value=0></td></tr>
<tr><td><input type=text size=20 name=product5
onChange="setProduct(5)"></td>
     <td><input type=text size=5 name=quantity5 value=0
onChange="checkInput(5)"></td>
     <td>$<input type=text size=5 name=total5 value=0></td></tr>
<tr><td></td><td align=right>Total</td>
     <td>$<input type=text size=5 name=total value=0></td></tr>
</table>
<br><input type=submit name=Submit value=Order!><input type=Reset
name=Clear value="Clear Input">
</form>

</BODY>
</HTML>
```

Review Questions

Answers to the review questions can be found in Appendix D.

1. There are a few cases in JavaScript where you multiply a string by 1. Why is this necessary?
2. Why is JavaScript a preferable choice over Java or CGI to perform form validation?

Exercises

1. The OCPMC was lucky; the state had decided not to tax its sales. Well, a new regime has taken over, and the OCPMC is now forced to charge 7 percent tax on all of its sales. Change the Total cell to a Subtotal cell and add a new Total cell below it. In addition to updating the Subtotal cell, `setTotal()` will have to update the Total cell, too. Make sure that you round the total off after you multiply it by .07 so that customers aren't charged a fraction of a cent.
2. OCPMC's owner calls to say that rather than examine the data after each field is altered, he prefers that it be examined all at once when the submit button is clicked. Alter the form to make him happy.
3. Currently, we don't have any function calls when a total field is modified. Can you imagine what would happen if a user changed the total field once a value was computed? Alter the order form so that a function is called whenever a total field is modified. Write a function named `checkTotal()` to grab all variables that it depends on and compute the total value. If the total value is different from the value shown, you will want to change the total value. *Hint:* Because this function is called whenever the total field is changed, you'll want to use the `OnChange` event handler.

CHAPTER 20

Creating a Control Panel

What's a control panel? For the purposes of this book, a *control panel* can control navigation through complex collections of documents, background color, the Netscape Exit option, and other browser features (much the way the Windows and Macintosh control panels control the features of the computer). JavaScript makes the creation and maintenance of a control panel possible, as you'll explore in this chapter.

Starting the Design Process with HTML

The first thing you need to do is create some files with different functions. Because this will be an example of using HTML frames, each file in the set has a different purpose. Specifically, you need to create these files:

- *main_fr.htm*, the main frame that combines the two frames you wanted to display. Here's the code:

```
<FRAMESET ROWS="135,*">
  <FRAME SRC="top_fr.htm"  NAME="frame1" SCROLLING="no" NORESIZE >
  <FRAME SRC="text.htm"  NAME="frame2" >
    </FRAMESET>
<NOFRAMES>
</NOFRAMES>
</FRAMESET>
```

  Figure 20.1 shows the main fr.htm frame.

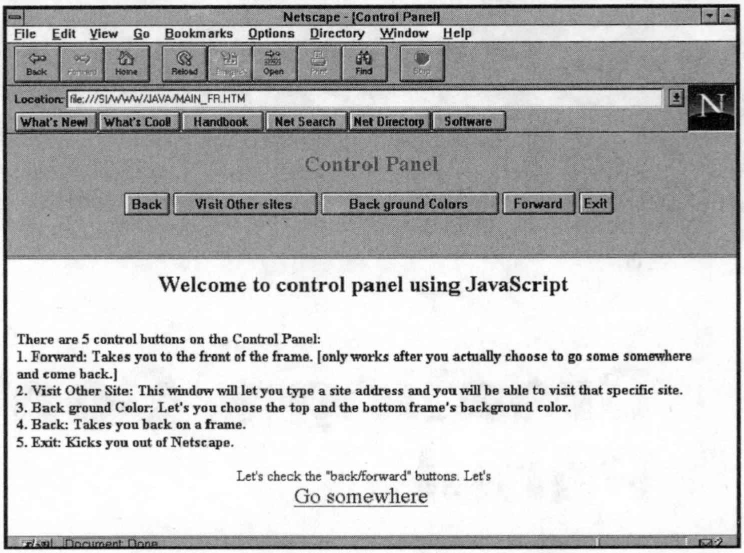

Figure 20.1
A simple two-frame example, from which you'll build a control panel (in the top frame).

- *top_fr.htm*, which contains all the buttons that will be used as control buttons.
- *text.htm*, the text file that gives you the idea of the page and describes what each of the control panel buttons do.
- *colors.htm*, which contains the script for the background color change.
- *visit.htm*, which contains the script for visiting other sites.

Coding in JavaScript

First, let's examine top_fr.htm, which contains all the buttons. This file uses five buttons total.

Back

The Back button takes you back one page in the lower frame. This button works only after you actually enter an URL, visit that site, and then move on to a new URL. Here's the code:

```
<input type="button" value="Back" onClick="parent.frame2.history.back()">
```

Notice that the `onClick` event does all the work. All you have to do is tell the function to go back one URL in the history list of `frame2`.

Visit Other Sites

By using this button, you can type a site address and be able to visit that specific site. Clicking this button opens a new window (or dialog box) to accept the destination URL. Figure 20.2 is an example of the button used when visiting a site.

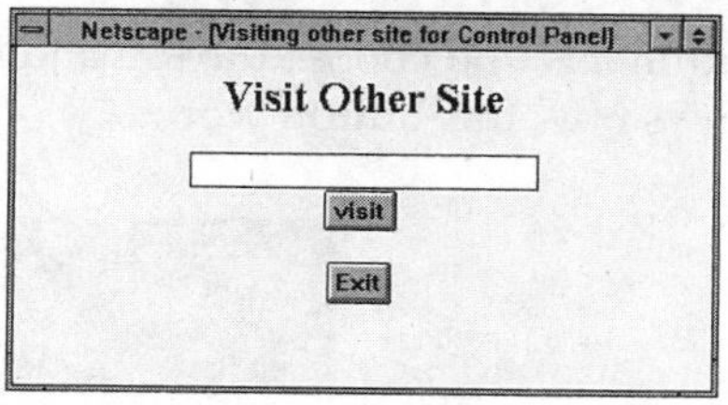

Figure 20.2
Visiting another site from the control panel.

Here's the code for this button:

```
<input type="button" Value="Visit Other sites" onClick="navi()">
```

Notice that `onClick` calls the `navi()` function, which contains the following codes:

```
function navi() {
    window.open('visit.htm', 'Visit', 'toolbar=no,location=no,
    ➥directories=no,status=no,menubar=no,scrollbars=no,
    ➥resizable=no,copyhistory=yes,width=400,height=200')
}
```

This function opens a new window (setting several of the window's properties, including toolbar, location, directions, and status), and loads the file visit.htm into it.

The visit.htm file creates two controls—a button and a text-input field:

- ♦ Text to put the site address. Here's the code:

```
<input type="text" name="site" size=50>
```

- ♦ A button to submit user's request. Here's the code:

```
<input type="button" name="submit_URL" value="visit"
➥onClick="window.close();visit('_go')">
```

When the user clicks the Visit button, the window that appeared when the Visit Other Sites button was clicked is closed. Also, the button calls another function, `visit(_go)`. This function has the following code:

```
function visit(frame) {
  if (frame == "_go")
    open (document.input_val.site.value, frame);
  return 0;
}
```

All this function is doing is taking the input from the text field "site" (as defined in the form) and placing the input in a new frame in the program. It then creates a new window.

Background Colors

This button lets you choose the top and bottom frames' background color. Figure 20.3 shows how this button works.

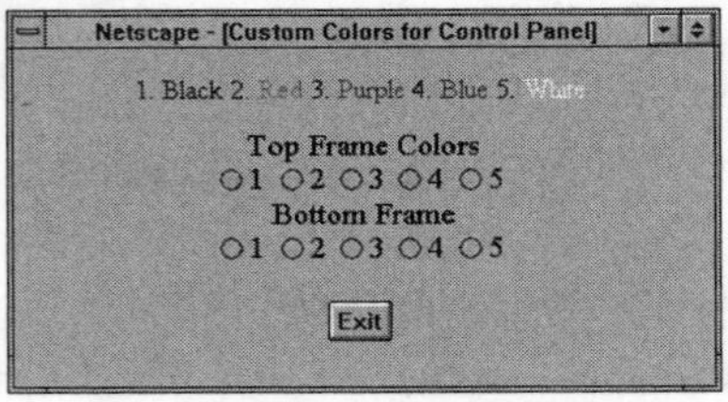

Figure 20.3
Using the Background Colors button to control the color of the frames.

Here's the code:

```
<input type="button" value="Back ground Colors" onClick="Customize()">
```

Notice that `OnClick` is calling the function `Customize()`. This is what `Customize()` does:

```
function Customize()
{
var PopWindow=window.open('colors.htm','Main', 'toolbar=no,
➥location=no,directories=no,status=no,menubar=no,scrollbars=no,
➥resizable=no,copyhistory=yes,width=400,height=200')
}
```

This function opens a new window (like the `navi()` function did), and loads the colors.htm file into it. In the colors.htm file are two options: changing the top frame and changing the bottom frame.

Changing the Top Frame

You need to create some radio buttons to provide possible color options for when the user clicks the top frame button. When the user chooses the specific radio button, the top frame background color changes. Here is a sample line of code:

```
<input type="radio" name="bgcolor" OnClick="creator.topColor('#000000')">
```

Notice that `OnClick` calls the `topColor()` function, and the value in that function is computed as `#000000`. You easily could use the color words (such as black) in place of `#000000`, if you prefer, but the hexadecimal values permit you more flexibility.

Now let's look at the `topColor()` function. All this function does is take the value from the passed parameter and put it in the `bgColor` property of `frame1`, which is your top frame. Here's the code (in top_fr.htm):

```
function topColor(newColor)
{
   window.parent.frames['frame1'].document.bgColor=newColor;
}
```

Changing the Bottom Frame

Just like in the top frame, you create some radio buttons for the bottom frame. When the user selects the specific radio button, the bottom frame background color changes. Here is a sample line of code:

```
<input type="radio" name="bgcolor"
onClick="creator.bottomColor('#000000')">
```

Notice that the `bottomColor()` function is called. This function isn't much different from the `topColor()` function. Like the `topColor()` function, all the `bottomColor()` function does is take the value from the form and put it in `frame2`, which is the bottom frame. Here's the code (located in top_fr.htm):

```
function bottomColor(newColor)
{
   window.parent.frames['frame2'].document.bgColor=newColor;
}
```

Forward

The Forward button takes you to the next URL of the frame, but it works only after you actually choose to go visit an URL and then return from the site using the Back button. Here's the code:

```
<input type="button"
   value="Forward" onClick="parent.frame2.history.go(1)">
```

Notice that the `onClick` event does all the work. All you have to do is tell the function to go forward one URL in the history list of `frame2`.

Exit

The Exit button does as its name implies—exits Netscape. Here's the code:

```
<input type="button" value="Exit" onClick="ConfirmClose()">
```

The `OnClick` event calls the `ConfirmClose()` function, which does two things:

- Asks whether the user really wants to close Netscape
- Exits Netscape if the user answers "Yes" to the preceding question; otherwise, nothing happens

In the `ConfirmClose()` function, the reserved word `confirm` and the built-in function `window.close()` do all the work:

```
function ConfirmClose() {
   if (confirm("Are you sure you want to exit Netscape?")) {
      window.close()
   }
```

Putting Everything Together

Listings 20.1 through 20.5 list all the codes for all the files, which you can find on the CD-ROM that accompanies this book. The listings show how your code would look after you put everything together that you have learned.

Listing 20.1 main_fr.htm

```
<HTML><TITLE>Control Panel</TITLE>
<FRAMESET ROWS="135,*">
  <FRAME SRC="top_fr.htm"  NAME="frame1" SCROLLING="no" NORESIZE >
  <FRAME SRC="text.htm"  NAME="frame2" >
</FRAMESET>
<NOFRAMES>
</NOFRAMES>
</HTML>
```

Listing 20.2 top_fr.htm

```
<html>
<head>
<TITLE>Control Panel</TITLE>
<SCRIPT LANGUAGE="JavaScript">

<!-- Beginning of JavaScript Applet -------------------

function bottomColor(newColor)
{
   window.parent.frames['frame2'].document.bgColor=newColor;
}
function topColor(newColor)
{
```

```
    window.parent.frames['frame1'].document.bgColor=newColor;
}

//visit Window
function navi() {
    window.open('visit.htm',
      'Visit',
      'toolbar=no,location=no,directories=no,
      status=no,menubar=no,scrollbars=no,
      resizable=no,copyhistory=yes,width=400,
      height=200')
 }

function Customize()
{
var PopWindow=window.open('colors.htm','Main',
    'toolbar=no,location=no,directories=no,status=no,
    menubar=no,scrollbars=no,resizable=no,copyhistory=yes,
    width=400,height=200')
PopWindow.creator=self
}

//Exit Window
function ConfirmClose() {
   if (confirm("Are you sure, you wish to exit Netscape?")) {
      window.close()
   }
}
// -- End of JavaScript code -------------- -->

</SCRIPT>
</HEAD>
<center>
<font color=red><h2>Control panel</h2>
<FORM>
<center>
<input type="button" value="Back"
   onClick="parent.frame2.history.back()">
<input type="button" Value="Visit Other sites"
   onClick="navi()">
<input type="button" value="Back ground Colors"
   onClick="Customize()">
<input type="button" value="Forward"
   onClick="parent.frame2.history.forward()">
<input type="button" value="Exit"
   onClick="ConfirmClose()">
</center></FORM>
</body>
</html>
```

Listing 20.3 text.htm

```
<HTML><TITLE>Control Panel Text</TITLE><body>
<body bgcolor="white">
<center>
<h2>Welcome to control panel using JavaScript</h2>
<br></center><b>
There are 5 control buttons on the control panel:<br>
   1. Forward: Takes you to the front of the frame.
      [only works after you actually choose to go some somewhere and come
back.]<br>
   2. Visit Other Site: This window will let you type a site address and
you will be able to visit that specific site.<br>
   3. Back ground Color: Let's you choose the top and the bottom frame's
background color.<br>
   4. Back: Takes you back on a frame.<br>
   5. Exit: Kicks you out of Netscape.<br>
<center></font>
<br> Let's check the "back/forward" buttons. Let's<Br>
<font size="+2"><a href="http://www.microsoft.com">Go somewhere</a>
</body>
</HTML>
```

Listing 20.4 colors.htm

```
<HTML>
<HEAD>
<TITLE>Custom Colors for control panel</TITLE>
</HEAD>
<FORM METHOD="POST" NAME="background">
<center><table><colspan='1'><td><tr>

1. <font color="#000000">Black</font> 2. <font color="#FF0235">Red</font>
3. <font color="#6600BA">Purple</font> 4. <font color="#3300CC">Blue</
font> 5. <font color="#FFFFFF">White</font>
</td></table>
<CENTER><FONT SIZE=4>Top Frame Colors<br>
<input type="radio" name="bgcolor"
ONCLICK="creator.topColor('#000000')">1
<input type="radio" name="bgcolor"
ONCLICK="creator.topColor('#FF0235')">2
<input type="radio" name="bgcolor"
ONCLICK="creator.topColor('#6600BA')">3
<input type="radio" name="bgcolor"
ONCLICK="creator.topColor('#3300CC')">4
<input type="radio" name="bgcolor"
ONCLICK="creator.topColor('#ffffff')">5
<br>
Bottom Frame<br>
```

```
<input type="radio" name="bgcolor"
ONCLICK="creator.bottomColor('#000000')">1
<input type="radio" name="bgcolor"
ONCLICK="creator.bottomColor('#FF0235')">2
<input type="radio" name="bgcolor"
ONCLICK="creator.bottomColor('#6600BA')">3
<input type="radio" name="bgcolor"
ONCLICK="creator.bottomColor('#3300CC')">4
<input type="radio" name="bgcolor"
ONCLICK="creator.bottomColor('#FFFFFF')">5
<p>
<input type="button" value="Exit" ONCLICK="window.close()">
</center></FORM>
</BODY>
</HTML>
```

Listing 20.5 visit.htm

```
<script language="JavaScript">
<!-----hiding----

function visit(frame) {
  if (frame == "_go")
    open (document.input_val.site.value, frame);
  return 0;
}

<!-----done hiding--->

</script>

<html>
<BODY  BGCOLOR= "#fffff0">
<title>Visiting other site for control panel</title>
</HEAD>
<center>
<h2><b>Visit Other Site</font></b></h2>
<form name="input_val" method="post">
<div align="center">
<input type="text" name="site" size=24><br>
<input type="button" name="othfull" value="visit"
onclick="window.close();visit('_go')">
</div>
<br>
<input type="button" value="Exit" ONCLICK="window.close()">
</form>
</body>
</html>
```

Summary

A control panel makes navigating a site easier for the user, and allows you to create custom button options that aren't built into the browser. In this chapter, you saw how to use frames to create a control window that's always available to users, no matter where they go. You also saw how to create custom input windows (dialogs) to accept specific types of information, based on the control buttons clicked.

Review Questions

Answers to the review questions can be found in Appendix D.

1. What is a control panel?
2. What are the steps you need to perform to create a control panel?
3. How can you create a custom dialog from within JavaScript?
4. What JavaScript object gives you access to the list of URLs the user has visited? How do you move through this list?

Exercise

1. Create another control panel using different variables. Try implementing buttons to display specific pages (a welcome page, an info page, a feedback page, and so forth).

CHAPTER 21

Sights and Sounds

This chapter discusses the use of audio and visual aids available for your Web page creation. You'll learn how to display a picture or graphic on your page, how to create custom background patterns for your page, and how visitors can hear sound files and music from your Web page.

To use some of the procedures and to be able to perform certain operations, you need to install plug-ins to your browser. In Netscape, open the Help menu and choose About Plug-Ins to view the plug-ins you have and to access the links to the available plug-ins.

> **Note:** You'll need to have a plug-in that handles AVI files in order to follow this chapter. The Crescendo! plug-in was used and is recommended.

Graphics

The inclusion of graphical images on your Web pages will help to enrich the overall appearance of the page and to provide a visual supplement to the text. You're familiar with the saying, "A picture is worth a thousand words"; the saying holds true for Web pages too. Just remember that too many graphics will slow the speed at which users can load your page, and the wait may become annoying.

Although JavaScript contains no additional features for graphical and sound manipulation and presentation, these features appeared with plug-ins that were made available about the same time, so it is a new and emerging area that merits some attention.

Included Graphic Images

You can include graphic images on your Web pages to help spice up the overall appearance and to provide visuals to supplement the text. A page with just plain text not only can be boring, but it can make it hard for users to find the information they want in a fast, effective manner. By placing an image with some logical representation to the subject matter being discussed next to the surrounding text, readers will intuitively scan the images to locate the area that interests them.

To place a graphical image on a Web page, use the `<IMG>` HTML tag. The syntax for the `<IMG>` tag is as follows:

```
<IMG SRC ="path/filename_of_image"
     ALIGN = "textAlignment"
     WIDTH = ##
     HEIGHT = ##
     ALT = "text"
     BORDER = ##>
```

The *path/filename_of_image* specifies the location of the image file you want to display.

> **Note:** As long as the files are located in the same directory as the loaded page, the full path doesn't need to be specified; the browser is "smart" enough to find them there.

The value of the `ALIGN` attribute can be one of the following: `left`, `center`, `right`, `middle`, `absmiddle`, `bottom`, `top`, `text`, or `baseline`. Choose one of these options to place the image in the appropriate part of the screen. You can see the different placements demonstrated in the images21.htm file on the companion CD.

The `WIDTH` and `HEIGHT` values (noted by the `##`) specify, in pixels, the dimensions of the image being displayed. By including the `HEIGHT` and `WIDTH` attributes for an image, you reserve space for the image while the rest of the page loads, thereby permitting users to browse some of the text while the image arrives in full detail. If the values you give for `WIDTH` and `HEIGHT` are different from the actual size of the image, the browser will stretch the image to fit these new values.

> **Caution:** Not specifying the `HEIGHT` and `WIDTH` attributes for *all* images on a page may cause any JavaScript code within that page to run erroneously and even crash. Therefore, you *always* want to include these two elements whenever you use an `<IMG>` tag to ensure that any errors encountered are scripting errors and not from improper image placement.
>
> You must also make sure that there's a `<BR>` tag at the end of the page, or it may cause errors to occur as well, such as a page that doesn't totally display an image (it appears cut off at the bottom of the screen and the user can't scroll down to see it), or even a crash.

The *text* specified in the ALT attribute displays if the specified image file in SRC is not found, or if the user is browsing with a text-only browser (such as Lynx). Also, newer browsers are displaying the text of the ALT attribute first, and then loading the image, providing the user with a quick preview of the purpose of the loading graphic.

The number specified by BORDER denotes the type of border around the placed image. This number represents the thickness of the border line (in pixels) drawn around the image. As the number increases, so does the thickness of the border. Zero, therefore, indicates no border. Omitting this attribute produces a default border of 2 pixels thick. These variations can be seen in the example from the images21.htm file on the companion CD and in figure 21.1.

Figure 21.1

Example of some of the things that can be accomplished through the use of graphics.

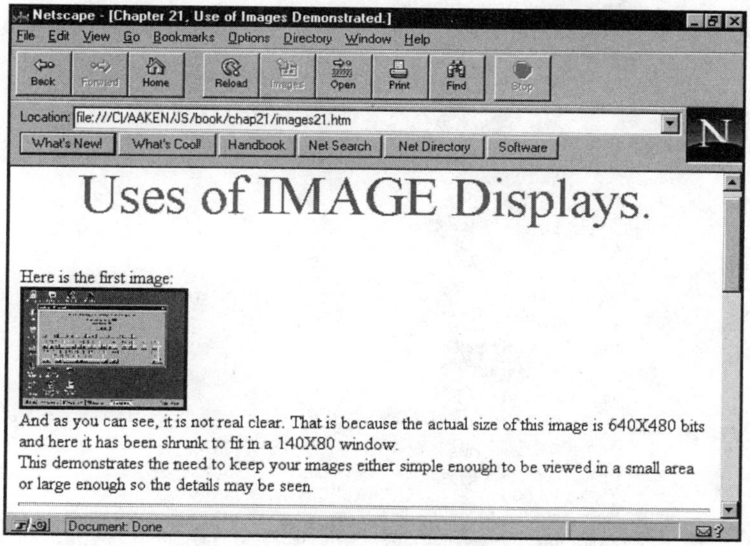

Listing 21.1 shows the code used to generate figure 21.1.

Listing 21.1

```
<html>
<head>
<title>Chapter 21, Use of Images Demonstrated.</title>
</head>
<body>
<bgcolor="white">
<center><font size="+6" color="#FF00FF">Uses of IMAGE Displays.
```

continues

Listing 21.1 Continued

```
</font></center>
<br><br>
Here is the first image:<br>
<img src="keyboard.gif"
     Align=top
     Width=140
     Heigth=80
     Border=3><br>
And as you can see, it is not real clear. That is because the actual size
of this image is 640X480 pixels and here it has been shrunk to fit in a
140X80 window.
<br>
This demonstrates the need to keep your images either simple enough to be
viewed in a small area or large enough so the details may be seen.<br>
<hr>
<br><br>
You may also include your company logo.<br>
<img src="loboso~1.gif"
     Align=center
     Width=500
     Height=219
     Border=1><br>
And thereby advertise.<br>
<hr>
<A HREF="http://home.netscape.com/comprod/mirror/index.html">
<img src="netscape.jpg"
     Align=text
     Width=75
     Height=25
     Border=2></a> You can also use a graphic to represent a link.<br>
Now all the user must do is click on that link to perform jump to that
page.<br>
You can notice too that the image can be any graphic format that your
browser will support, so keep that in mind when placing images so they
will be viewable by every visitor to your page.<br>
<hr>
<img src="intro.gif"
     Align=left
     Width=100
     Height=25
     Border=0><br>
You can also use a graphic to catch people's attention to a certain
area.<br>
Once you have their attention, tell them what it is they need to know or
do.<br>
<hr>
It is even possible to include comic pictures
<img src="bath.gif"
     Align=baseline
     Width=200
     Height=114
```

```
      Border=4> in your page!!<br>
   <hr>
   <br>
   </body>
   </html>
```

The first image displayed illustrates that a picture (of 640×480 pixels in this example) can be compressed into a border smaller than its original size (140×80 pixels). However, there's a loss of clarity within the image. Images must be simple enough to be viewed in a small area, or large enough so that details may be seen. Although it's possible to increase the size of the display area for the image, displaying complex images in larger windows slows the load time of the page and doesn't let the user see much of the rest of the page (unless the `WIDTH` and `HEIGHT` attributes are specified for the image, freeing the browser from having to load the entire image before it can format the page). Simple graphic images thereby need to be used as a general rule.

Backgrounds Using Graphic Images

You can use graphics to form the background of a Web page. This way, you have unlimited options for varied color schemes beyond the given basic (solid) colors listed in Appendix C. It provides a way to create a background with a marbled effect, or any other pattern you may choose.

Setting the background to a graphic image instead of one of the usual colors is accomplished through the following command format:

```
<BODY BACKGROUND="path/filename-of-desired-background">
```

Just like placing a graphic within the document, placing an image as the background pattern requires that you specify the location of the desired file. Often it will be of the form

```
http://server/~account/remaining-path/filename
```

> **Note:** In the HTML files on the companion CD, references to images in `SRC` and `BACKGROUND` attributes appear in the form
>
> ```
> filename
> ```
>
> No path is specified because it's assumed that the graphic files are in the same directory as the .HTM file. If you copy the .HTM files to another location, be sure to either copy the graphic and other support files also, or modify the .HTM source to include a full path to the location of the given graphics files.

Also, if the background graphic is smaller than the screen, the browser tiles the graphic, repeating it over and over. Although this makes it possible to create attractive backgrounds that don't consist of *very* large image files, care must be taken that the graphic tiles well (that is, no seams are visible between repetitions of the image).

The following script files demonstrate the use of images to form background patterns, or pictures. You can follow each progression by executing bgnd21-1.htm on the companion CD. (From there is a link to the next file, so you don't need to enter each new name; it will flow just as it appears in the book.)

The bgnd21-1.htm script produces the results in figure 21.2. Listing 21.2 shows the code that produces these results.

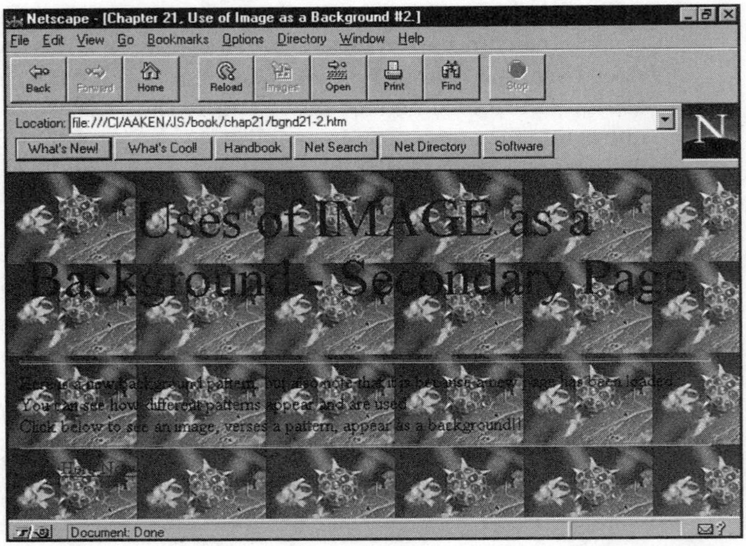

Figure 21.2
This graphic file used as the page's background produces a marbled effect.

Listing 21.2

```
<html>
<head>
<title>Chapter 21, Use of Image as a Background #1.</title>
</head>
<body>
<body background="paper.gif" >
<center><font size="+6" color="red">Uses of IMAGE as a Background -
Initial Page.</font></center>
<br><br>
<hr>
Notice the variety it adds to a page.<br>
Currently, background cannot be changed dynamically once a page is
established.<br>
The page must be reloaded to facilitate a change in background color or
design.
<hr>
```

```
<a href="bgnd21-2.htm">Click Here to View Next Background</a>
<br>
</body>
</html>
```

About the only command that should be new to you at this point is the line

```
<body background="paper.gif" >
```

This places the image as the background pattern. Remember that for a pattern on a Web page, the reference will need to be one the user can access, such as

```
<body background="http://www.server.com/~account/directory-for-images/
paper.gif" >
```

or

```
<body background="paper.gif" >
```

if the HTML file is located in the same directory as the graphic.

> **Note:** This line is given only as an example; don't type it in exactly as it appears. You must substitute the appropriate server name, account, directory, and file name.

Click the link to go to the next file, which yields the results in figure 21.3.

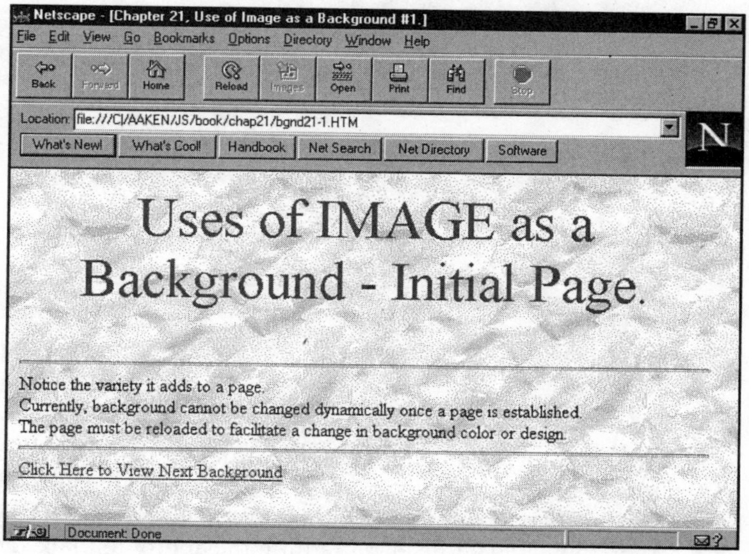

Figure 21.3

An example of *tiling* the background, where the graphic is replicated to fill the screen.

The only main difference in this script and the one that produced figure 21.2 is the line

```
<body background="winlogo.gif" >
```

A different file is specified for the background. The pattern of this image can easily be detected and it can be seen how the pattern will repeat.

Click the link at the bottom of the page to see a demonstration of the use of a full-screen sized image as the background (see fig. 21.4).

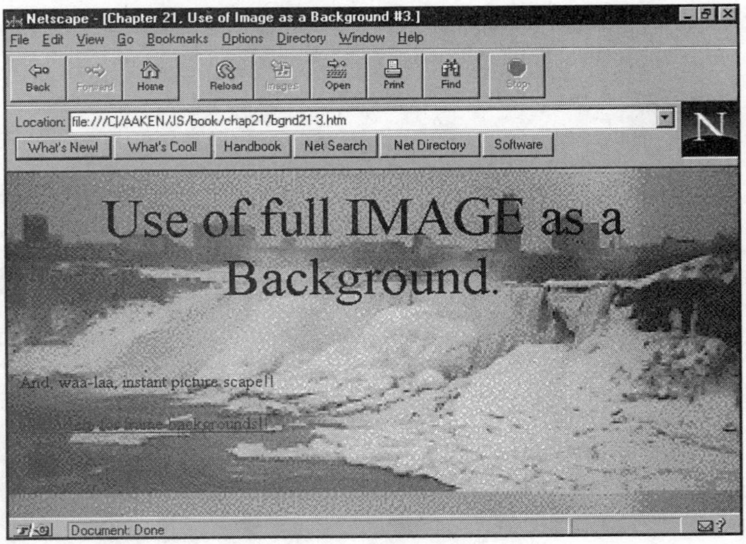

Figure 21.4
Example of a full-screen image for the background instead of a pattern.

The code to produce this is similar to the preceding two scripts, except for the line

```
<body background="belle1.gif" >
```

which refers to an image whose size is larger than the screen area of the browser.

> **Note:** Because the graphic is a full-screen image, you need to be cautious with text placement as well as text color to ensure that the words will be visible to all readers.

The ability to display a graphic larger than the screen can be valuable for placing a company logo, name, or emblem as the center background on the page. This is true especially if the image is a light gray on white—thus permitting the background to remain visible while also granting the ability to place text over it.

> **Note:** Microsoft's Internet Explorer has an extension to HTML that supports centering a background (as well as one that creates a background that doesn't scroll with the screen, or a *watermark*). Because Internet Explorer doesn't support JavaScript, however, this chapter won't cover those attributes.

Clicking the frame background link will produce what you see in figure 21.5.

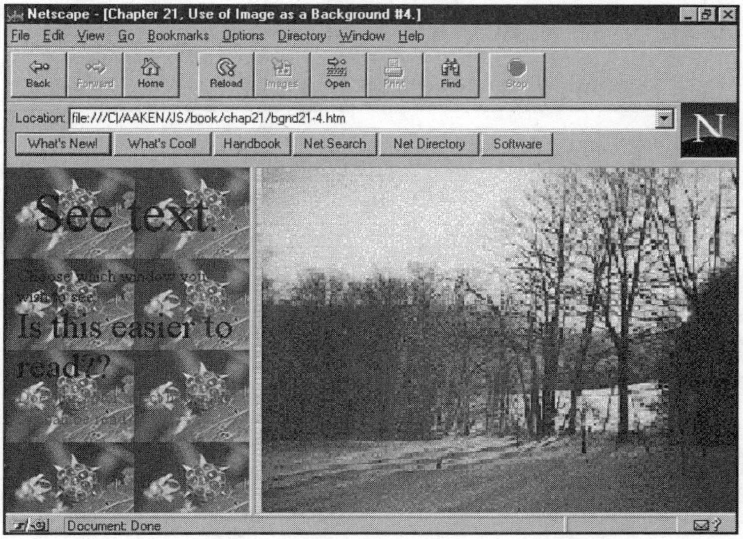

Figure 21.5
By creating different background images in different frames, you can have one frame contain a repeating pattern and another frame simultaneously contain a full-frame image.

Three files were needed to generate the results in figure 21.5. Listing 21.3 shows bgnd21-4.htm, which creates the frames (named "one" and "two") and then calls bgnd21-5.htm and bgnd21-6.htm to fill the frames. Listing 21.4 shows bgnd21-5.htm, which fills the first frame with a pattern image. bgnd21-5.htm also uses different text styles and colors to demonstrate text "readability" over a strong, colored background. Finally, listing 21.5 shows bgnd21-6.htm, a very simple file that fills the second frame with just a full-frame image (no text is included).

Listing 21.3 bgnd21-4.htm

```
<html>
<head>
<title>Chapter 21, Use of Image as a Background #4.</title>
</head>
<FRAMESET ROWS="70%">
```

continues

Listing 21.3 Continued

```
<FRAMESET COLS="34%,66%">
<FRAME SRC="bgnd21-5.htm" SCROLLING="NO" NAME="one">
<FRAME SRC="bgnd21-6.htm" SCROLLING="auto" NAME="two">
</FRAMESET>
<body>
This shows the use of images as backgrounds within frames.
<br>
</body>
</html>
```

Listing 21.4 bgnd21-5.htm

```
<html>
<head>
<title>Chapter 21, Use of Image as a Background #5.</title>
</head>
<body>
<body background="psu.gif" >
<center><font size="+6" color="black">See text.</font></center>
<br>
Choose which window you wish to see.
<br>
<font size="+3">Is this easier to read??</font>
<br>
<font color="red">Does the color affect how easy this can be read??
</font>
<br>
</body>
</html>
```

Listing 21.5 bgnd21-6.htm

```
<html>
<head>
<title>Chapter 21, Use of Image as a Background #6.</title>
</head>
<body>
<body background="calvin.gif" >
</body>
</html>
```

> **Note:** In the bgnd21-6.htm file, you also could place the full image in the second frame in a `HEIGHT` and `WIDTH` area as an included graphic. But then you wouldn't be able to place text over the image, if you so desired.

There are no more links to click because the basics of using an image as a background have been covered. All that remains is for you to experiment with these concepts.

Sounds

You can incorporate sound on a Web page in various ways. Depending on the type of sound file being played and the plug-in that plays the file, a pop-up window may appear with buttons for play, stop, forward, reverse, and others similar to CD player controls. Other plug-ins simply play the sound file in the background and require no special efforts on the user's part.

Because the latter of these two methods normally will be the more desirable one (the less the user needs to do, the better), attention shall be focused there. The plug-in used in the example shown here is used with the Crescendo! plug-in, which is produced by LiveUpdate (**http://www.liveupdate.com/**) and is designed to play MIDI files.

Adding Sounds to Pages

Figure 21.6 shows a CD player box from the Media Player of Windows 95 for an .AU sound format file (at the top of the screen). The Crescendo! box will be explained later, because it's the result of another sound file (in MIDI format) being played simultaneously. To create this scenario, open the MIDI file as described later, and then open the buglrev.au file (select All Files (*.*) from the Files of Type drop-down list to find the file on the CD-ROM). This example shows that it's possible to have multiple sound files (of different types) being played at the same time.

Figure 21.6
One uses a CD player type control box; the other loads into a plug-in and plays. Both can play simultaneously, because they're of separate audio formats.

With the Crescendo! plug-in installed, you can open a MIDI file directly into the browser. To open a file in such manner, follow these steps:

1. Open the File menu and choose Open File in Browser. The Open dialog box appears.
2. Set the Files of Type to LiveUpdate! MIDI (*.mid).
3. Select the appropriate directory for the MIDI file location, and then select the file you want to hear.

Figure 21.7 shows the Open dialog box, right before the sound file is selected.

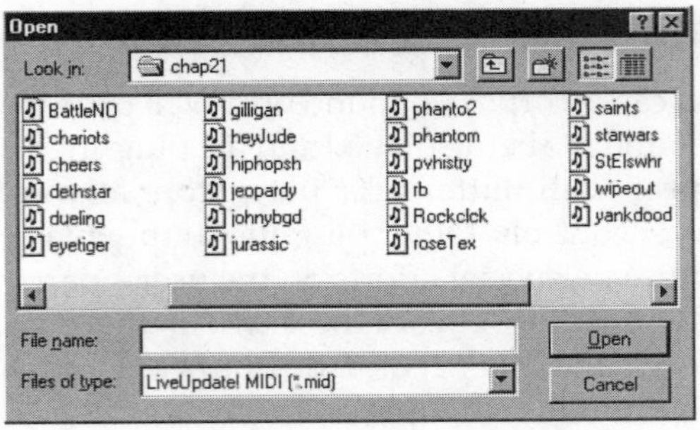

Figure 21.7

Selecting a MIDI file from Netscape's Navigator.

Doing this, however, is more work on users than having them click a sound player's play button and is therefore undesirable. It's possible to create links to automatically open such files, as discussed later. After learning to access sounds by links, you'll see how to embed the sounds so they automatically play in the background, and also how to control the sounds as they play. Let's first look at playing sound files by links.

Setting Up a Jukebox

As you surf the Net and find a cluster of MIDI files, they'll often be grouped and presented through a "jukebox" setup, where a list of available files is given and you select the one you want to hear.

The code in listing 21.6 is from jukebox.htm on the companion CD. The file produces a jukebox of all the MIDI files included on the companion CD (see fig. 21.8). Clicking the desired sound title will produce a screen like figure 21.6. After you hear enough of the sound file, select the browser's Back button to return to the jukebox.

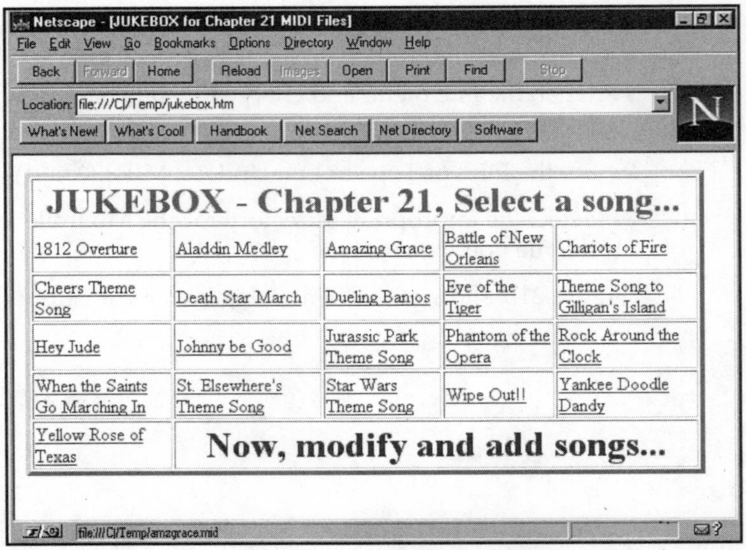

Figure 21.8

The jukebox as it appears in the file jukebox.htm. To list all the MIDI files that can be played, simply click the link.

Listing 21.6

```
<html>
<head>
<title>JUKEBOX for Chapter 21 MIDI Files</title>
</head>
<body>
<center><table border= "4">
<tr>
<th colspan="5"><font color="red" size="6">JUKEBOX - Chapter 21,
Select a song...</font></th>
</tr>
<tr>
<td><A HREF="1812over.mid">1812 Overture</td>
<td><A HREF="aladdin.mid">Aladdin Medley</td>
<td><A HREF="amzgrace.mid">Amazing Grace</td>
<td><A HREF="battleno.mid">Battle of New Orleans</td>
<td><A HREF="chariots.mid">Chariots of Fire</td></A>
</tr>
<tr>
<td><A HREF="cheers.mid">Cheers Theme Song</td>
<td><A HREF="dethstar.mid">Death Star March</td>
<td><A HREF="dueling.mid">Dueling Banjos</td>
<td><A HREF="eyetiger.mid">Eye of the Tiger</td>
<td><A HREF="gilligan.mid">Theme Song to Gilligan's Island</td></A>
</tr>
<tr>
<td><A HREF="heyjude.mid">Hey Jude</td>
<td><A HREF="johnybgd.mid">Johnny be Good</td>
<td><A HREF="jurassic.mid">Jurassic Park Theme Song</td>
<td><A HREF="phantom.mid">Phantom of the Opera</td>
<td><A HREF="rockclck.mid">Rock Around the Clock</td></A>
</tr>
<tr>
<td><A HREF="saintmch.mid">When the Saints Go Marching In</td>
<td><A HREF="stelswhr.mid">St. Elsewhere's Theme Song</td>
<td><A HREF="starwars.mid">Star Wars Theme Song</td>
<td><A HREF="wipeout.mid">Wipe Out!!</td>
<td><A HREF="yankdood.mid">Yankee Doodle Dandy</td></A>
</tr>
<tr>
<td><A HREF="rosetex.mid">Yellow Rose of Texas</td>
<th colspan="4"><font color="blue" size="6">Now, modify and add
songs...</font></th>
</tr></A>
</table></center>
</body>
</html>
```

Note: It's possible that your Web server isn't configured to correctly transmit MIDI files to the user's browser (in which case, the browser will attempt to interpret the files as text, producing a page of "garbage"). If you encounter this problem, check with your Internet provider to determine what needs to be changed on the server.

To control the playing file, right-click the Crescendo! icon. A pop-up menu will appear (see fig. 21.9). Note that control is limited only to playing or stopping the file. This is less control than afforded a user through a CD-type control box, because you can't forward or reverse through a song.

Figure 21.9
Controlling the Crescendo! plug-in MIDI player.

Embedding Sound

Now that you understand how to access sound via links, embedding a sound so that it will automatically play when a Web page loads shall be considered.

The embed21.htm file on the companion CD adds an embedded file to the jukebox created with jukebox.htm. The two files are similar, except that embed21.htm has the following additional command, which causes a MIDI file to begin execution on page startup:

```
<embed src="jeopardy.mid"  Width=2   Height=2>
```

This line, included just before the closing `</body>` tag, places the table containing the jukebox entries on the page first and then begins execution of the jeopardy.mid file.

> **Note:** The inclusion of height and width attributes keeps the Crescendo! box from appearing in full size. You can still control the playing file by clicking just the created 2×2 pixel image. Try it.

The sound doesn't have to begin only when a page loads, as it can be stopped or changed through the establishment of user controls on the page.

Summary

Adding graphics and sound to your Web pages can make them sparkle and dance, keeping the users' attention (and drawing them back again and again). Graphics are implemented with the HTML `<IMG>` tag, which allows you to control both the size and placement of the image.

Sound is often implemented through a *plug-in*, a special application that extends the brower's capabilities and permits other types of files (such as sound files) to be processed. By using the HTML `<EMBED>` tag, you can force a sound to be played whenever users load the page.

Review Questions

Answers to the review questions can be found in Appendix D.

1. True or false: It is possible to play multiple sound files of different formats at the same time.
2. True or false: The Crescendo! plug-in will spawn a new window in order to play a MIDI file.
3. True or false: Once a sound file has started playing through Crescendo!, it can't be stopped until a new one is loaded.
4. The control panel for the Crescendo! plug-in contains which options/commands for controlling the sound file?
5. To access the control panel for Crescendo!, you must do what?
6. Explain how to set a MIDI file so that it plays in the background of a page.

Exercise

1. Create your own jukebox. Begin by modifying the given example to include additional sound clips. Now, design your own, or find a creative way to allow users to choose which sound file to play (maybe use graphics for the href instead of text).

CHAPTER 22

Creating a Scientific Calculator

Now that you have a good idea of how to use JavaScript, it's time to create something more difficult—a scientific calculator. Before I actually explain all the functions and codes, let me tell you how easy it is to create such a calculator using JavaScript. By using JavaScript, you can just create buttons like the ones on a physical calculator. You name the buttons and call JavaScript functions when the buttons are clicked or pressed. When the functions are called, they'll perform the operation and return a value. It's that easy!

Starting the Design Process with HTML

With HTML, the first thing you need to do is create a display for the user to see all the calculations, just like on a regular calculator. Next, you need to create several buttons for all the numbers (1, 2, 3, and so on) and operations (such as + and –). For the example in this chapter, I've also created a reset button to reset all the values. The program asks the user to do that at the beginning of the program like an "on" button on a physical calculator. There's also an = button to finish the calculation.

With JavaScript, when you use "buttons," you use the `OnClick` event as explained in Chapter 4, "Understanding Events." For a quick review, here's an example on how to create a button called 0 for the calculator:

```
<input type="button" value='0'
 onClick="addChar(this.form.display,'0')">
```

> **Note:** The example program has a button called Stack. This is a "hidden" button that keeps track of the last input.

Getting Up with JavaScript

To create this scientific calculator, the two main code components you'll need are functions (which perform the desired calculations) and variables (which provide "work areas" for the functions). The following two sections are a review of these components.

Variables

The program uses two Boolean variables, one integer variable, and one float variable:

- `computed` Keeps track of whether the program had computed `display.value` since the last digit the user entered into the calculator.
- `button` Keeps track of whether the button is clicked.
- `operator` An integer variable that keeps track of what the requested operation is (0=equal, 1=plus, 2=minus, 3=multiply, and 4=divide).
- `temp` Keeps the value of `display`. Because the displayed value can be a decimal number, this is a float variable.

Functions

The program uses the following functions:

- `pushStack()` Keeps track of the last input.
- `reset()` Resets all the functions.
- `addChar()` Adds a character in the display.
- `deleteChar()` Deletes a character when the ← button is clicked.
- `goOperation()` The "main engine" function that performs the operation now on the stack when a new operation button is clicked.
- `add()` Performs addition.
- `subtract()` Performs subtraction.
- `multiply()` Performs multiplication.

- `divide()` Performs division.
- `equals()` Finishes the calculation.
- `tan()` Finds the tangent of the display value.
- `cos()` Finds the cosine of the display value.
- `sin()` Finds the sine of the display value.
- `atan()` Finds the arctangent of the display value.
- `acos()` Finds the arccosine of the display value.
- `asin()` Finds the arcsine of the display value.
- `abs()` Returns the absolute value of the display value.
- `sqrt()` Figures the square root of the display value.
- `exp()` Returns the exponent of the display value.
- `pi()` Returns the value of pi (π).
- `ln2()` Returns the value of the natural logarithm of 2.
- `e()` Returns Euler's constant.
- `sqrt1_2()` Returns the square root of one-half.
- `log()` Figures the natural logarithm of the display value.
- `changeSign()` Changes – to + and + to – of a number.

If you want to review these functions, see Chapter 14, "Miscellaneous Methods and Functions."

pushStack()

For this function, you need to set the `stack` value equal to the `display` value. The code is as follows:

```
function pushStack(form)
{
    form.stack.value = form.display.value
    form.display.value=0
    computed = false
}
```

Notice that when you call the function, you include `form` because the value is coming from the form in your HTML document. Also notice that the variable `computed` is set to false, because no computation is being done in this function.

reset()

For this function, set the `stack`, `display`, and `reset` values to 0. The code is as follows:

```
function reset(form)
{
     form.stack.value=0
     form.display.value=0
     computed = false
     operator = 0
     button = false
}
```

Because you want to make sure that all the values in memory are initialized to zero before the user starts clicking calculator buttons, `reset()` should be called first. To encourage this, the display field of the calculator is loaded with the phrase `Please Press Reset To Start`, as in

```
<input name="display"
   size=40 value="Please Press Reset To Start">
```

addChar()

This function builds the input field one character at a time, saving the current display (if it has been computed) or adding to it (if the user is completing an expression). The code is as follows:

```
function addChar(input, character)
{
    // auto-push the stack if the last value was computed
    if (computed == true) pushStack(input.form)

    // see if the new value starts a new string
    if(input.value == null ¦¦ input.value == "0")
        input.value = character
    else
             input.value += character
     computed = false
      button = false
}
```

deleteChar()

For this function, take the length of the input value and delete 1 each time the function is called. The code is as follows:

```
function deleteChar(input)
{
    input.value = input.value.substring(0, input.value.length - 1)
}
```

goOperation()

The first thing you do in this function is take the `display` value and put it in a `temp` value. Then you perform the operation according to the user's button push of +, –, /, or *. The code is as follows:

```
function goOperation(form)
{
     temp = parseFloat(form.display.value)
     if (operator == 1) {
          form.display.value = parseFloat(form.stack.value)
                              + parseFloat(form.display.value)
     } else if (operator == 2) {
          form.display.value = parseFloat(form.stack.value)
                              - parseFloat(form.display.value)
     } else if (operator == 3) {
          form.display.value = parseFloat(form.stack.value)
                              * parseFloat(form.display.value)
     } else if (operator == 4) {
          if (form.display.value == 0) {
               form.display.value = "divide by zero"
               form.stack.value = 0
               operator = 0
          } else {
               form.display.value = parseFloat(form.stack.value)
                              / parseFloat(form.display.value)
          }
     }
     if (button == false) form.stack.value = temp
     computed = true
     button = true
}
```

Notice some issues about this function:

- In the division operation, the function makes sure that the number is divided by a non-zero number.
- If the `button` is false (not clicked), the function dumps the `temp` value in the `stack` value. This is considered a Boolean.
- Because this function evaluates the expression keyed in, `computed` is set to true.
- When you do any computation, you take the `parseFloat()` of the variable or field *before* you perform the operation. This makes sure that if the value is a float, it keeps it a float value.

To complete the rest of the code, you'll need to compose code for all the math functions as covered in Chapter 10, "Math Methods." The following is a list of the ones you'll need to write code for:

```
tan()    acos()    ln2()

cos()    abs()     e()
```

```
sin()     sqrt()    sqrt1_2()
atan()    exp()     log()
asin()    pi()      changeSign()
```

Putting Everything Together

Now that you've reviewed the math methods, you're ready to create the scientific calculator. Listing 22.1 shows the code for the calculator, and figure 22.1 shows the calculator in action. You'll find comment lines above parts of the code describing what function or method is being used. This program is also on the CD-ROM accompanying your book.

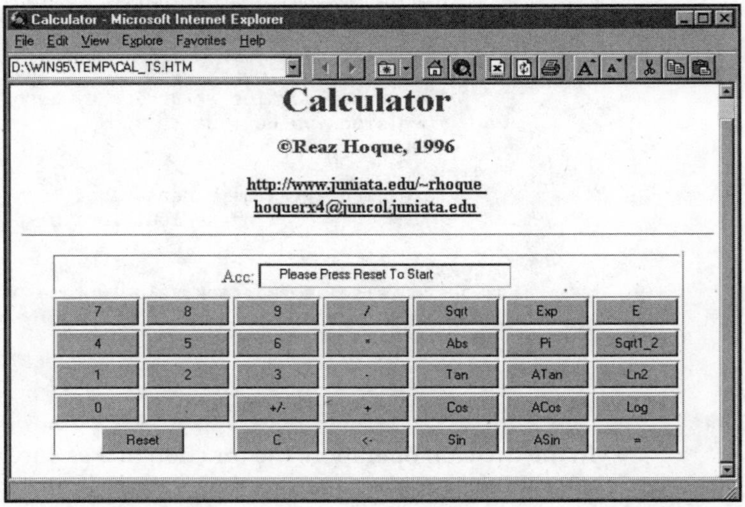

Figure 22.1

The calculator in action.

Listing 22.1

```
<html>
<body>
<head><title>Calculator</title>
<body bgcolor=ffffff></body>
<script language="JavaScript">
<!-- hide this script tag's contents from old browsers
//--------------------variables------------------------------------
var computed = false
// keep track of whether we just computed display.value
var button = false//if the button is pressed
var operator = 0 // 0=equal, 1:plus, 2:minus, 3:multiply, 4:divide
//--------function to keep track of the last input-----------------
```

```
function pushStack(form)
{
     form.stack.value = form.display.value
     form.display.value=0
     computed = false
}
//-----------------function to reset all---------------------
function reset(form)
{
      form.stack.value=0
      form.display.value=0
      computed = false
      operator = 0
      button = false
}
//--------function to add a new character to the display------
function addChar(input, character)
{
     // auto-push the stack if the last value was computed
     if (computed == true) pushStack(input.form)
     // make sure input.value is a string
     if(input.value == null || input.value == "0")
         input.value = character
     else
              input.value += character
      computed = false
       button = false
}
//--------------function to delete character--------------------
function deleteChar(input)
{
     input.value = input.value.substring(0, input.value.length - 1)
}
function goOperation(form)
{
      temp = parseFloat(form.display.value)
      if (operator == 1) {
           form.display.value = parseFloat(form.stack.value)
                              + parseFloat(form.display.value)
      } else if (operator == 2) {
           form.display.value = parseFloat(form.stack.value)
                              - parseFloat(form.display.value)
      } else if (operator == 3) {
           form.display.value = parseFloat(form.stack.value)
                              * parseFloat(form.display.value)
      } else if (operator == 4) {
           if (form.display.value == 0) {
                form.display.value = "error"
                form.stack.value = 0
                operator = 0
           } else {
```

continues

Listing 22.1 Continued

```
                form.display.value = parseFloat(form.stack.value)
                                  / parseFloat(form.display.value)
          }
     }
     if (button == false) form.stack.value = temp
     computed = true
     button = true
}
//---------------addition--------------------------
function add(form)
{
     goOperation(form)
     operator = 1
}
//----------------subtraction--------------------
function subtract(form)
{
     if (button == false)
          goOperation(form)
     operator = 2
}
//-------------------multiplication------------------
function multiply(form)
{
     goOperation(form)
     operator = 3
}
//----------------------division--------------------
function divide(form)
{
     goOperation(form)
     operator = 4
}
//----------------------equals-----------------------
function equals(form)
{
     goOperation(form)
     operator = 0
}
//-----------------------tan-------------------------
function tan(form)
{
    form.display.value=Math.tan(form.display.value);
    computed = true
}
//----------------------cos--------------------------
function cos(form)
{
    form.display.value=Math.cos(form.display.value);
    computed = true
}
//----------------------sin--------------------------
```

```
function sin(form)
{
    form.display.value=Math.sin(form.display.value);
    computed = true
}
//--------------------atan---------------------------
function atan(form)
{
    form.display.value=Math.atan(form.display.value);
    computed = true
}
//----------------------asin---------------------------
function asin(form)
{
    form.display.value=Math.asin(form.display.value);
    computed = true
}
//--------------------acos-----------------------------
function acos(form)
{
    form.display.value=Math.acos(form.display.value);
    computed = true
}
//--------------------abs-----------------------------
function abs(form)
{
    form.display.value=Math.abs(form.display.value);
    computed = true
}
//--------------------sqrt-----------------------------
function sqrt(form)
{
    form.display.value=Math.sqrt(form.display.value);
    computed = true
}
//--------------------exp-----------------------------
function exp(form)
{
    form.display.value=Math.exp(form.display.value);
    computed = true
}
//------------------------pi------------------------------
function pi(form)
{
    form.display.value=Math.PI;
    computed = true
}
//------------------------ln2------------------------------
function LN2(form)
{
    form.display.value=Math.LN2;
```

continues

Listing 22.1 Continued

```
    computed = true
}
//------------------------e-----------------------------
function e(form)
{
    form.display.value=Math.E;
    computed = true
}
//------------------------sqrt1_2-----------------------------
function sqrt1_2(form)
{
    form.display.value=Math.sqrt1_2;
    computed = true
}
//------------------------log-----------------------------
function log(form)
{
    form.display.value=Math.log(form.display.value);
    computed = true
}
//---------------------change sign---------------------
function changeSign(input)
{
    // could use input.value = 0 - input.value,
    // but let's show off substring
    if(input.value.substring(0, 1) == "-")
        input.value = input.value.substring(1, input.value.length)
    else
        input.value = "-" + input.value
}
<!-- done hiding from old browsers -->
</script>
</head>
<body><center>
<FONT COLOR="RED">
<h1> Calculator</h1>
<hr>
<form method="post">
<table border="1" align=center>
<tr align="center">
<td colspan = 7>
<table border="0">
<INPUT
   TYPE="hidden"
   NAME="stack"
   [VALUE="0"]>
<tr>
<td align=middle>Acc:</td>
<td><input name="display" size=40 value="Please Press Reset To Start">
</td>
</tr>
```

```
</table>
</td>
</tr>
<tr align=center>
<td>
<input type="button" value=" 7 "
  onClick="addChar(this.form.display, '7')">
</td>
<td>
<input type="button" value=" 8 "
  onClick="addChar(this.form.display, '8')">
</td>
<td>
<input type="button" value=" 9 "
  onClick="addChar(this.form.display, '9')">
</td>
<td>
<input type="button" value=" / "
  onClick="divide(this.form)">
</td>
<td>
<input type="button" value=" Sqrt "
  onClick="sqrt(this.form)">
</td>
<td>
<input type="button" value="  Exp  "
  onClick="exp(this.form)">
</td><td>
<input type="button" value="     E     "
  onCick="e(this.from)">
</td>
</tr>
<tr align=center>
<td>
<input type="button" value=" 4 "
  onClick="addChar(this.form.display, '4')">
</td>
<td>
<input type="button" value=" 5 "
  onClick="addChar(this.form.display, '5')">
</td>
<td>
<input type="button" value=" 6 "
  onClick="addChar(this.form.display, '6')">
</td>
<td>
<input type="button" value=" * "
  onClick="multiply(this.form)">
</td>
<td>
<input type="button" value=" Abs "
  onClick="abs(this.form)">
```

continues

Listing 22.1 Continued

```
</td>
<td>
<input type="button" value="   Pi     "
  onClick="pi(this.form)"> </td><td>
<input type="button" value="Sqrt1_2"
  onClick="sqrt1_2(this.form)">
</td>
</tr>
<tr align=center>
<td>
<input type="button" value=" 1 "
  onClick="addChar(this.form.display, '1')">
</td>
<td>
<input type="button" value=" 2 "
  onClick="addChar(this.form.display, '2')">
</td>
<td>
<input type="button" value=" 3 "
  onClick="addChar(this.form.display, '3')">
</td>
<td>
<input type="button" value=" - "
  onClick="subtract(this.form)">
</td>
<td>
<input type="button" value=" Tan "
  onClick="tan(this.form)">
</td>
<td>
<input type="button" value=" ATan "
  onClick="atan(this.form)"></td><td>
<input type="button" value="   Ln2    "
  onClick="ln2(this.form)">
</td>
</tr>
<tr align=center>
<td>
<input type="button" value=" 0 "
  onClick="addChar(this.form.display, '0')">
</td>
<td>
<input type="button" value=" . "
  onClick="addChar(this.form.display, '.')">
</td>
<td>
<input type="button" value="+/-"
  onClick="changeSign(this.form.display)">
</td>
<td>
```

```
<input type="button" value=" + "
  onClick="add(this.form)">
</td>
<td>
<input type="button" value=" Cos "
  onClick="cos(this.form)">
</td>
<td>
<input type="button" value=" ACos "
  onClick="acos(this.form)"></td><td>
<input type="button" value="   Log    "
  onClick="log(this.form)">
</td>
</tr>
<tr align=center>
<td colspan="2">
<input type="button" value=" Reset "
  onClick="reset(this.form)">
</td>
<td>
<input type="button" value=" C "
  onClick="reset(this.form)">
</td>
<td>
<input type="button" value=" <- "
  onClick="deleteChar(this.form.display)">
</td>
<td>
<input type="button" value=" Sin "
  onClick="sin(this.form)">
</td>
<td>
<input type="button" value=" ASin "
  onClick="asin(this.form)">
</td>
<td>
<input type="button" value="     =      "
  onClick="equals(this.form)">
</td>
</tr>
</table>
</form>
</body>
</html>
```

Summary

This chapter looked at the implementation of a scientific calculator through a combination of JavaScript and HTML. With HTML, the visual "look" of the calculator was created as a form, which provided the necessary input fields and button objects for performing the computations. The supporting JavaScript code performed the actual computations and display updates.

Review Questions

Answers to the review questions can be found in Appendix D.

1. What are the main components of the code for the calculator?
2. Before you perform math operations on user-entered fields, what must you do to the field data?

Exercises

1. See whether you can use different code to create the scientific calculator.
2. The `OnLoad` event handler allows you to execute JavaScript after a page is loaded. Modify the calculator example to automatically call `reset()` when users load the page (rather than have them do so manually).
3. *Advanced:* Although this is a scientific calculator, it could be modified to perform financial operations. Try adding additional buttons (and code) to perform calculations such as loan amortization, compound interest, and so forth.

CHAPTER 23

Creating a 1040 Tax Form

So far in this book, you've built some pretty small programs, such as a control panel, a scientific calculator, and a form-entry checker. Because I'm writing this chapter as April 15th nears, taxes are on my mind. So let's create a program that you could use in real life over the Net—a 1040 tax form. The code used in this chapter is also on the CD-ROM that accompanies this book.

Getting Started with HTML

First, you need to create the form in which the user can input numbers. You will use a table to make sure that the input boxes are flush right and that the text for what to enter in each line of the tax form is flush left. Using the first line of a tax form where you fill in a dollar amount (line 7), listing 23.1 shows how the HTML tag for a typical input field on this form will look.

Listing 23.1

```
<INPUT TYPE=text NAME="line7" SIZE=15
       ONFOCUS="this.select();"
       ONCHANGE="processChange(this);">
```

In listing 23.1, the input box, `line7`, is defined as a `text` object and its size is set to 15. Because the size will be important for the program (to replicate the layout of the 1040 tax form), all the text boxes will be set to `SIZE=15`.

To make the table "work" (input fields flush right, text flush left), you need to take advantage of several attributes available in HTML. Each line in the table consists of two columns wrapped in a <TR>...</TR> tag pair, with each column wrapped in a <TD>...</TD> tag pair. To make certain that the column containing the input boxes will always be just large enough for the box (no matter the size of the browser window), its width is "fixed" with the WIDTH attribute:

```
<TD WIDTH=130 VALIGN=BOTTOM>
   <INPUT TYPE=text name="line7" ...>
</TD>
```

which forces the width to 130 pixels. The addition of the VALIGN attribute ensures that when the browser window is reduced in size (causing the text in the left column to wrap to multiple lines), the input box is always positioned at the bottom of the cell (just as with a regular tax form).

> **Note:** Any pixel sizes specified in this chapter were determined on a Windows-based computer. Macintosh and UNIX users may find that they need to "play" with these values to produce a more pleasing display.

Using JavaScript in the Program

Let's continue with the input field `line7` from the preceding section. Notice that listing 23.1 uses two JavaScript event handlers:

- `OnChange` calls a `processChange()` function, which verifies the validity of the data entered and updates the rest of the form appropriately.
- `OnFocus` to forces the selection of the entire contents of the field when the user tabs into it. This makes the form behave more like a spreadsheet and, therefore, is much easier for the user to work with.

The `processChange()` function isn't really a function—rather, it's a collection of several functions that all have the same purpose:

- Verify the field data is valid
- If valid, call the "tally it up" function for the section
- If not, select the data in the field for easy deletion or editing

Each section of the tax form will have its own `processChange()` function, but each has the format shown in listing 23.2.

Listing 23.2

```
function processIncome(field) {
    if(!checkNum(field.value)) {
        field.focus();
        field.select();
    } else {
        field.value = exact(dollar(field.value), 15, 2);
        income(field);
    }
}
```

The only thing that will change from one section to another (apart from the name of the function itself) is the line that calls the "tally" function (in the Income section, `income()` is called, whereas in the Credits section a `credit()` function is called).

Because a tax form is much like a spreadsheet (entries made in any given section result in values changing in all the sections following), each section's tally function will also—after finishing its totals—call the tally function of the next section. This effectively updates the information in the tax form no matter where the user makes changes. These functions are covered in more detail in the next sections.

Functions

Several functions are used in this program:

- `checkNum()` checks to see whether the input is a string or number.
- `exact()` displays the number with two decimal places, a dollar sign ($) preceding, and commas (,) grouping the numbers in the familiar dollars-and-cents format. `exact()` also pads the number with blanks to right-justify it in the display field.
- `dollar()` takes a "display value" (generated by `exact()`) and converts it back to a valid decimal for computation purposes.
- `income()` calculates the total income.
- `adjust()` calculates the total adjustment to income (deductions would go in this function).
- `gross()` calculates adjusted gross income.
- `computation()` calculates the tax computation.
- `credit()` calculates credits, such as the Earned Income Credit.
- `otherTaxes()` calculates the total tax.
- `payment()` calculates what you've already paid in taxes (such as withholdings and quarterly payments).

- `owe()` calculates the amount you owe or the refund you should get.
- `refund()` and `estimate()` calculate how much of your refund you want to keep or apply to next year's taxes

The *checkNum()* Function

Because dollar signs ($) and commas (,) are valid input characters on a tax form, using JavaScript's built-in `parseFloat()` method wouldn't work (these characters aren't interpreted as parts of numbers by `parseFloat()`). Therefore, it's necessary to write your own validation function—`checkNum()`.

This function, shown in listing 23.3, uses the `length` property of the JavaScript string object to find the length of the input string and to make sure that the string isn't 0, `""` (an empty string), or null; if it is, it returns `false`. Then a `for` loop is used to step through the input string character-by-character to ensure that no invalid characters have been entered. If anything except a digit (0, 1, … 9), a period (.), a dollar sign ($), or a comma (,) is found, the user sees a message warning of the invalid input and the function returns `false`. If all characters are valid, the function returns `true`. The `checkNum()` function is used to verify the value in each input field in this program.

Listing 23.3

```
function checkNum(str) {
   if(str.length == 0 || str == "" ||
      str == null) {
      str = 0.0;
      return false;
   }

   // skip over any leading blanks
   // (added for) right-justification
   //
   var j = 0;
   for(var i=0; i<str.length;i++) {
      if(str.substring(i, i+1) != ' ') {
         j = i;
         break;
      }
   }

   for (var i = j; i < str.length; i++) {
      var ch = str.substring(i, i + 1)

      if ((ch < "0" || "9" < ch) && ch != '.' &&
          ch != '$' && ch != ',') {
         alert("Try a valid input, please.");
         return false;
```

```
      }
    }

    return true;
}
```

The *exact()* Function

Because of the inaccuracies encountered in JavaScript when doing decimal math, it's necessary to "tweak" any decimal values to make sure that they keep to 2 decimal places. The `exact()` function works much like the built-in `round()` method of the `Math` object, except that it rounds to a given number of decimal places *and* handles "money characters" (dollar signs and commas) that may be encountered. The parameters of `exact()` are as follows:

- `val`, which replaces the input
- `len`, the length of the input (usually 15)
- `decimal`, the number of digits to the right of the decimal point

Listing 23.4 shows the code.

Listing 23.4

```
function exact(val, len, decimal) {
   if(decimal == null)
      decimal = 1;

   scale = Math.pow(10, decimal+1);

   tStr = "" + Math.round(parseFloat(val) * scale);

   if(tStr.length == 0 || tStr == "0") {
      tStr = "0";

      for(var i=0; i<=decimal; i++)
         tStr += "0";
   }

   str = "."
      + tStr.substring(tStr.length-decimal-1,
                       tStr.length);

   for(i=tStr.length-decimal-2, j=0 ; i>=0; i--) {
      if(++j > 3) {
         str = "," + str;
         j = 0;
      }
```

continues

Listing 23.4 Continued

```
        str = tStr.substring(i, i+1) + str;
    }

    str = "$" + str;
    i = len - str.length;

    if (scale != 1)
        i--;

    while(0 < i--)
        str = " " + str;

    return str;
}
```

The function first creates a variable named `scale` and assigns 1 to it. Next, `exact()` makes sure that if the `decimal` parameter wasn't specified, a "default" of 1 decimal place is assumed. The variable `scale` is then set to 10 taken to the `decimal+1` power (for example, if `decimal` were 2, `scale` would be set to 100). Next, the parameter `val` is converted to a float and multiplied by `scale`, the result being rounded and assigned to a new variable, `tStr`. For example, if `val` were 2388.90 and `decimal` were 2, `tStr` would be assigned a value of 238890.

If the length of `tStr` comes out to be 0 or the string stored in `tStr` is `"0"`, the function sets the value of `tStr` to a sequence of zeros (0) `decimal+1` characters long. Now the reconstruction process starts.

A new variable, `str`, is initialized to a decimal point (.) and the last `decimal` characters of `tStr` (or .90, using the running example). You now work from this end of `tStr` to the first character, moving characters to the front of `str` and inserting commas for every three digits transferred (which, using the example, would result in `str` containing 2,388.90). Finally, a $ is tacked onto the front of `str`.

When the new dollar value is constructed, spaces are added to the front of the string to bring its total `length` to `len` characters long. This final result is returned.

The *dollar()* function

Whereas `exact()` takes a decimal number and converts it into dollars-and-cents format, the `dollar()` function works in the opposite direction, converting dollars-and-cents format back into decimal numbers for use in the tally functions.

The operation of `dollar()` (see listing 23.5) is very straightforward. Looping through the parameter `str` one character at a time, a new string, `tStr`, is built from only the digits and decimal point from `str`. Once built, `eval()` is used to convert `tStr` to a true numeric value.

Listing 23.5

```
function dollar(str) {
   tStr = "";

   for(var i=0; i<str.length; i++) {
      ch = str.substring(i, i + 1);

      if((ch >= '0' && ch <= '9') || ch == '.')
         tStr += ch;
   }

   return eval(tStr);
}
```

The *income()* Function

The `income()` function adds up all the income information the user has entered on the form. This function, shown in listing 23.6, retrieves the values from form fields `line7` though `line21`, adds them, and assigns the result to `line22` after using `exact()` to convert it to display (dollar-and-cents) format.

Listing 23.6

```
function income(input) {
   var form = input.form;
   var temp = dollar(form.line7.value)
            + dollar(form.line8a.value)
            + dollar(form.line8b.value)
            + dollar(form.line10.value)
            + dollar(form.line11.value)
            + dollar(form.line12.value)
            + dollar(form.line13.value)
            + dollar(form.line14.value)
            + dollar(form.line15a.value)
            + dollar(form.line15b.value)
            + dollar(form.line16a.value)
            + dollar(form.line16b.value)
            + dollar(form.line17.value)
            + dollar(form.line18.value)
            + dollar(form.line19.value)
            + dollar(form.line20a.value)
            + dollar(form.line20b.value)
            + dollar(form.line21.value);

   form.line22.value = exact(temp, 15, 2);
   gross(input);
}
```

To ensure that any changes in the Income section reflect through the rest of the form, `income()` calls `gross()` as its last operation (to update the displayed adjusted gross income).

The *adjust()* Function

The next section of the tax form is Income Adjustments, which is tallied by the `adjust()` function. This function, shown in listing 23.7, adds up the values in form fields `line23a` though `line29` and assigns the result to `line30`. As with the `income()` function, `exact()` is used to make sure that the output is properly displayed.

Listing 23.7

```
function adjust(input) {
   var form = input.form;
   var temp = dollar(form.line23a.value)
            + dollar(form.line23b.value)
            + dollar(form.line24.value)
            + dollar(form.line25.value)
            + dollar(form.line26.value)
            + dollar(form.line27.value)
            + dollar(form.line28.value)
            + dollar(form.line29.value);

   form.line30.value = exact(temp, 15, 2);
   gross(input);
}
```

Again, as with `income()`, `gross()` is called once the tallying is done to reflect the new adjustments down the rest of the form.

The *gross()* Function

The AGI, or adjusted gross income, is computed by the `gross()` function. This function, shown in listing 23.8, subtracts `line30` from `line22` and assigns it to `line31`.

Listing 23.8

```
function gross(input) {
   var form = input.form;
   var temp = dollar(form.line22.value)
            - dollar(form.line30.value);

   form.line31.value = exact(temp, 15, 2);
   computation(input);
}
```

As before, the next section's tally function (`computation()`, in this case) is called to reflect the new figures down the rest of the form.

The *computation()* Function

The `computation()` function works on the fields in the Tax Computation section of the form. This function, shown in listing 23.9, subtracts the value in `line34` (total allowed deductions) from the value in `line32` (adjusted gross) and assigns it to `line35`. Then it subtracts `line36` (exemptions) from `line35` and puts the result in `line37` (taxable income). If the subtraction is negative, the function ignores the result. Next, it takes the sum of `line39` (additional taxes) and `line38` (base tax) and assigns it to `line40` (total taxes).

Listing 23.9

```
function computation(input) {
    var form = input.form;
    var temp = 0;

    form.line32.value = form.line31.value;

    temp  = dollar(form.line32.value)
          - dollar(form.line34.value);
    form.line35.value = exact(temp, 15, 2);

    temp  = dollar(form.line35.value)
          - dollar(form.line36.value);
    if(temp <= 0)
       temp = 0;      //ignore negative value

    form.line37.value = exact(temp, 15, 2);

    temp  = dollar(form.line38.value)
          + dollar(form.line39.value);
    form.line40.value = exact(temp, 15, 2);
    credit(input);
}
```

Any changes in the Tax Computation section will reflect through the rest of the form, so the `credit()` function is called to continue the update process.

The *credit()* Function

Totalling the Credits part of the form is the job of the `credit()` function. This function, shown in listing 23.10, adds the values in fields `line41` through `line44` and puts the result in `line45`. Then it subtracts `line45` from `line40` and puts *that* result in `line46`. Any negative value is ignored.

Listing 23.10

```
function credit(input) {
   var form = input.form;
   var temp = dollar(form.line41.value)
            + dollar(form.line42.value)
            + dollar(form.line43.value)
            + dollar(form.line44.value);

   form.line45.value = exact(temp, 15, 2);

   var temp = dollar(form.line40.value)
            - dollar(form.line45.value);
   if(temp <= 0)
      temp = 0;      //ignore negative value

   form.line46.value = exact(temp, 15, 2);
   otherTaxes(input);
}
```

Because the section after Credits is Other Taxes, `credit()` calls `otherTaxes()` to reflect updates down the form.

The *otherTaxes()* Function

The next section on the tax form, Other Taxes, is handled by the `otherTaxes()` function. This function, shown in listing 23.11, retrieves the values from `line47` though `line53`, adds them, and then assigns the total to `line54`. As with all the other display manipulation functions, `exact()` is used to make sure that the output is properly displayed.

Listing 23.11

```
function otherTaxes(input) {
   var form = input.form;
   temp  = dollar(form.line46.value)
         + dollar(form.line47.value)
         + dollar(form.line48.value)
         + dollar(form.line49.value)
         + dollar(form.line50.value)
         + dollar(form.line51.value)
         + dollar(form.line52.value)
         + dollar(form.line53.value);

   form.line54.value = exact(temp, 15, 2);
   payment(input);
}
```

Like all the other tally functions, `otherTaxes()` passes control to `payment()`, the tally function for the next section in the form.

The *payment()* Function

The Payments section of the tax form is managed by the `payment()` function. This function, shown in listing 23.12, tallies up the input fields `line55` though `line60`, calls `exact()` to format the total, and stores the result in `line61`.

Listing 23.12

```
function payment(input) {
   var form = input.form;
   temp  = dollar(form.line55.value)
         + dollar(form.line56.value)
         + dollar(form.line57.value)
         + dollar(form.line58.value)
         + dollar(form.line59.value)
         + dollar(form.line60.value);

   form.line61.value = exact(temp, 15, 2);
   owe(input);
}
```

After `line61` is updated, `owe()` is called to compute the refund or tax owed.

The *owe()* Function

This function, shown in listing 23.13, computes the size of the owed tax or refund. If the value of `line61` is bigger than that of `line54`, the difference is stored in `line62` (with `line65` being cleared, because you don't get a refund if you owe taxes). Otherwise, `line62` is cleared (no tax owed), and the difference is stored in `line65` (the refund). If a refund is in order, `owe()` assumes that you want all of it, so `line63` is set to the total of the refund.

Listing 23.13

```
function owe(input) {
   var form = input.form;

   form.line63.value = "";
   form.line64.value = "";

   if (dollar(form.line61.value) >=
       dollar(form.line54.value)) {
      // you get a refund
      var refund = dollar(form.line61.value)
                 - dollar(form.line54.value);
      form.line62.value = exact(refund, 15, 2);
      form.line63.value = exact(refund, 15, 2);
      form.line65.value = "";
   } else {
```

continues

Listing 23.13 Continued

```
      // you owe money
      var tax = dollar(form.line54.value)
              - dollar(form.line61.value);
      form.line62.value = "";
      form.line65.value = exact(tax, 15, 2);
   }
}
```

If a refund is in order, one last computation set is called—the `refund()` function.

The *refund()* and *estimate()* Functions

If a refund has been computed, you can do three things with the money: get it back from the government, apply it to next year's taxes, or a combination of the two. The `refund()` and `estimate()` functions (see listing 23.14) are called by the `OnChange` event handlers of `line63` and `line64` respectively, and work in tandem to make certain that the total of `line63` and `line64` matches that of `line62`. The functions also make sure that you don't get a larger refund (or application to next year's taxes) than you're entitled to.

Listing 23.14

```
function refund(input) {
   var form = input.form;

   if(dollar(form.line63.value) >
      dollar(form.line62.value))
      form.line63.value =
         exact(dollar(form.line62.value), 15, 2);

   var temp = dollar(form.line62.value)
            - dollar(form.line63.value);

   form.line64.value = exact(temp, 15, 2);
}

function estimate(input) {
   var form = input.form;

   if(dollar(form.line64.value) >
      dollar(form.line62.value))
      form.line64.value =
         exact(dollar(form.line62.value), 15, 2);

   var temp = dollar(form.line62.value)
            - dollar(form.line64.value);

   form.line63.value = exact(temp, 15, 2);
}
```

This wraps up the computations for the tax form.

Putting Everything Together

Listing 23.15 shows the full code of the program.

Listing 23.15

```
<HTML>
<HEAD>
   <TITLE>1040 Tax form</TITLE>

<SCRIPT LANGUAGE="JavaScript">
<!--hide from non-JavaScript browsers

function checkNum(str) {
   if (str.length == 0 || str == "" ||
       str == null) {
      str = 0.0;
      return false;
   }

   // skip over any leading blanks
   //(added for) from right-justification
   //
   var j = 0;
   for(var i=0; i<str.length;i++) {
      if(str.substring(i, i+1) != ' ') {
         j = i;
         break;
      }
   }

   for (var i = j; i < str.length; i++) {
      var ch = str.substring(i, i + 1)

      if ((ch < "0" || "9" < ch) && ch != '.' &&
          ch != '$' && ch != ',') {
         alert("Try a valid input, please.");
         return false;
      }
   }

   return true;
}

function exact(val, len, decimal) {
   if(decimal == null)
      decimal = 1;
```

continues

Listing 23.15 Continued

```
   scale = Math.pow(10, decimal+1);

   tStr = "" + Math.round(parseFloat(val) * scale);

   if(tStr.length == 0 ¦¦ tStr == "0") {
      tStr = "0";

      for(var i=0; i<=decimal; i++)
         tStr += "0";
   }

   str = "."
      + tStr.substring(tStr.length-decimal-1,
                       tStr.length);

   for(i=tStr.length-decimal-2, j=0 ; i>=0; i--) {
      if(++j > 3) {
         str = "," + str;
         j = 0;
      }

      str = tStr.substring(i, i+1) + str;
   }

   str = "$" + str;
   i = len - str.length;

   if (scale != 1)
      i--;

   while(0 < i--)
      str = " " + str;

   return str;
}

function dollar(str) {
   tStr = "";

   for(var i=0; i<str.length; i++) {
      ch = str.substring(i, i + 1);

      if((ch >= '0' && ch <= '9') ¦¦ ch == '.')
         tStr += ch;
   }

   return eval(tStr);
}

function income(input) {
   var form = input.form;
```

```
    var temp = dollar(form.line7.value)
             + dollar(form.line8a.value)
             + dollar(form.line8b.value)
             + dollar(form.line10.value)
             + dollar(form.line11.value)
             + dollar(form.line12.value)
             + dollar(form.line13.value)
             + dollar(form.line14.value)
             + dollar(form.line15a.value)
             + dollar(form.line15b.value)
             + dollar(form.line16a.value)
             + dollar(form.line16b.value)
             + dollar(form.line17.value)
             + dollar(form.line18.value)
             + dollar(form.line19.value)
             + dollar(form.line20a.value)
             + dollar(form.line20b.value)
             + dollar(form.line21.value);

    form.line22.value = exact(temp, 15, 2);
    gross(input);
}

function adjust(input) {
    var form = input.form;
    var temp = dollar(form.line23a.value)
             + dollar(form.line23b.value)
             + dollar(form.line24.value)
             + dollar(form.line25.value)
             + dollar(form.line26.value)
             + dollar(form.line27.value)
             + dollar(form.line28.value)
             + dollar(form.line29.value);

    form.line30.value = exact(temp, 15, 2);
    gross(input);
}

function gross(input) {
    var form = input.form;
    var temp = dollar(form.line22.value)
             - dollar(form.line30.value);

    form.line31.value = exact(temp, 15, 2);
    computation(input);
}

function computation(input) {
    var form = input.form;
    var temp = 0;

    form.line32.value = form.line31.value;
```

continues

Listing 23.15 Continued

```
   temp  = dollar(form.line32.value)
         - dollar(form.line34.value);
   form.line35.value = exact(temp, 15, 2);

   temp  = dollar(form.line35.value)
         - dollar(form.line36.value);
   if(temp <= 0)
      temp = 0;     //ignore negative value

   form.line37.value = exact(temp, 15, 2);

   temp  = dollar(form.line38.value)
         + dollar(form.line39.value);
   form.line40.value = exact(temp, 15, 2);
   credit(input);
}

function credit(input) {
   var form = input.form;
   var temp = dollar(form.line41.value)
            + dollar(form.line42.value)
            + dollar(form.line43.value)
            + dollar(form.line44.value);

   form.line45.value = exact(temp, 15, 2);

   var temp = dollar(form.line40.value)
            - dollar(form.line45.value);
   if(temp <= 0)
      temp = 0;     //ignore negative value

   form.line46.value = exact(temp, 15, 2);
   otherTaxes(input);
}

function otherTaxes(input) {
   var form = input.form;
   temp  = dollar(form.line46.value)
         + dollar(form.line47.value)
         + dollar(form.line48.value)
         + dollar(form.line49.value)
         + dollar(form.line50.value)
         + dollar(form.line51.value)
         + dollar(form.line52.value)
         + dollar(form.line53.value);

   form.line54.value = exact(temp, 15, 2);
   payment(input);
}

function payment(input) {
```

```
    var form = input.form;
    temp  = dollar(form.line55.value)
          + dollar(form.line56.value)
          + dollar(form.line57.value)
          + dollar(form.line58.value)
          + dollar(form.line59.value)
          + dollar(form.line60.value);

    form.line61.value = exact(temp, 15, 2);
    owe(input);
 }

 function owe(input) {
    var form = input.form;

    form.line63.value = "";
    form.line64.value = "";

    if (dollar(form.line61.value) >=
        dollar(form.line54.value)) {
       // you get a refund
       var refund = dollar(form.line61.value)
                  - dollar(form.line54.value);
       form.line62.value = exact(refund, 15, 2);
       form.line63.value = exact(refund, 15, 2);
       form.line65.value = "";
    } else {
       // you owe money
       var tax = dollar(form.line54.value)
               - dollar(form.line61.value);
       form.line62.value = "";
       form.line65.value = exact(tax, 15, 2);
    }
 }

 function refund(input) {
    var form = input.form;

    if(dollar(form.line63.value) >
       dollar(form.line62.value))
       form.line63.value =
          exact(dollar(form.line62.value), 15, 2);

    var temp = dollar(form.line62.value)
             - dollar(form.line63.value);

    form.line64.value = exact(temp, 15, 2);
 }

 function estimate(input) {
    var form = input.form;
```

continues

Listing 23.15 Continued

```
   if(dollar(form.line64.value) >
      dollar(form.line62.value))
      form.line64.value =
         exact(dollar(form.line62.value), 15, 2);

   var temp = dollar(form.line62.value)
           - dollar(form.line64.value);

   form.line63.value = exact(temp, 15, 2);
}

function processIncome(field) {
   if(!checkNum(field.value)) {
      field.focus();
      field.select();
   } else {
      field.value =
         exact(dollar(field.value), 15, 2);
      income(field);
   }
}

function processAdjust(field) {
   if(!checkNum(field.value)) {
      field.focus();
      field.select();
   } else {
      field.value =
         exact(dollar(field.value), 15, 2);
      adjust(field);
   }
}

function processComputation(field) {
   if(!checkNum(field.value)) {
      field.focus();
      field.select();
   } else {
      field.value =
         exact(dollar(field.value), 15, 2);
      computation(field);
   }
}

function processCredit(field) {
   if(!checkNum(field.value)) {
      field.focus();
      field.select();
   } else {
      field.value =
         exact(dollar(field.value), 15, 2);
```

```
        credit(field);
    }
}

function processOTax(field) {
    if(!checkNum(field.value)) {
        field.focus();
        field.select();
    } else {
        field.value =
            exact(dollar(field.value), 15, 2);
        otherTaxes(field);
    }
}

function processPayment(field) {
    if(!checkNum(field.value)) {
        field.focus();
        field.select();
    } else {
        field.value =
            exact(dollar(field.value), 15, 2);
        payment(field);
    }
}

function processOwe(field) {
    if(!checkNum(field.value)) {
        field.focus();
        field.select();
    } else {
        field.value =
            exact(dollar(field.value), 15, 2);
        owe(field);
    }
}

function processRefund(field) {
    if(!checkNum(field.value)) {
        field.focus();
        field.select();
    } else {
        field.value =
            exact(dollar(field.value), 15, 2);
        refund(field);
    }
}

function processEstimate(field) {
    if(!checkNum(field.value)) {
        field.focus();
        field.select();
```

continues

Listing 23.15 Continued

```
      } else {
         field.value =
            exact(dollar(field.value), 15, 2);
         estimate(field);
      }
   }

// end hiding -->
</SCRIPT>
</HEAD>
<BODY BGCOLOR=#ffffff TEXT=#000000>

<H2>1040 Tax Form</H2>

<HR>

<FORM>
<TABLE WIDTH="100%" CELLPADDING="2" border>

<TR><TD VALIGN=BOTTOM COLSPAN=2>
   <FONT SIZE=+2><B><BR>Income</B></FONT>
</TD></TR>

   <TR>
      <TD>
         7. Total wages, salaries, and tips. This
         should be shown in box 1 of your W-2 form(s).
         Attach your W-2 forms(s)
      </TD>
      <TD WIDTH=130 VALIGN=BOTTOM>
         <INPUT TYPE=text NAME="line7" SIZE=15
                ONFOCUS="this.select();"
                ONCHANGE="processIncome(this)">
      </TD>
   </TR>
   <TR>
      <TD>
         8a. Taxable interest income(see page 15).
         Attach Schedule B if over $400
      </TD>
      <TD WIDTH=130 VALIGN=BOTTOM>
         <INPUT TYPE=text NAME="line8a" SIZE=15
                ONFOCUS="this.select();"
                ONCHANGE="processIncome(this)">
      </TD>
   </TR>
   <TR>
      <TD>
         8b. Tax-exempt interest (see page 15).
         Don't include on line 2a
      </TD>
```

```
    <TD WIDTH=130 VALIGN=BOTTOM>
       <INPUT TYPE=text NAME="line8b" SIZE=15
              ONFOCUS="this.select();"
              ONCHANGE="processIncome(this)">
    </TD>
 </TR>
 <TR>
    <TD>
       9. Dividend income. Attach Schedule B
       if over $400
    </TD>
    <TD WIDTH=130 VALIGN=BOTTOM>
       <INPUT TYPE=text NAME="line9" SIZE=15
              ONFOCUS="this.select();"
              ONCHANGE="processIncome(this)">
    </TD>
 </TR>
 <TR>
    <TD>
       10. Taxable refunds, credits, or offsets
       of state and local income taxes
       (see page 15)
    </TD>
    <TD WIDTH=130 VALIGN=BOTTOM>
       <INPUT TYPE=text NAME="line10" SIZE=15
              ONFOCUS="this.select();"
              ONCHANGE="processIncome(this)">
    </TD>
 </TR>
 <TR>
    <TD>
       11. Alimony received
    </TD>
    <TD WIDTH=130 VALIGN=BOTTOM>
       <INPUT TYPE=text NAME="line11" SIZE=15
              ONFOCUS="this.select();"
              ONCHANGE="processIncome(this)">
    </TD>
 </TR>
 <TR>
    <TD>
       12. Business income or (loss).
       Attach Schedule C or C-EZ
    </TD>
    <TD WIDTH=130 VALIGN=BOTTOM>
       <INPUT TYPE=text NAME="line12" SIZE=15
              ONFOCUS="this.select();"
              ONCHANGE="processIncome(this)">
    </TD>
 </TR>
 <TR>
    <TD>
```

continues

Listing 23.15 Continued

```
            13. Capital gain or (losses).
            If required, attach Schedule D
            (see page 16)
         </TD>
         <TD WIDTH=130 VALIGN=BOTTOM>
            <INPUT TYPE=text NAME="line13" SIZE=15
                   ONFOCUS="this.select();"
                   ONCHANGE="processIncome(this)">
         </TD>
      </TR>
      <TR>
         <TD>
            14. Other gains or (losses).
            Attach Form 4797
         </TD>
         <TD WIDTH=130 VALIGN=BOTTOM>
            <INPUT TYPE=text NAME="line14" SIZE=15
                   ONFOCUS="this.select();"
                   ONCHANGE="processIncome(this)">
         </TD>
      </TR>
      <TR>
         <TD>
            15a. Total IRA distributions
         </TD>
         <TD WIDTH=130 VALIGN=BOTTOM>
            <INPUT TYPE=text NAME="line15a" SIZE=15
                   ONFOCUS="this.select();"
                   ONCHANGE="processIncome(this)">
         </TD>
      </TR>
      <TR>
         <TD>
            15b. Taxable amount(see page 16)
         </TD>
         <TD WIDTH=130 VALIGN=BOTTOM>
            <INPUT TYPE=text NAME="line15b" SIZE=15
                   ONFOCUS="this.select();"
                   ONCHANGE="processIncome(this)">
         </TD>
      </TR>
      <TR>
         <TD>
            16a. Total pensions and annuities
         </TD>
         <TD WIDTH=130 VALIGN=BOTTOM>
            <INPUT TYPE=text NAME="line16a" SIZE=15
                   ONFOCUS="this.select();"
                   ONCHANGE="processIncome(this)">
         </TD>
      </TR>
```

```
<TR>
   <TD>
      16b. Taxable amount(see page 16)
   </TD>
   <TD WIDTH=130 VALIGN=BOTTOM>
      <INPUT TYPE=text NAME="line16b" SIZE=15
             ONFOCUS="this.select();"
             ONCHANGE="processIncome(this)">
   </TD>
</TR>
<TR>
   <TD>
      17. Rental real estate, royalties,
      partnerships, S corporations, trusts,
      etc., Attach Schedule E
   </TD>
   <TD WIDTH=130 VALIGN=BOTTOM>
      <INPUT TYPE=text NAME="line17" SIZE=15
             ONFOCUS="this.select();"
             ONCHANGE="processIncome(this)">
   </TD>
</TR>
<TR>
   <TD>
      18. Farm income or (loss).
      Attach Schedule F
   </TD>
   <TD WIDTH=130 VALIGN=BOTTOM>
      <INPUT TYPE=text NAME="line18" SIZE=15
             ONFOCUS="this.select();"
             ONCHANGE="processIncome(this)">
   </TD>
</TR>
<TR>
   <TD>
      19. Unemployment compensation
      (see page 17)
   </TD>
   <TD WIDTH=130 VALIGN=BOTTOM>
      <INPUT TYPE=text NAME="line19" SIZE=15
             ONFOCUS="this.select();"
             ONCHANGE="processIncome(this)">
   </TD>
</TR>
<TR>
   <TD>
      20a. Social Security benefits
   </TD>
   <TD WIDTH=130 VALIGN=BOTTOM>
      <INPUT TYPE=text NAME="line20a" SIZE=15
             ONFOCUS="this.select();"
             ONCHANGE="processIncome(this)">
```

continues

Listing 23.15 Continued

```
      </TD>
   </TR>
   <TR>
      <TD>
         20b. Taxable amount (see page 18)
      </TD>
      <TD WIDTH=130 VALIGN=BOTTOM>
         <INPUT TYPE=text NAME="line20b" SIZE=15
                ONFOCUS="this.select();"
                ONCHANGE="processIncome(this)">
      </TD>
   </TR>
   <TR>
      <TD>
         21. Other income (see page 18)
      </TD>
      <TD WIDTH=130 VALIGN=BOTTOM>
         <INPUT TYPE=text NAME="line21" SIZE=15
                ONFOCUS="this.select();"
                ONCHANGE="processIncome(this)">
      </TD>
   </TR>
   <TR>
      <TD>
         22. Add the amounts in the far right column
         for <B>lines 7-21</B>. This is your
         <B>total income</B>
      </TD>
      <TD WIDTH=130 VALIGN=BOTTOM>
         <INPUT TYPE=text NAME="line22" SIZE=15
                ONFOCUS="this.select();"
                ONCHANGE="processIncome(this)">
      </TD>
   </TR>

<TR><TD VALIGN=BOTTOM COLSPAN=2>
   <FONT SIZE=+2><B><BR>Adjustements to income</B></FONT>
</TD></TR>

   <TR>
      <TD>
         23a. Your IRA deduction (see page 19)
      </TD>
      <TD WIDTH=130 VALIGN=BOTTOM>
         <INPUT TYPE=text NAME="line23a" SIZE=15
                ONFOCUS="this.select();"
                ONCHANGE="processAdjust(this)">
      </TD>
   </TR>
   <TR>
      <TD>
```

```
      23b. Spouse's IRA deduction (see page 19)
   </TD>
   <TD WIDTH=130 VALIGN=BOTTOM>
      <INPUT TYPE=text NAME="line23b" SIZE=15
             ONFOCUS="this.select();"
             ONCHANGE="processAdjust(this)">
   </TD>
</TR>
<TR>
   <TD>
      24. Moving expenses. Attach Form 3903 or 3903-F
   </TD>
   <TD WIDTH=130 VALIGN=BOTTOM>
      <INPUT TYPE=text NAME="line24" SIZE=15
             ONFOCUS="this.select();"
             ONCHANGE="processAdjust(this)">
   </TD>
</TR>
<TR>
   <TD>
      25. One-half of self-employment tax
   </TD>
   <TD WIDTH=130 VALIGN=BOTTOM>
      <INPUT TYPE=text NAME="line25" SIZE=15
             ONFOCUS="this.select();"
             ONCHANGE="processAdjust(this)">
   </TD>
</TR>
<TR>
   <TD>
      26. Self-employed health insurance deduction
      (see page 21)
   </TD>
   <TD WIDTH=130 VALIGN=BOTTOM>
      <INPUT TYPE=text NAME="line26" SIZE=15
             ONFOCUS="this.select();"
             ONCHANGE="processAdjust(this)">
   </TD>
</TR>
<TR>
   <TD>
      27. Keogh &amp; self-employed SEP plans.
   </TD>
   <TD WIDTH=130 VALIGN=BOTTOM>
      <INPUT TYPE=text NAME="line27" SIZE=15
             ONFOCUS="this.select();"
             ONCHANGE="processAdjust(this)">
   </TD>
</TR>
<TR>
   <TD>
      28. Penalty on early withdrawal of savings
```

continues

Listing 23.15 Continued

```
        </TD>
        <TD WIDTH=130 VALIGN=BOTTOM>
           <INPUT TYPE=text NAME="line28" SIZE=15
                  ONFOCUS="this.select();"
                  ONCHANGE="processAdjust(this)">
        </TD>
     </TR>
     <TR>
        <TD>
           29. Alimony paid
        </TD>
        <TD WIDTH=130 VALIGN=BOTTOM>
           <INPUT TYPE=text NAME="line29" SIZE=15
                  ONFOCUS="this.select();"
                  ONCHANGE="processAdjust(this)">
        </TD>
     </TR>
     <TR>
        <TD>
           30. Add <B>lines 23a through 29.</B>. These
           are your <B>total Adjustments</B>
        </TD>
        <TD WIDTH=130 VALIGN=BOTTOM>
           <INPUT TYPE=text NAME="line30" SIZE=15
                  ONFOCUS="this.select();"
                  ONCHANGE="processAdjust(this)">
        </TD>
     </TR>

  <TR><TD VALIGN=BOTTOM COLSPAN=2>
     <FONT SIZE=+2><B><BR>Adjusted Gross Income</B></FONT>
  </TD></TR>

     <TR>
        <TD>
           31. Subtract line <B>30 from line 22</B>.
           This is your <B>Adjusted Gross Income</B>.
           If less than $26,673 and a child lived with
           you (less than $9,230 if a child did not live
           with you), see "Earned Income Credit" on
           page 27
        </TD>
        <TD WIDTH=130 VALIGN=BOTTOM>
           <INPUT TYPE=text NAME="line31" SIZE=15
                  ONFOCUS="this.select();"
                  ONCHANGE="gross(this); computation(this);">
        </TD>
     </TR>

  <TR><TD VALIGN=BOTTOM COLSPAN=2>
     <FONT SIZE=+2><B><BR>Tax Computation</B></FONT>
  </TD></TR>
```

```
<TR>
   <TD>
      32. Amount from line 31 (adjusted gross income)
   </TD>
   <TD WIDTH=130 VALIGN=BOTTOM>
      <INPUT TYPE=text NAME="line32" SIZE=15
             ONFOCUS="this.select();"
             ONCHANGE="processComputation(this)">
   </TD>
</TR>
<TR>
   <TD>
      33a. Check if:
      <INPUT TYPE=checkbox NAME="c33a" VALUE="on">You
      were 65 or older
      <INPUT TYPE=checkbox NAME="c33b" VALUE="on">Blind
      <INPUT TYPE=checkbox NAME="c33c" VALUE="on">Your
      spouse was 65 or older
      <INPUT TYPE=checkbox NAME="c38d" VALUE="on">Blind
   </TD>
</TR>
<TR>
   <TD>
      33b. If your parents (or some else) can claim you
      as a dependent, check here:
      <INPUT TYPE=checkbox NAME="c33e" VALUE="on">
   </TD>
</TR>
<TR>
   <TD>
      33c. If you are married filling separately and
      your spouse itemizes deductions or you are a
      dual-status alien, see page 23 and
      check here:
      <INPUT TYPE=checkbox NAME="c33f" VALUE="on">
   </TD>
</TR>
<TR>
   <TD>
      34. Enter the larger of your: Itemized
      deductions from Schedule A, line 28 or Standard
      deduction shown below for your filing status.
      But if you checked any box on line 33a or b,
      go to page 23 to find your standard
      deduction. If you checked box 33c, your
      standard deduction is zero.
   </TD>
   <TD WIDTH=130 VALIGN=BOTTOM>
      <INPUT TYPE=text NAME="line34" SIZE=15
             ONFOCUS="this.select();"
```

continues

Listing 23.15 Continued

```
              ONCHANGE="processComputation(this)">
    </TD>
</TR>
<TR>
    <TD>
        35. Subtract line 34 from line 32
    </TD>
    <TD WIDTH=130 VALIGN=BOTTOM>
        <INPUT TYPE=text NAME="line35" SIZE=15
              ONFOCUS="this.select();"
              ONCHANGE="processComputation(this)">
    </TD>
</TR>
<TR>
    <TD>
        36. If line 32 is $86,025 or less, multiply
        $2,500 by the total number of exemptions
        claimed on line 6e. If line 32 is over
        $86,025, see the worksheet on page 23, for
        the amount to enter
    </TD>
    <TD WIDTH=130 VALIGN=BOTTOM>
        <INPUT TYPE=text NAME="line36" SIZE=15
              ONFOCUS="this.select();"
              ONCHANGE="processComputation(this)">
    </TD>
</TR>
<TR>
    <TD>
        37. Taxable income. Subtract line 36 from line
        35. If line 36 is more than line 35, enter -0-
    </TD>
    <TD WIDTH=130 VALIGN=BOTTOM>
        <INPUT TYPE=text NAME="line37" SIZE=15
              ONFOCUS="this.select();"
              ONCHANGE="processComputation(this)">
    </TD>
</TR>
<TR>
    <TD>
        38. Tax. check if from
        <B>a</B><INPUT TYPE=checkbox NAME="c38a"
        VALUE="off" ONFOCUS="this.select();"
        ONCHANGE="processComputation(this)">Tax Table,

        <B>b</B><INPUT TYPE=checkbox NAME="c38b"
        VALUE="off" ONFOCUS="this.select();"
        ONCHANGE="processComputation(this)">Tax Rate
        Schedules,

        <B>c</B><INPUT TYPE=checkbox NAME="c38c"
```

```
            VALUE="on" ONFOCUS="this.select();"
            ONCHANGE="processComputation(this)">Capital
            Gain Tax worksheet or

            <B>d</B><INPUT TYPE=checkbox NAME="c38d"
            VALUE="on" ONFOCUS="this.select();"
            ONCHANGE="processComputation(this)">Form
            8615 (see page 24).

            Amount From Form(s) 8814
            <INPUT TYPE=text NAME="c38e" SIZE=15
                   ONFOCUS="this.select();"
                   ONCHANGE="processComputation(this)">
         </TD>
         <TD WIDTH=130 VALIGN=BOTTOM>
            <INPUT TYPE=text NAME="line38" SIZE=15
                   ONFOCUS="this.select();"
                   ONCHANGE="processComputation(this)">
         </TD>
      </TR>
      <TR>
         <TD>
            39. Additional taxes. Check if from
            <B>a</B><INPUT TYPE=checkbox NAME="c39a"
            VALUE="off">Form 4970,
            <B>b</B><INPUT TYPE=checkbox NAME="c39b"
            VALUE="off">Form 4972
         </TD>
         <TD WIDTH=130 VALIGN=BOTTOM>
            <INPUT TYPE=text NAME="line39" SIZE=15
                   ONFOCUS="this.select();"
                   ONCHANGE="processComputation(this)">
         </TD>
      </TR>
      <TR>
         <TD>
            40. Add lines 38 and 39
         </TD>
         <TD WIDTH=130 VALIGN=BOTTOM>
            <INPUT TYPE=text NAME="line40" SIZE=15
                   ONFOCUS="this.select();"
                   ONCHANGE="processComputation(this)">
         </TD>
      </TR>

   <TR><TD VALIGN=BOTTOM COLSPAN=2>
      <FONT SIZE=+2><B><BR>Credits</B></FONT>
   </TD></TR>

      <TR>
         <TD>
            41. Credit for child and dependent care
            expenses. Attach Form 2441
```

continues

Listing 23.15 Continued

```
    </TD>
    <TD WIDTH=130 VALIGN=BOTTOM>
       <INPUT TYPE=text NAME="line41" SIZE=15
              ONFOCUS="this.select();"
              ONCHANGE="processCredit(this);">
    </TD>
 </TR>
 <TR>
    <TD>
       42. Credit for elderly or disabled.
       Attach Schedule R
    </TD>
    <TD WIDTH=130 VALIGN=BOTTOM>
       <INPUT TYPE=text NAME="line42" SIZE=15
              ONFOCUS="this.select();"
              ONCHANGE="processCredit(this);">
    </TD>
 </TR>
 <TR>
    <TD>
       43. Foreign tax credit. Attach Form 1116
    </TD>
    <TD WIDTH=130 VALIGN=BOTTOM>
       <INPUT TYPE=text NAME="line43" SIZE=15
              ONFOCUS="this.select();"
              ONCHANGE="processCredit(this);">
    </TD>
 </TR>
 <TR>
    <TD>
       44. Other credits(see page 25). Check if from
       <B>a</B><INPUT TYPE=checkbox NAME="c44a"
       VALUE="off">Form 4255,
       <B>b</B><INPUT TYPE=checkbox NAME="c44"
       VALUE="off">Form 8611,
       <BR><B>c</B><INPUT TYPE=checkbox NAME="c44c"
       VALUE="off">Form (specify)<INPUT TYPE=text
       NAME="c44d" SIZE=10>
    </TD>
    <TD WIDTH=130 VALIGN=BOTTOM>
       <INPUT TYPE=text NAME="line44" SIZE=15
              ONFOCUS="this.select();"
              ONCHANGE="processCredit(this);">
    </TD>
 </TR>
 <TR>
    <TD>
       45. Add lines 41 through 44
    </TD>
    <TD WIDTH=130 VALIGN=BOTTOM>
```

```
            <INPUT TYPE=text NAME="line45" SIZE=15
                    ONFOCUS="this.select();"
                    ONCHANGE="processCredit(this);">
         </TD>
      </TR>
      <TR>
         <TD>
            46. Subtract line 45 from line 40. If line
            45 is more than line 40, enter -0-
         </TD>
         <TD WIDTH=130 VALIGN=BOTTOM>
            <INPUT TYPE=text NAME="line46" SIZE=15
                    ONFOCUS="this.select();"
                    ONCHANGE="processCredit(this);">
         </TD>
      </TR>

   <TR><TD VALIGN=BOTTOM COLSPAN=2>
      <FONT SIZE=+2><B><BR>Other Taxes</B></FONT>
   </TD></TR>

      <TR>
         <TD>
            47. Self-employment tax. Attach
            Schedule SE
         </TD>
         <TD WIDTH=130 VALIGN=BOTTOM>
            <INPUT TYPE=text NAME="line47" SIZE=15
                    ONFOCUS="this.select();"
                    ONCHANGE="processOTax(this);">
         </TD>
      </TR>
      <TR>
         <TD>
            48. Alternative minimum Tax. Attach
            Form 6251
         </TD>
         <TD WIDTH=130 VALIGN=BOTTOM>
            <INPUT TYPE=text NAME="line48" SIZE=15
                    ONFOCUS="this.select();"
                    ONCHANGE="processOTax(this);">
         </TD>
      </TR>
      <TR>
         <TD>
            49. Recapture taxes. Check if from
            <B>a</B><INPUT TYPE=checkbox NAME="c49a"
            VALUE="off">Form 4255,
            <B>b</B><INPUT TYPE=checkbox NAME="c49b"
            VALUE="off">Form 8611,
            <B>c</B><INPUT TYPE=checkbox NAME="c49c"
            VALUE="off">Form 8828
```

continues

Listing 23.15 Continued

```
      </TD>
      <TD WIDTH=130 VALIGN=BOTTOM>
         <INPUT TYPE=text NAME="line49" SIZE=15
                ONFOCUS="this.select();"
                ONCHANGE="processOTax(this);">
      </TD>
   </TR>
   <TR>
      <TD>
         50. Social security and Medicare tax on tip
         income not reported to employer. Attach
         Form 4137
      </TD>
      <TD WIDTH=130 VALIGN=BOTTOM>
         <INPUT TYPE=text NAME="line50" SIZE=15
                ONFOCUS="this.select();"
                ONCHANGE="processOTax(this);">
      </TD>
   </TR>
   <TR>
      <TD>
         51. Tax on qualified retirement plans,
         including IRAs. If required, attach
         Form 5329.
      </TD>
      <TD WIDTH=130 VALIGN=BOTTOM>
         <INPUT TYPE=text NAME="line51" SIZE=15
                ONFOCUS="this.select();"
                ONCHANGE="processOTax(this);">
      </TD>
   </TR>
   <TR>
      <TD>
         52. Advance earned income credit payments
         from Form W-2
      </TD>
      <TD WIDTH=130 VALIGN=BOTTOM>
         <INPUT TYPE=text NAME="line52" SIZE=15
                ONFOCUS="this.select();"
                ONCHANGE="processOTax(this);">
      </TD>
   </TR>
   <TR>
      <TD>
         53. Household employment taxes. Attach
         Schedule H
      </TD>
      <TD WIDTH=130 VALIGN=BOTTOM>
         <INPUT TYPE=text NAME="line53" SIZE=15
                ONFOCUS="this.select();"
                ONCHANGE="processOTax(this);">
```

```
        </TD>
    </TR>
    <TR>
        <TD>
            54. Add lines 46 through 53. This is your
            total tax
        </TD>
        <TD WIDTH=130 VALIGN=BOTTOM>
            <INPUT TYPE=text NAME="line54" SIZE=15
                   ONFOCUS="this.select();"
                   ONCHANGE="processOTax(this);">
        </TD>
    </TR>

<TR><TD VALIGN=BOTTOM COLSPAN=2>
    <FONT SIZE=+2><B><BR>Payments</B></FONT>
</TD></TR>

    <TR>
        <TD>
            55. Federal income tax withheld. If any is
            from Form(s), check here:<INPUT TYPE=checkbox
            NAME="c55" VALUE="off">
        </TD>
        <TD WIDTH=130 VALIGN=BOTTOM>
            <INPUT TYPE=text NAME="line55" SIZE=15
                   ONFOCUS="this.select();"
                   ONCHANGE="processPayment(this);">
        </TD>
    </TR>
    <TR>
        <TD>
            56. 1995 estimated tax payments and amount
            applied from 1994 return
        </TD>
        <TD WIDTH=130 VALIGN=BOTTOM>
            <INPUT TYPE=text NAME="line56" SIZE=15
                   ONFOCUS="this.select();"
                   ONCHANGE="processPayment(this);">
        </TD>
    </TR>
    <TR>
        <TD>
            57. Earned income credit. Attach Schedule EIC
            if you have a qualifying child. Nontaxable
            earned income:
            amount <INPUT TYPE=text NAME="line57a" SIZE=15>
            and
            type <INPUT TYPE=text NAME="line57b">
        </TD>
        <TD WIDTH=130 VALIGN=BOTTOM>
            <INPUT TYPE=text NAME="line57" SIZE=15
```

continues

Listing 23.15 Continued

```
                ONFOCUS="this.select();"
                ONCHANGE="processPayment(this);">
        </TD>
    </TR>
    <TR>
        <TD>
            58. Amount paid with Form 4868
            (extension request)
        </TD>
        <TD WIDTH=130 VALIGN=BOTTOM>
            <INPUT TYPE=text NAME="line58" SIZE=15
                ONFOCUS="this.select();"
                ONCHANGE="processPayment(this);">
        </TD>
    </TR>
    <TR>
        <TD>
            59. Excess social security and RRTA tax
            withheld (see page 32)
        </TD>
        <TD WIDTH=130 VALIGN=BOTTOM>
            <INPUT TYPE=text NAME="line59" SIZE=15
                ONFOCUS="this.select();"
                ONCHANGE="processPayment(this);">
        </TD>
    </TR>
    <TR>
        <TD>
            60. Other payments. Check if from
            <B>a</B><INPUT TYPE=checkbox NAME="c60a"
            VALUE="off">Form 2439,
            <B>b</B><INPUT TYPE=checkbox NAME="c60b"
            VALUE="on">Form 4136
        </TD>
        <TD WIDTH=130 VALIGN=BOTTOM>
            <INPUT TYPE=text NAME="line60" SIZE=15
                ONFOCUS="this.select();"
                ONCHANGE="processPayment(this);">
        </TD>
    </TR>
    <TR>
        <TD>
            61. Add lines 55 through 60. these are your
            total payments
        </TD>
        <TD WIDTH=130 VALIGN=BOTTOM>
            <INPUT TYPE=text NAME="line61" SIZE=15
                ONFOCUS="this.select();"
                ONCHANGE="processPayment(this);">
        </TD>
    </TR>

<TR><TD VALIGN=BOTTOM COLSPAN=2>
```

```
    <FONT SIZE=+2><B><BR>Refund or Amount You Owe</B></FONT>
</TD></TR>

    <TR>
        <TD>
            62. If line 61 is more than line 54,
            subtract line 54 from line 61. This is the
            amount you <B>overpaid</B>
        </TD>
        <TD WIDTH=130 VALIGN=BOTTOM>
            <INPUT TYPE=text NAME="line62" SIZE=15
                   ONFOCUS="this.select();"
                   ONCHANGE="processOwe(this);">
        </TD>
    </TR>
    <TR>
        <TD>
            63. Amount of line 62 you want
            <B>Refunded to you</B>
        </TD>
        <TD WIDTH=130 VALIGN=BOTTOM>
            <INPUT TYPE=text NAME="line63" SIZE=15
                   ONFOCUS="this.select();"
                   ONCHANGE="processRefund(this);">
        </TD>
    </TR>
    <TR>
        <TD>
            64. Amount of line 62 you want <B>applied to
            your 1996 estimated tax</B>
        </TD>
        <TD WIDTH=130 VALIGN=BOTTOM>
            <INPUT TYPE=text NAME="line64" SIZE=15
                   ONFOCUS="this.select();"
                   ONCHANGE="processEstimate(this);">
        </TD>
    </TR>
    <TR>
        <TD>
            65. If line 54 is more than line 61, subtract
            line 61 from line 54. This is the <B>amount
            you owe</B>
        </TD>
        <TD WIDTH=130 VALIGN=BOTTOM>
            <INPUT TYPE=text NAME="line65" SIZE=15
                   ONFOCUS="this.select();"
                   ONCHANGE="processOwe(this);">
        </TD>
    </TR>
</TABLE>

</FORM>
</BODY>
</HTML>
```

Exercises

1. Go through this program on the CD-ROM and fill out your tax return.
2. Extend the tax return model to include other tax forms.

CHAPTER 24

Late-Breaking News

As with everything else in the computer industry, JavaScript also is going through many changes. This chapter updates you on some of the latest changes coming to JavaScript, some even having started during the time this book was being written.

Netscape Navigator

At the time of this writing, Netscape's new Navigator (code-named *Atlas*) was still in beta testing. Many of the scripts in the book have already been tested on the new Navigator 3.0 for compatibility. Except in some rare instances, the scripts worked just fine. Those rare instances were written in the text to reflect the problems.

> **Note:** If you'll recall from Chapter 2, "JavaScript's Uniqueness and Limitations," *beta testing* is the release of new software to a limited number of persons, strictly for testing purposes. The code may still be too unstable for general public use. I recommend that you always have the latest public release of Navigator. Your friends may all have the "latest beta," but if you're concerned about stability, you'd better not be using a beta for general use.

Frame Navigation

A new feature of Navigator 3.0 is the behavior of the Back navigation button. In Navigator 2.0, if you came upon a page that used frames, clicking the Back button would return you to the *referring page* (the page you came from), not the previous document in the frame (an irritant for people trying to navigate through online zines). To navigate back in a frame, you had to right-click and choose the Back in Frame option from a popup menu.

In Navigator 3.0, when you click a link that updates a frame, clicking the Back button returns you to the previous state of the frame.

MIME Types and Plug-Ins

I've very briefly covered MIME types in my discussions. MIME types represent standards for the Internet. If I have a plain page of text that has a MIME type of plain / text and your software supports the MIME plain / text type, we can share that page. HTML pages have a particular MIME type—plain / html. Figure 24.1 shows the MIME types installed in my personal copy of Navigator 2.0.

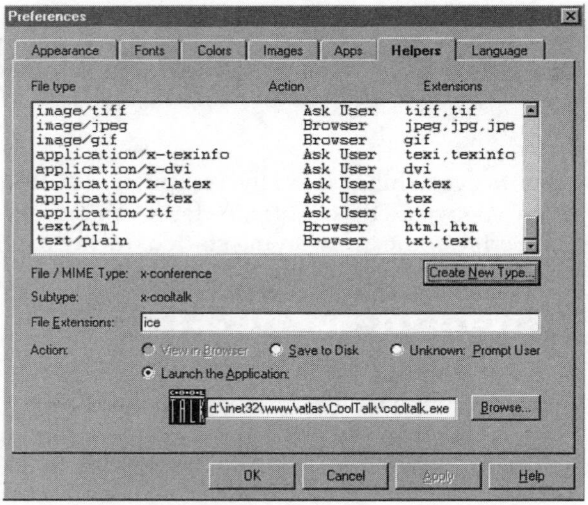

Figure 24.1
Example of MIME types supported by Navigator.

Netscape mentions helper apps and plug-ins. *Helper apps*, such as the RealAudio sound software, run outside the Netscape environment (they pop up their own window of controls). *Plug-ins*, such as the QuickTime plug-in, directly influence the content of the current browser window (their controls appear to be embedded directly into the document).

Netscape knows which helper or plug-in to activate based on the relationship established between MIME types and the associated application. If you click a link to newsound.au, Netscape reads the associations and sees that the Netscape Audio Player handles this type of file. You can use the associations to "create" your own MIME types.

For example, my company uses Microsoft Word as its primary word processor. Because I want to distribute the company's documents via a Web server, I create links to the .DOC files. Navigator sees the .DOC file and tries to load it into the browser window. If this were a plain-text file, this would be tolerable. However,

Word .DOC files contain markup language and don't view very well in the Navigator browser. One workaround would be to download the application to a local file, start Word, and then open the file—a bit of a production, wouldn't you say?

So let's try a different approach. I'll create an association between .DOC files and Word. If all the user needs to do is read the file, it would be better to use the Microsoft Word reader helper app (which is smaller and faster). Now all Netscape handles is the downloading of the file, the opening of Word (or its reader), and the passing of the file to the application.

But what if the visitor doesn't have Word or the Word reader software? Can you warn him before he downloads it? Yes, you could put a warning on the page that links to the file, but would this really slow them down?

I discuss the `navigator` object in Chapter 8, "JavaScript Objects." The Navigator authors have added two new properties to the `navigator` object with Navigator 3.0.

The new properties, `mimeTypes` and `plugins`, are both arrays. The `mimeTypes` property is an array of all MIME types supported by the client. Each element of the array is a `mimeTypes`, which has properties for its type, description, and file extensions. The `plugins` property is also an array of all plug-ins now installed on the client. Each element of the array is a `plugins` type, which has properties for its name and description, as well as a subarray of `mimeTypes` supported by that plug-in.

As an example, the Shockwave for Director plug-in by Macromedia (**http://www.macromedia.com/**) is popular for placing multimedia in a Web page. If a user has Shockwave installed, one of the entries in `plugins` will have the `name` property set to `Shockwave`. I could use a function like the following,

```
function pluginInstalled(strPlugin) {
  for(var i=0; i<navigator.plugins.length; i++) {
    if (navigator.plugins[i].name.indexOf(strPlugin) != -1)
    {
      return true;
    }
  }
  return false;
}
```

to check for the presence of the plug-in:

```
if(pluginInstalled("Shockwave")) {
   // Shockwave's installed!  Go ahead and load the file!
} else {
   // Shockwave's NOT installed!  Warn the user!
}
```

Now when users visit my page—provided they're using Navigator 3.0 (but I can check for that also)—I can verify that they have the correct software to handle the file my server is about to ship to them. But wait! With the dynamic creation of HTML, I can check for the appropriate software *before* users even know there's a file to download. If the software is installed, I create a page with the appropriate links to my files. If it isn't installed, I create a page with a link to the helper app or plug-in.

Table Colors

Navigator 3.0 also supports separate backgrounds for each table cell, similar to the HTML extensions supported by Microsoft's Internet Explorer. You can specify that a background color be used when displaying table cells. To specify a table background color, use the `bgcolor` attribute. Nested tables inherit background colors. The `bgcolor` attribute specifies one of the supported color names and can be used with the following tags: `<table>`, `<td>`, `<th>`, and `<tr>`.

Here's an example of how to use the bgcolor attribute within a table:

```
<TABLE ALIGN=RIGHT BORDER=1 WIDTH=20%>
 <CAPTION CENTER Valign=BOTTOM>Color Cells</CAPTION>
 <TR><TD BGCOLOR=#ffdddd>One Color</TD></TR>
 <TR><TD BGCOLOR=#ccffff>Another Color</TD></TR>
</TABLE>
```

Microsoft Internet Explorer

Microsoft, as normally is the case, is being very quiet about its plans for JavaScript's future. As you've seen in this book, Microsoft supports JavaScript with its Internet Explorer 3.0 browser. Only Microsoft knows what new features are proposed for its implementation of JavaScript.

However, Microsoft is pushing for the use of the <embed> tag, which currently can be used to call up plug-ins or helper apps to handle specific files. The software giant would like to see the <embed> tag replace the <script> tag. I have to agree with Microsoft on this, because <embed> already uses the SRC parameter for pulling information from other files. Also, if Microsoft helps push a tag for embedding objects into HTML, it will force other browsers to include embedded object support.

Wrapping It Up

By now, you should have a fairly stable understanding of JavaScript. Although this is only an introductory-level book, you've seen some intermediate and advanced material as well. I hope to see your site listed on the Web soon.

Appendixes

What's on the CD?

This book includes a CD-ROM that contains the following:

- All the code from the examples in the text
- The complete text of Que's *Special Edition Using JavaScript*
- Other tools and utilities

The CD has been assembled around an HTML interface; simply load the file INDEX.HTM into your favorite browser and follow the appropriate links. For example, in Netscape, open the File menu and choose Open File (or press Ctrl+O). In the Open dialog box, choose the drive corresponding to your CD-ROM drive, select the INDEX.HTM file from the root directory of the CD-ROM, and click Open.

The following sections describe the specific organization and contents of the CD-ROM.

Code Examples

The code examples are in directories according to the chapter they appear in. For example, all the code from Chapter 12 is contained in a CHAP12 directory. The actual code snippets are contained in separate HTML files within these directories and are named according to the order they appear in the chapter. For example, the third code listing in Chapter 12 will be stored in the following file:

\CHAP12\CODE12_3.HTM

To see the code in action, click the appropriate link in the INDEX.HTM file. To look at or use the code, copy the appropriate file from the CD into your HTML editor and cut and paste into a new file.

> **Tip:** To see the actual code source in your browser, open Netscape's View menu and choose Document Source, or open Microsoft Internet Explorer's View menu and choose Source.

Special Edition Using JavaScript

The entire text of Que's complete reference to JavaScript is on the enclosed CD-ROM. This text will be useful as a reference to the JavaScript language after you learn the fundamentals.

To view the text of the book, load the INDEX.HTM file from the CD and follow the *Special Edition Using JavaScript* link.

Useful Tools and Utilities

The CD-ROM also contains several tools and utilities that are mentioned in the text of this book.

- *W3e* is a powerful and friendly HTML editor.
- *Map This!* is a utility that allows you to easily create image maps for your HTML pages.
- *Cool Edit* is an audio editor for assembling audio content for your HTML pages.
- *Crescendo!* is a Netscape plug-in that allows background playing of MIDI files on your HTML pages.

To use these utilities, load INDEX.HTM from the CD-ROM and click the appropriate link to copy the application to your local hard drive. Unzip the file or run the executable program and follow the instructions contained in the individual packages.

APPENDIX B

Reserved Words

The following is a list of words that can't be used in naming variables in JavaScript. These words have special duties in JavaScript.

```
abstract      float         public
boolean       for           return
break         function      short
byte          goto          static
case          if            super
catch         implements    switch
char          import        synchronized
class         in            this
const         instanceof    throw
continue      int           throws
default       interface     transient
do            long          true
double        native        try
else          new           var
extends       null          void
false         package       while
final         private       with
finally       protected
```

APPENDIX C

Colors

The following table lists the predefined JavaScript colors. The official name is given, along with the decimal equivalents of the red, green, and blue components, and the hexadecimal RGB code.

You might find the decimal component numbers helpful when working in a paint program that supports the RGB color model. Simply enter the color values in the palette to create a matching color. The hexadecimal number is valuable when assigning background colors to your documents.

Color	*Red*	*Green*	*Blue*	*Hexadecimal Triplet*
`aliceblue`	240	248	255	f0f8ff
`antiquewhite`	250	235	215	faebd7
`aqua`	0	255	255	00ffff
`aquamarine`	127	255	212	7fffd4
`azure`	240	255	255	f0ffff
`beige`	245	245	220	f5f5dc
`bisque`	255	228	196	ffe4c4
`black`	0	0	0	000000
`blanchedalmond`	255	235	205	ffebcd
`blue`	0	0	255	0000ff

continues

continued

Color	*Red*	*Green*	*Blue*	*Hexadecimal Triplet*
blueviolet	138	43	226	8a2be2
brown	165	42	42	a52a2a
burlywood	222	184	135	deb887
cadetblue	95	158	160	5f9ea0
chartreuse	127	255	0	7fff00
chocolate	210	105	30	d2691e
coral	255	127	80	ff7f50
cornflowerblue	100	149	237	6495ed
cornsilk	255	248	220	fff8dc
crimson	220	20	60	dc143c
cyan	0	255	255	00ffff
darkblue	0	0	139	00008b
darkcyan	0	139	139	008b8b
darkgoldenrod	184	134	11	b8860b
darkgray	169	169	169	a9a9a9
darkgreen	0	100	0	006400
darkkhaki	189	183	107	bdb76b
darkmagenta	139	0	139	8b008b
darkolivegreen	85	107	47	556b2f
darkorange	255	140	0	ff8c00
darkorchid	153	50	204	9932cc
darkred	139	0	0	8b0000
darksalmon	233	150	122	e9967a
darkseagreen	143	188	143	8fbc8f
darkslateblue	72	61	139	483d8b
darkslategray	47	79	79	2f4f4f
darkturquoise	0	206	209	00ced1

Color	*Red*	*Green*	*Blue*	*Hexadecimal Triplet*
`darkviolet`	148	0	211	9400d3
`deeppink`	255	20	147	ff1493
`deepskyblue`	0	191	255	00bfff
`dimgray`	105	105	105	696969
`dodgerblue`	30	144	255	1e90ff
`firebrick`	178	34	34	b22222
`floralwhite`	255	250	240	fffaf0
`forestgreen`	34	139	34	228b22
`fuchsia`	255	0	255	ff00ff
`gainsboro`	220	220	220	dcdcdc
`ghostwhite`	248	248	255	f8f8ff
`gold`	255	215	0	ffd700
`goldenrod`	218	165	32	daa520
`gray`	128	128	128	808080
`green`	0	128	0	008000
`greenyellow`	173	255	47	adff2f
`honeydew`	240	255	240	f0fff0
`hotpink`	255	105	180	ff69b4
`indianred`	205	92	92	cd5c5c
`indigo`	75	0	130	4b0082
`ivory`	255	255	240	fffff0
`khaki`	240	230	140	f0e68c
`lavender`	230	230	250	e6e6fa
`lavenderblush`	255	240	245	fff0f5
`lawngreen`	124	252	0	7cfc00
`lemonchiffon`	255	250	205	fffacd

continues

continued

Color	*Red*	*Green*	*Blue*	*Hexadecimal Triplet*
`lightblue`	173	216	230	add8e6
`lightcoral`	240	128	128	f08080
`lightcyan`	224	255	255	e0ffff
`lightgoldenrodyellow`	250	250	210	fafad2
`lightgreen`	144	238	144	90ee90
`lightgrey`	211	211	211	d3d3d3
`lightpink`	255	182	193	ffb6c1
`lightsalmon`	255	160	122	ffa07a
`lightseagreen`	32	178	170	20b2aa
`lightskyblue`	135	206	250	87cefa
`lightslategray`	119	136	153	778899
`lightsteelblue`	176	196	222	b0c4de
`lightyellow`	255	255	224	ffffe0
`lime`	0	255	0	00ff00
`limegreen`	50	205	50	32cd32
`linen`	250	240	230	faf0e6
`magenta`	255	0	255	ff00ff
`maroon`	128	0	0	800000
`mediumaquamarine`	102	205	170	66cdaa
`mediumblue`	0	0	205	0000cd
`mediumorchid`	186	85	211	ba55d3
`mediumpurple`	147	112	219	9370db
`mediumseagreen`	60	179	113	3cb371
`mediumslateblue`	123	104	238	7b68ee
`mediumspringgreen`	0	250	154	00fa9a
`mediumturquoise`	72	209	204	48d1cc
`mediumvioletred`	199	21	133	c71585

Color	Red	Green	Blue	Hexadecimal Triplet
midnightblue	25	25	112	191970
mintcream	245	255	250	f5fffa
mistyrose	255	228	225	ffe4e1
moccasin	255	228	181	ffe4b5
navajowhite	255	222	173	ffdead
navy	0	0	128	000080
oldlace	253	245	230	fdf5e6
olive	128	128	0	808000
olivedrab	107	142	35	6b8e23
orange	255	165	0	ffa500
orangered	255	69	0	ff4500
orchid	218	112	214	da70d6
palegoldenrod	238	232	170	eee8aa
palegreen	152	251	152	98fb98
paleturquoise	175	238	238	afeeee
palevioletred	219	112	147	db7093
papayawhip	255	239	213	ffefd5
peachpuff	255	218	185	ffdab9
peru	205	133	63	cd853f
pink	255	192	203	ffc0cb
plum	221	160	221	dda0dd
powderblue	176	224	230	b0e0e6
purple	128	0	128	800080
red	255	0	0	ff0000
rosybrown	188	143	143	bc8f8f
royalblue	65	105	225	4169e1

continues

continued

Color	*Red*	*Green*	*Blue*	*Hexadecimal Triplet*
saddlebrown	139	69	19	8b4513
salmon	250	128	114	fa8072
sandybrown	244	164	96	f4a460
seagreen	46	139	87	2e8b57
seashell	255	245	238	fff5ee
sienna	160	82	45	a0522d
silver	192	192	192	c0c0c0
skyblue	135	206	235	87ceeb
slateblue	106	90	205	6a5acd
slategray	112	128	144	708090
snow	255	250	250	fffafa
springgreen	0	255	127	00ff7f
steelblue	70	130	180	4682b4
tan	210	180	140	d2b48c
teal	0	128	128	008080
thistle	216	191	216	d8bfd8
tomato	255	99	71	ff6347
turquoise	64	224	208	40e0d0
violet	238	130	238	ee82ee
wheat	245	223	179	f5deb3
white	255	255	255	ffffff
whitesmoke	245	245	245	f5f5f5
yellow	255	255	0	ffff00
yellowgreen	154	205	50	9acd32

APPENDIX D

Answers to the Review Questions

Chapter 1

1. *What is JavaScript? What is it not?*

JavaScript is a scripting language, a type of programming language that is interpreted, not compiled. It's object-based, with objects built into the language. It's platform-independent and runs on Macintosh, Windows, and UNIX alike. It's also event-driven and responds to user input (such as mouse clicks and keystrokes). Finally, it's secure and doesn't permit reading or writing to the user's computer or the server.

JavaScript is *not* Java, Perl, LiveWire, or any other language that provides server-side control of the flow of information.

2. *What browsers currently support JavaScript?*

Netscape Navigator 2.0, Navigator 3.0, and Internet Explorer 3.0.

3. *What is Java?*

Java is a full-blown, object-oriented programming language that extends both the client and server capabilities of the Web.

4. *How are JavaScript and Java similar? How are they different?*

Java and JavaScript are both built on the principles of object programming. JavaScript, however, is object-*based* and doesn't have the advanced object-*oriented* methodologies of Java. Whereas JavaScript is interpreted, a Java program must be compiled before it can be used.

5. *What's the difference between object-oriented and object-based?*

An object-based language is a special category of object-oriented languages and has predefined objects already built into the language itself.

6. *What is an event? How does this relate to JavaScript?*

An event is "something that happens." Within the context of JavaScript, events are things that the user does when interacting with a Web page, such as mouse clicks, text entry, and keystrokes. Loading and unloading pages and submitting forms are also events.

7. *What is a scripting language?*

A scripting language is a type of programming language that's interpreted (by a special program called an *interpreter*) rather than compiled into the native format of the computer. Scripting languages appear (even in final form) as "pseudo-English," with the interpreter handling the job of translating the English-like statements into a form the computer can understand.

8. *What is LiveWire?*

LiveWire is a collection of tools that allow a Webmaster running the Netscape FastTrack Server to more easily maintain the server. It includes a browser/editor (Navigator Gold) and the capability to create JavaScript scripts that run on the server.

Chapter 2

1. *What makes JavaScript unique among current Web technologies?*

JavaScript makes it possible for Web designers to create dynamic pages (pages that change with time or user selections) without having to resort to CGI or other server-side programming.

2. *What's a plug-in?*

A plug-in is a special program that hooks (plugs) into the browser. It's designed to manage a specific type of data (such as a sound or animation file) that the browser wasn't programmed to handle. Because it's plugged into the browser, it makes the data it's handling appear to be part of the document (instead of a new window being opened just to display the new information).

3. *What browsers support JavaScript? What are some of the browsers that don't?*

JavaScript is currently supported by Netscape Navigator 2.0, Navigator 3.0, and Internet Explorer 3.0. Other popular browsers that *don't* support JavaScript include Mosaic, WinWeb, AOL, and Lynx, to name a few.

4. *What's an alpha release? a beta release?*

When a program is first put together and released for people to "kick the tires," it's called an alpha. Alpha releases are usually very buggy and will probably change greatly in appearance and behavior over time.

After most of the bugs are eliminated and the product is considered relatively stable, it's called a beta. Beta releases are usually close enough to the final version that the only things that might change are the fixing of internal bugs and smoothing out the rough spots.

5. *What's an example of a platform-related limitation of JavaScript?*

Under JavaScript 2.0, the `random()` method of the `Math` object is supported only on the UNIX platform, and generates an error in Windows and Macintosh.

6. *How is JavaScript a "secure" environment?*

JavaScript can't read from or write to the user's local hard disk. Nor can it transmit information about the user's private files back to the server or another e-mail account.

7. *What hardware do you need to run JavaScript?*

Any system capable of running a browser that supports JavaScript (such as Navigator or Internet Explorer 3.0) will also run JavaScript.

8. *What's a good set of software packages for a "JavaScript starter kit"?*

A JavaScript-enabled browser, a simple text editor, and a good graphics program are an excellent trio of starter applications for JavaScript development.

Chapter 3

1. *What HTML tag is used to identify JavaScript? What is its syntax?*

In an HTML document, JavaScript is bracketed by a `<SCRIPT>...</SCRIPT>` tag pair. The `<SCRIPT>` tag takes two attributes: the `LANGUAGE` attribute to identify the scripting language, and the `SRC` attribute for loading the source from another file.

2. *Why does the `<SCRIPT>` tag need the `LANGUAGE` attribute?*

With the appearance of Microsoft's own scripting language, VBScript, the `LANGUAGE` attribute becomes necessary for the browser to determine whether the scripting language inside the `<SCRIPT>` tag is one it can interpret.

3. *What will the* `SRC` *attribute be used for?*

   It will allow JavaScript source code to reside in an external file that will be loaded when the page loads. This will allow for "libraries" of common routines to be easily created and maintained.

4. *What does* `document.write()` *do?*

   `document.write()` sends the text within the parentheses to the HTML document, as though it were typed inside the `<BODY>` tag of the document.

5. *How can you get input from the user with JavaScript?*

   You can get input from the user through two different built-in JavaScript dialogs: `confirm()` and `prompt()`. The `confirm()` dialog can get yes/no answers from the user, whereas the `prompt()` dialog can retrieve a complete string.

6. *How can you hide your code from browsers that don't support JavaScript?*

   You can hide your code from non-JavaScript browsers by placing `<!--` immediately after the `<SCRIPT>` tag, and `// -->` immediately before the `</SCRIPT>` tag. This places the code inside a comment that the browser ignores (but the JavaScript interpreter doesn't).

7. *What have you learned about printing?*

   There are several different ways to answer this question. The key point to remember, though, is that Navigator 2.0 doesn't properly print pages that are built with JavaScript, whereas Internet Explorer 3.0 does.

Chapter 4

1. *What is an event?*

   An *event* is "something that happens." In the context of JavaScript, events are anything the user does when interacting with a document, such as clicking with the mouse, pressing a button, entering/editing text, and submitting forms.

2. *How many events are now available to JavaScript programmers?*

   JavaScript makes nine different events available to programmers: `OnClick`, `OnMouseOver`, `OnSubmit`, `OnLoad`, `OnUnload`, `OnSelect`, `OnFocus`, `OnChange`, and `OnBlur`.

3. *The* `OnClick` *handler can be applied to how many types of objects?*

   `OnClick` is supported by three types of objects: links, check boxes, and buttons.

4. *How do you know whether an object is in focus?*

Focus is shown by the object being outlined on the page, or by the insertion cursor flashing (in the case of a text field).

5. *Where would you use an `OnUnload` event handler?*

Whenever you need to do something just before a user leaves a page, such as disconnect a timer or display a warning message.

6. *The `OnSubmit` handler can be used with which object type?*

It's supported by the `Form` object.

7. *Which represents the more economical event handler—`OnBlur` or `OnChange`?*

The `OnChange` handler is more economical, because it would be called only when a field's value changes. `OnBlur`, on the other hand, is called every time a field loses focus.

8. *What danger can there be in using the `OnFocus` event handler improperly?*

If a dialog (such as `alert()`) is used within the `OnFocus` code, a "lock-up" can occur because focus is lost when the dialog appears and is restored when the dialog is closed (thus refiring the handler). The only way to get out of this loop is to shut down the browser.

9. *What could you use the `OnSubmit` event for?*

`OnSubmit` allows you to check the validity of form data before it's sent to the server. If the data isn't valid, you can return a value of `false` to prevent the form from being submitted (a value of `true` would submit the form).

Chapter 5

1. *Name three characters that aren't permitted in a variable's name.*

With the exception of the underscore, punctuation isn't allowed in a variable name, so you could have named any three of these characters: `+ - \ ¦ * / ( ) [ ] < > "` or `'`.

2. *Where do you declare a global variable? a local variable?*

Global variables are declared outside the body of all functions and are available to any function that needs them. Local variables are declared inside the function body and are only "seen."

3. *How many data types does JavaScript support?*

JavaScript supports numeric, logical (Boolean), string, and null data types.

4. *Give an example of a special character you can use within a string.*

   Special characters are those that are converted into something else, such as `\n` (newline), `\r` (carriage return), `\t` (tab), `\f` (formfeed), and `\b` (backspace).

Chapter 6

1. *What are the three kinds of expressions?*

   Arithmetic, logical (Boolean), and string.

2. *What is an operator? an operand?*

   Operators are special symbols that control how an expression is to be evaluated (such as `+`, `-`, `/`, and `*`). Operands are pretty much anything else in an expression (such as variables, constants, and other expressions).

3. *What is a Boolean?*

   A "Boolean" is something that can have only one of two possible values: true or false.

4. *What are unary operators? binary operators?*

   Unary operators require a single operand, either before or after the operator. A binary operator requires two operands, one before the operator and one after.

5. *Name some of the different types of operators. Give an example of each.*

   Arithmetic operators: `+`, `-`, `*`, `/`, `%`, `--`, `++`, and `-` (negation)

   Comparison operators: `==`, `!=`, `>`, `<`, `>=`, and `<=`

   The string operator: `+`

   Logical operators: `&&`, `||`, and `!`

   Bitwise operators: `&`, `|`, `^`, `~`, `<<`, `>>`, and `>>>`

6. *Give an example of a "shorthand" operator.*

   A shorthand operator combines an operator and an equate. Some examples are `+=`, `-=`, `*=`, `<<=`, `|=`, and `&=`.

7. *How do comparison operators handle strings?*

   Comparison operators try to alphabetize the two strings being compared. A string is less than (<) another string if it would come before it alphabetically. Likewise, a string that's greater than (>) another is one that comes after it alphabetically.

8. *What is operator precedence? Give an example of how it works.*

Operator precedence controls the order in which operations are performed on a complex (multioperator) expression. For example, 5 * 4 + 3 would evaluate to 23, not 60 (because multiplication has higher precedence than addition).

9. *What is a statement? a reserved word?*

A statement is a sequence of keywords, operators, operands, and/or expressions, terminated by a semicolon (`;`). A reserved word is a word that's used internally by JavaScript (such as `if`, `return`, and `function`). Reserved words can't be used for variable or function names.

10. *What are the four types of statements in JavaScript? Give an example of each.*

The four types of statements are as follows:

- Comments:

```
// this is a comment
```

- Conditional:

```
if(a > 3) {
  b = 5;
}
```

- Loop:

```
for(var i=0; i<10; i++) {
  document.write("Hello");
}
```

- Object manipulation:

```
var myDate = new Date();
```

Chapter 7

1. *What's the definition of an object?*

An object is an element in a piece of software that has properties and specific behavior.

2. *How does inheritance work?*

Inheritance is the obtaining of certain characteristics from an object's class.

3. *What is "data hiding"? How does it work?*

Data hiding involves restricting the access to the properties of an object through methods only (rather than direct manipulation of the properties).

4. *Why are classes important?*

   Classes allow the programmer to reuse objects.

5. *Why do subclasses exist?*

   Subclasses exist to further divide the classes into more specific instances.

Chapter 8

1. *What are the properties of the `navigator` object?*

   They are `appName`, `appVersion`, `appCodename`, and `userAgent`.

2. *What are some of the objects that are part of a form?*

   Some form objects include `select`, `text`, `textarea`, `password`, `button`, `radio`, and `checkbox`.

3. *How can you store information in a form without displaying it to the user?*

   By using a `hidden` object.

4. *What's one use for the `submit` object (and the `OnSubmit` event)?*

   The verification of data within the form before actually sending it to the server.

Chapter 9

1. *Is it possible to edit the values in the anchors array?*

   The values in the anchors array are read-only and can't be changed.

2. *What array property defines the size of the array?*

   The `length` property holds the length or size of the array in an integer value.

3. *What result is returned if a location greater than the array's size is queried?*

   The interpreter returns the value `<undefined>`.

4. *What are examples of built-in JavaScript arrays?*

   Some of the built-in JavaScript arrays are `anchors[]` and `frames[]`.

Chapter 10

1. *What is the range of numbers valid for use by the `sqrt()` method?*

   Any positive number is valid.

2. *What is the return value of the `log()` method if the argument is a negative number?*

Given a negative number, `log()` returns 0.

3. *What can the `floor()` method be used for?*

To truncate a decimal into its integer component.

4. *Can the `random()` method be used on a Windows NT system?*

Under JavaScript 2.0, no (it generates an error). With JavaScript 3.0 (meaning using Navigator 3.0), `random()` will work.

5. *Explain the differences between the `round()`, `ceil()`, and `floor()` methods.*

`round()` rounds a decimal to the nearest integer (either up or down, depending on the decimal). `floor()` always rounds down (the `floor()` of 3.5 is 3, but the `floor()` of –3.5 is –4), whereas `ceil()` always rounds up (the `ceil()` of 3.5 is 4, but the `ceil()` of –3.5 is 3).

6. *Name the output ranges for the six trigonometry methods.*

`sin()` outputs a value between –1 and +1.

`cos()` outputs a value between –1 and +1.

`tan()` has no limit for its output.

`asin()` outputs a value between $-\pi/2$ and $+\pi/2$.

`acos()` outputs a value between 0 and π.

`atan()` outputs a value between $-\pi/2$ and $+\pi/2$.

7. *Why does `Math.sin(Math.asin(radians))` return the value that it does?*

Although this should return the value *`radians`*, it's slightly off because of the computer's limited capability to handle decimal numbers.

Chapter 11

1. *What are the six types of string methods?*

Navigational, size, positional, attribute, manipulation, and case.

2. *How can you draw the user's attention to part of your site?*

By displaying text that's a different color, a different size, or blinking.

3. *What are some of the methods that allow you to control the visual display of text?*

Some of the manipulation methods are `big()`, `small()`, `bold()`, `italics()`, `fontcolor()`, and `fontsize()`.

4. *How can you convert the case of a string?*

By using `toLowerCase()` or `toUpperCase()`.

5. *What is an example use for a fixed-pitch font?*

To display source code.

6. *How can you "extract" part of a string from a larger string?*

By using `substring()`.

7. *What is an anchor? a link?*

An anchor is a tagged element in an HTML document that can be referenced through an URL with the hash character (#). A link is a special type of anchor that points to another document (or somewhere else in the same document).

Chapter 12

1. *What are the three types of date methods?*

Set, get, and conversion.

2. *What are two examples of the use of date methods?*

There are many possible answers to this question. Two possibilities are

- To display the current date and time on a page
- To compute the amount of time until a holiday

3. *What is a locale?*

A locale is "where the user is." With respect to date objects, it means the time zone the user is in.

4. *What is GMT? What's another name for it?*

Greenwich Mean Time is also called Coordinated Universal Time, or UTC.

5. *How do you convert a date to local time? to GMT?*

The `toLocaleString()` creates a local time string, whereas the `toGMTString()` converts to GMT.

6. *Why would you want to convert a date to GMT?*

By using GMT for all internal date computations, you avoid computing mistakes when computations span time zones.

Chapter 13

1. *What are the three "simple" windows you can create with JavaScript?*

   The `alert()`, `confirm()`, and `prompt()` dialog boxes.

2. *What are the possible values returned by the `confirm()` method?*

   The `confirm()` method returns a value of either true or false because it's a Boolean operator.

3. *True or false: A new window can be created from any other window.*

   This is actually a trick question. If you count the `alert()`, `prompt()`, and `confirm()` dialogs as windows, the answer is false. A new window can't be created from any other window because some windows are used to display messages only. However, ignoring the three dialogs, the answer is true. Any browser window can be made to create new windows (with JavaScript).

4. *What kind of response could be held in the variable containing the results from a `prompt()` method?*

   Numeric, alphanumeric, or text (in short, there is no restriction on type).

5. *What are the possible options facing a user when an alert window appears?*

   There are no options. All the user can do is choose OK.

6. *What may be considered the most critical window method?*

   The `open()` method is probably the most critical window method because it sets a window's attributes.

7. *What features can you control when you create a window?*

   Some of the features are `toolbar`, `location`, `status`, `menubar`, `scrollbars`, `resizable`, `width`, and `height`.

Chapter 14

1. *How do you access the browser's history list?*

   Through the `history` object.

2. *What are three different objects that can take user input?*

   Possible answers include `text`, `textarea`, `password`, `select`, or any other object that's part of a `form`.

3. *What are the components of a `select` object?*

   `length`, `name`, `options[]` (an array), and `selectedIndex`.

4. *How do you define a* `select` *object where you can select more than one option?*

By including the `MULTIPLE` attribute in the `<SELECT>` tag.

5. *What are three functions that can be used to convert a string to a numeric representation?*

`parseInt()`, `parseFloat()`, and `eval()`.

6. *How do you convert from ASCII to characters?*

By using the `escape()` method.

7. *True or false: System functions vary depending on which operating system they are executed under.*

False. System functions will *not* vary depending on which operating system they're executed under because they're part of JavaScript and made to run on multiple platforms.

8. *True or false: The* `length` *function applies only to the* `select` *object.*

False. The `length` function applies to *many* objects.

9. *Describe the operation of the* `escape()` *function.*

The `escape()` function returns the escape (ASCII) value of a character entered between its parentheses.

10. *How does the value returned by the* `unescape()` *function relate to the* `escape()` *function?*

The `unescape()` function returns the character of an ASCII value produced by the `escape()` function.

11. *True or false:* `NaN` *will be a return value that occurs only under a Windows operating system.*

False. `NaN` will *not* be a return value that occurs under a Windows operating system. Only the UNIX platform returns `NaN` (all others return 0 instead).

12. *What are the three properties of a* `password` *object?*

The three properties are `defaultValue`, `name`, and `value`.

13. `blur()`*,* `focus()`*, and* `select()` *are all methods of which objects?*

They are methods for the `password`, `select`, `text`, and `textarea` objects.

Chapter 15

1. *What is a property?*

A property is a variable attached to a JavaScript object that defines a particular attribute of the object.

2. *What properties contain information about a document?*

   `alinkColor`, `anchors[]`, `bgColor`, `cookie`, `fgColor`, `forms[]`, `lastModified`, `linkColor`, `links[]`, `location`, `referrer`, `title`, and `vlinkColor`.

3. *How do you reference the elements of a form?*

   By the name specified with the `NAME` attribute of the particular object (as in `form.objText`).

4. *How can you control the color of a document?*

   With the `bgColor`, `alinkColor`, `fgColor`, `linkColor`, and `vlinkColor` properties.

5. *True or false: All the properties of objects can be changed using JavaScript at any time—that's why JavaScript is such a powerful language.*

   False. While most properties can be changed, not all can be changed once a page is loaded.

6. *True or false: `alinkColor` and `linkColor` are the same property.*

   False. `alinkColor` specifies the color of the *active* (clicked) link, whereas `linkColor` specifies the color of a *normal* (not selected) link.

7. *When you set the background color using an HTML tag, you can change it by using which property?*

   By using the `bgColor` property.

Chapter 16

1. *How are cookies transported?*

   They're transported in the HTTP headers, which contain other information useful for the communications between the server and the client.

2. *What are the only two required attributes of a cookie?*

   The `name` and `value` attributes.

3. *Which system reads the cookie—the server or the client?*

   The client system reads the cookie from storage and delivers it to the server.

4. *Where is the cookie stored?*

   Cookies are stored in a file called cookies.txt found in Navigator's \program subdirectory.

5. *What are the minimum number of cookies a client should be ready to receive?*

   A client should be prepared to receive 300 cookies at any one time. However, only 20 cookies are permitted from each domain.

6. *Can cookie names have spaces in them?*

   No. The same limits imposed on naming variables apply to cookies also.

7. *Can a page loaded from the HTTP server at www.gatech.com set a cookie with a* `DOMAIN` *attribute valid for only www.psu.com?*

   No. The `DOMAIN` attribute sets the limits of the cookie.

Chapter 17

1. *What's a marquee?*

   Our working definition of a marquee is a location on-screen with scrolling text.

2. *Name a problem with the status bar marquees.*

   Status bar marquees present two primary problems—they're resource-intensive, and they obscure real Navigator messages.

3. *How are marquees implemented with Internet Explorer?*

   Internet Explorer uses the `<MARQUEE>` HTML tag to identify marquees.

4. *What line of code determines whether you create a form-based marquee or a status bar marquee?*

```
window.status = scroll.out
```

Chapter 19

1. *There are a few cases in JavaScript where you multiply a string by 1. Why is this necessary?*

   JavaScript variables are *loosely typed,* which means that you don't have to associate a variable with a specific type. It also means that you can have a variable that you think is an integer, but somewhere during its life becomes a string.

   When a field's value is grabbed from a text field of a form, it's always grabbed as a string. If, however, you multiply it by an integer, it will be treated as an integer in that calculation and will become an integer. Because 1 is the identity element for multiplication, the variable will be converted to an integer but will have the same value.

2. *Why is JavaScript a preferable choice over Java or CGI to perform form validation?*

   The answer to this question is actually twofold. This chapter discussed CGI, and I left Java for you to figure out yourself. JavaScript is a preferable choice over CGI because the JavaScript validation is performed client-side. Therefore, the user isn't forced to wait while a server-side CGI checks over his input.

Java actually could be used in this situation, but it would take much more time to develop and could make the form more confusing. Users are very familiar with HTML forms, and if you were to develop a Java solution, your page could look very different. Users are more likely to deal with a form if they understand it fully.

Chapter 20

1. *What is a control panel?*

For our purposes, a control panel is a window on-screen that contains controls used to manipulate variables and settings in other windows.

2. *What are the steps you need to perform to create a control panel?*

To use a control panel, you must use variables rather than hard code within all your other windows so that the values can be changed.

3. *How can you create a custom dialog from within JavaScript?*

By opening a new window (with the `open()` method), specifying its size, and turning off all other browser features (such as status and menu bars, toolbars, and scroll bars). Then create a form in the window with the fields and buttons you need.

4. *What JavaScript object gives you access to the list of URLs the user has visited? How do you move through this list?*

The "history list" is available through the `history` object. You use the `go()`, `forward()`, and `back()` methods to move through it.

Chapter 21

1. *True or false: It is possible to play multiple sound files of different formats at the same time.*

True.

2. *True or false: The Crescendo! plug-in will spawn a new window in order to play a MIDI file.*

True.

3. *True or false: Once a sound file has started playing through Crescendo!, it can't be stopped until a new one is loaded.*

   False. Once a sound file has started playing through Crescendo!, you can stop it by using the control panel.

4. *The control panel for the Crescendo! plug-in contains which options/commands for controlling the sound file?*

   Play and Stop.

5. *To access the control panel for Crescendo!, you must do what?*

   Right-click.

6. *Explain how to set a MIDI file so it plays in the background of a page.*

   Use the `<embed src="filename">...</embed>` tag pair.

Chapter 22

1. *What are the main components of the code for the calculator?*

   The calculator consists of functions that manipulate the `total.value`.

2. *Before you perform math operations on user-entered fields, what must you do to the field data?*

   Make certain that the field is numeric by using `eval()`, `parseInt()`, or `parseFloat()`.

APPENDIX E

Common Internet MIME Types

Table E.1 lists the more commonly used MIME types. MIME types and how they relate to plug-ins are discussed in Chapter 21, "Sights and Sounds." To see what MIME types are associated with your browser, you need to check your helper application's settings.

Table E.1 Content Types and Subtypes

Type	*Subtype*
text	plain richtext enriched tab-separated-values
multipart	mixed alternative digest parallel appledouble header-set
message	rfc822 partial external-body news

continues

Table E.1 Continued

Type	*Subtype*
application	octet-stream
	postscript
	oda
	atomicmail
	andrew-inset
	slate
	wita
	dec-dx
	dca-rft
	activemessage
	rtf
	applefile
	mac-binhex40
	news-message-id
	news-transmission
	wordperfect5.1
	pdf
	zip
	macwriteii
	msword
	remote-printing
image	jpeg
	gif
	ief
	tiff
audio	basic
video	mpeg
	quicktime

Index

Symbols

A

D

E

F

G

H

I

J

K

L

N

P

Q-R

S

T

U

X-Y-Z

Complete and Return this Card for a *FREE* Computer Book Catalog

Thank you for purchasing this book! You have purchased a superior computer book written expressly for your needs. To continue to provide the kind of up-to-date, pertinent coverage you've come to expect from us, we need to hear from you. Please take a minute to complete and return this self-addressed, postage-paid form. In return, we'll send you a free catalog of all our computer books on topics ranging from word processing to programming and the internet.

☐ Mrs. ☐ Ms. ☐ Dr. ☐

ne (first) ☐☐☐☐☐☐☐☐☐☐☐ (M.I.) ☐ (last) ☐☐☐☐☐☐☐☐☐☐☐☐☐☐☐

dress ☐☐☐☐☐☐☐☐☐☐☐☐☐☐☐☐☐☐☐☐☐☐☐☐☐☐☐☐☐☐☐☐☐☐☐☐☐

☐☐☐☐☐☐☐☐☐☐☐☐☐☐☐☐☐☐☐☐☐☐☐☐☐☐☐☐☐☐☐☐☐☐☐☐☐

y ☐☐☐☐☐☐☐☐☐☐☐☐☐☐☐ State ☐☐ Zip ☐☐☐☐☐ ☐☐☐☐

ne ☐☐☐ ☐☐☐ ☐☐☐☐ Fax ☐☐☐ ☐☐☐ ☐☐☐☐

npany Name ☐☐☐☐☐☐☐☐☐☐☐☐☐☐☐☐☐☐☐☐☐☐☐☐☐☐☐☐☐☐☐☐☐

nail address ☐☐☐☐☐☐☐☐☐☐☐☐☐☐☐☐☐☐☐☐☐☐☐☐☐☐☐☐☐☐☐☐☐☐

Please check at least (3) influencing factors for purchasing this book.

nt or back cover information on book .... ☐
cial approach to the content .... ☐
npleteness of content .... ☐
hor's reputation .... ☐
lisher's reputation .... ☐
ok cover design or layout .... ☐
ex or table of contents of book .... ☐
e of book .... ☐
cial effects, graphics, illustrations .... ☐
er (Please specify): ________________ ☐

How did you first learn about this book?

in Macmillan Computer Publishing catalog .... ☐
ommended by store personnel .... ☐
the book on bookshelf at store .... ☐
ommended by a friend .... ☐
eived advertisement in the mail .... ☐
an advertisement in: ________________ ☐
d book review in: ________________ ☐
er (Please specify): ________________ ☐

How many computer books have you purchased in the last six months?

s book only .... ☐ 3 to 5 books .... ☐
oks .... ☐ More than 5 .... ☐

4. Where did you purchase this book?

Bookstore .... ☐
Computer Store .... ☐
Consumer Electronics Store .... ☐
Department Store .... ☐
Office Club .... ☐
Warehouse Club .... ☐
Mail Order .... ☐
Direct from Publisher .... ☐
Internet site .... ☐
Other (Please specify): ________________ ☐

5. How long have you been using a computer?

☐ Less than 6 months ☐ 6 months to a year
☐ 1 to 3 years ☐ More than 3 years

6. What is your level of experience with personal computers and with the subject of this book?

	With PCs	With subject of book
New	☐	☐
Casual	☐	☐
Accomplished	☐	☐
Expert	☐	☐

Source Code ISBN: 0-7897-0813-2

7. Which of the following best describes your job title?

- Administrative Assistant ☐
- Coordinator ☐
- Manager/Supervisor ☐
- Director ☐
- Vice President ☐
- President/CEO/COO ☐
- Lawyer/Doctor/Medical Professional ☐
- Teacher/Educator/Trainer ☐
- Engineer/Technician ☐
- Consultant ☐
- Not employed/Student/Retired ☐
- Other (Please specify): ____________ ☐

8. Which of the following best describes the area of the company your job title falls under?

- Accounting ☐
- Engineering ☐
- Manufacturing ☐
- Operations ☐
- Marketing ☐
- Sales ☐
- Other (Please specify): ____________ ☐

9. What is your age?

- Under 20 ☐
- 21-29 ☐
- 30-39 ☐
- 40-49 ☐
- 50-59 ☐
- 60-over ☐

10. Are you:

- Male ☐
- Female ☐

11. Which computer publications do you read regularly? (Please list)

____

Comments: ____________________

Fold here and scotch-tape to m

BUSINESS REPLY MAIL

FIRST-CLASS MAIL PERMIT NO. 9918 INDIANAPOLIS IN

POSTAGE WILL BE PAID BY THE ADDRESSEE

ATTN MARKETING
MACMILLAN COMPUTER PUBLISHING
MACMILLAN PUBLISHING USA
201 W 103RD ST
INDIANAPOLIS IN 46290-9042

NO POSTAGE
NECESSARY
IF MAILED
IN THE
UNITED STATES

Licensing Agreement

By opening this package, you are agreeing to be bound by the following:

The software contained on this CD is in many cases copyrighted, and all rights are reserved by the individual software developer and / or publisher. You are bound by the individual licensing agreements associated with each piece of software contained on the CD. THIS SOFTWARE IS PROVIDED FREE OF CHARGE, AS IS, AND WITHOUT WARRANTY OF ANY KIND, EITHER EXPRESSED OR IMPLIED, INCLUDING BUT NOT LIMITED TO THE IMPLIED WARRANTIES OF MERCHANTABILITY AND FITNESS FOR A PARTICULAR PURPOSE. Neither the book publisher nor its dealers and distributors assumes any liability for any alleged or actual damages arising from the use of this software. (Some states do not allow exclusion of implied warranties, so the exclusion may not apply to you.)